DATE DUE

DEMCO 38-296

Literacy, Access, and Libraries among the Language Minority Population

Edited by
Rebecca Constantino

The Scarecrow Press, Inc.
Lanham, Md., & London
1998

SCARECROW PRESS, INC.

Published in the United States of America
by Scarecrow Press, Inc.
4720 Boston Way
Lanham, Maryland 20706

British Library Cataloguing in Publication Information Available

Library of Congress Cataloging-in-Publication Data

Literacy, access, and libraries among the language minority community / edited
 by Rebecca Constantino.
      p. cm.
 Includes bibliographical references and index.
 ISBN 0-8108-3418-9 (cloth : alk. paper)
   1. Libraries—Services to linguistic minorities—United States.
 Z711.8.L58   1997
 027.6'3—dc21   97-24393
                                                                         CIP

ISBN 0-8108-3418-9 (cloth : alk. paper)

♾ᵀᴹ The paper used in this publication meets the minimum requirements of
American National Standard for Information Sciences—Permanence of
Paper for Printed Library Materials, ANSI Z39.48–1984.
Manufactured in the United States of America.

Contents

Acknowledgments

This book is the culmination of the work and passion of the numerous authors. I am grateful for their fine research contributions to the area of literacy. It is my hope that their essays contribute to the literacy environment of the diverse populations discussed.

Special thanks goes to Stephen Krashen and Christian Faltis, two professors who encouraged me to delve more deeply into the area of literacy, reading and writing.

Also, I am grateful to my mother who provided me with an abundance of books and siblings to model reading them.

Lastly, thanks to Steve.

Foreword

Every once in a while a book is published that addresses an issue in education that few others have considered. This is one of those books. There are hundreds of books written about reading and writing and literacy. As a nation, we are obsessed with literacy. We want to know how it works and how to help children and adolescents become literate. But if you take a close look at most of the books on literacy, you will find that they assume that the learners are English speakers who are surrounded by reading materials and, in most cases, have knowledge of how to get reading materials. Rebecca Constantino and the group of contributors in this book know better. By the year 2000, it is conservatively estimated that more than 3.5 million school–aged children will be speakers of languages other than English. What will they read? What role will libraries play in meeting their needs?

Children and adolescents need access to books in their own language to become avid readers and ultimately to succeed in school. Stephen Krashen points out in the introduction that libraries and books may be the most important source of comprehensible language, and of language acquisition available to children and adolescents who are becoming bilingual. And yet, as Rebecca exclaims: Too many immigrant and language minority students have not been invited into the world of books and libraries.

This book is a project that has concerned Rebecca for many years. I recall when she was a graduate student in one of my courses nearly ten years ago, she presented her research paper on some work she did with immigrant parents. She was interested in involving them in using the library. At that time, there were few books or other reading materials available in languages other than English, and the local public

library had little interest in acquiring any. She reported that the
librarians would not help the parents, and that the parents knew very
little about how libraries worked. I was impressed then, and I am even
more impressed now because Rebecca has not given up. This book
represents one more battle against the inequities that exist for immigrant
and language minority communities in the United States.

I commend Rebecca and the contributors to this book for their
commitment to literacy and justice for all, and for bringing the role of
libraries in supporting literacy in any language to the forefront.

Christian J. Faltis, Professor
Arizona State University

Introduction

Why Consider the Library and Books?

Stephen Krashen

There is a powerful circumstantial case for the role of the library in helping children develop literacy. Research shows that more free voluntary reading consistently means more literacy development, that children read more when they have more access to books, and that children get a significant percentage of the books they read from libraries. In this paper, I briefly review this research, and then examine whether this circumstantial evidence is supported by studies of the effect of libraries on literacy development. The good news is that the case for libraries is strongly supported.

Free Reading > Literacy

Research done over the last fifty years consistently shows that reading, especially free voluntary reading, is a powerful means of developing literacy: Those who have read more also read better, write better, and have larger vocabularies (Krashen, 1993). There is also very good evidence that other means proposed for literacy development, such as direct instruction, are not effective: The system to be acquired is too complex to be taught and consciously learned. In addition, many people have developed high levels of literacy without instruction, and studies probing the effectiveness of instruction have in general found very small and short-lived effects (Krashen, 1993, 1994).

Access > Free Reading

If free reading is the path to literacy development, a major issue is how we can encourage children to read. The most obvious way has been the most neglected: Making sure children have access to good books and a quiet, comfortable place to read them. There is strong research evidence supporting this common–sense hypothesis (Krashen, 1993). Of particular interest is Houle and Montmarquette (1984), who reported that students take more books out of school libraries that have more books, and that stay open longer.

Where Do Children Get Books?

Children get a surprising percentage of their books from some kind of library, the percentage reported in the research literature ranging from 30 percent (Gaver, 1963) to 97 percent (Ingram, 1981). (Additional research is reviewed in Krashen, 1993).

Libraries and Reading Achievement

If all this is true, we would expect that the availability of books in libraries would be a good predictor of children's reading achievement. This prediction is supported by the research. In the survey presented here, we will see that the quantity of books in school libraries is a consistent predictor of reading achievement. What makes this research particularly impressive is the fact that the same results occur in a variety of situations. The research is presented in chronological order.

Gaver (1963): The New Jersey Study

Gaver (1963) was, to my knowledge, the first published empirical investigation of the relationship between school libraries and literacy development. Gaver studied schools in New Jersey that fell into three categories, with two schools in each category: (1) schools with libraries; (2) schools without school libraries, but with "centralized book collections" without librarians; (3) schools with only classroom libraries.

Table 1–1 presents Gaver's findings, which are consistent with the hypothesis that school libraries have an impact on literacy development. These results, however, must be considered as only suggestive: A small number of schools was studied, and other factors, such as socio-economic class, were not controlled. We will see later, however, that this result has been replicated and holds even when other factors are controlled.

Table 1-1. School Libraries and Literacy Development

Type of Library	Skills tested	
	Vocabulary	Reading
School Library with librarian	25.50	28.00
Centralized collection but no librarian	21.67	23.84
Classroom library only	19.93	21.22

Test Scores: Differences between sixth and fourth grade scores on Iowa test of Basic Skills. (From Gaver, 1963).

Farris and Hancock (1991): The Rural Study

Farris and Hancock (1991) examined library use in 38 elementary schools in the United States. All the schools in their sample were in areas populated by 150 inhabitants or less per square mile and had enrollments of under 500 students. The measure of reading achievement used was sixth graders' performance on the Iowa Test of Basic Skills.

Students' mean reading scores (69th percentile) and the average number of volumes per student in the libraries studied (24.2) are well above the national average, which is consistent with the hypothesis that access to books and reading ability are related. The average number of volumes in the libraries, 5,616, was, however, below the national average of 7,386 (White, 1990). In addition, Farris and Hancock reported no significant differences in reading achievement between schools with more than 25 volumes per child and schools with fewer than 25 volumes per child.

Twenty-seven schools reported circulation data: The average circulation was 25.64 volumes per student per year. In comparison, Los Angeles middle schools report an average circulation of about five books per year (see below). Schools reporting a circulation of greater than 30 volumes per year had significantly higher reading scores than schools reporting circulation of fewer than 30 volumes per year.

Elley (1992): How in the World do Children Read?

Elley (1992) was a survey of reading ability of a total of "210,000 nine- and fourteen-year-old children in 32 countries." The measure used probed ability to understand narrative and expository prose, as well as documents. Table 1–2 gives readers an idea of the range of scores:

Table 1–2. Sample Reading Scores

	nine-year-olds	fourteen-year-olds
Finland	569	560
U.S.	547	535
Ireland	509	511
Cyprus	481	497
Venezuela	383	417

mean=500   standard deviation=100
Source: Elley, 1992.

(Note that contrary to what one reads and hears in the media, the United States scored quite well. Nine-year-olds in the United States ranked second, behind Finland, among the 32 countries, and fourteen-year-olds ranked ninth but scored quite close to the leader, Finland.)

Elley computed, for each country, a "Composite Development Index," (CDI), a measure of economic development. The CDI took into consideration the Gross National Product, public expenditures per student on education, life expectancy, the percentage of adult literacy, newspapers, and percent of children born with low birth weight. There was, as expected, a clear relationship between CDI measures and reading ability (table 1–3).

Among the predictors of reading ability, the school library did very well. For both nine-year-olds and fourteen-year-olds, countries that reported more books in their school library reported higher reading scores. Elley grouped the countries into quarters, according to the size of the school library. As shown in table 1–4, for all countries studied, and for countries with lower CDIs, there was a clear relationship between library size and reading achievement. For high CDI countries, the relationship was much weaker. As Elley notes (p. 67), there appears to be a "threshold of advantage": Beyond a certain CDI level, the library makes a much smaller contribution. Apparently, children from wealthier countries have other sources of books.

*Table 1–3. Correlations between Developmental Indices and Reading
        Ability*

Indicator	Correlation of reading ability	
	nine–year–olds	fourteen–year–olds
GNP	.60	.64
Expenditures for education	.46	.51
Life expectancy	.73	.73
Percentages with		
low birth rate	−.69	−.69
Newspaper circulation	.47	.61
Percentage of adult literacy	.64	.70

n=32; all correlations significant at .01, one tail test.
Source: Elley, 1992.

Table 1–4. Library Size and Reading Achievement

Library size	lowest quarter	2nd quarter	3rd quarter	4th quarter
high CDI countries	521	525	536	535
all countries	492	500	504	515
low CDI countries	445	452	454	474

Source: Elley, 1992.

The data in table 1–4 thus suggests that the school library plays an especially important role when other sources of books are not available, and it suggests that the school library can make up a significant part of the gap between reading scores in richer and poorer countries.

Foertsch (1992): The NAEP Study

The NAEP (National Association for Educational Progress) study investigated reading achievement in a nationally representative sample of 4th, 8th, and 12th graders. One of the many variables considered was library use (no distinction was made between public and school libraries). Table 1-5 presents the results.

Table 1-5. Students' Reported Use of the Library ("How often do you take books out of the library yourself?")

grade		daily	weekly	monthly	yearly	never
4	percent	6	60	16	7	10
	test score	214	238	244	228	210
8	percent	5	19	33	23	20
	test score	258	264	267	263	245
12	percent	3	9	27	36	25
	test score	280	292	296	291	277

Source: Foertsch, 1992.

Foertsch found some relationship between voluntary library use and reading scores, but the relationship was not perfect. Clearly, those who never used the library performed the lowest on the reading test. For the older students, however, differences among the other groups are very small. (The finding that those who use the library daily are not the best readers is not a problem: Very few students did so, and one wonders what kind of a life they had if they were in the library every day.) Table 1-5 also reveals that library use declines dramatically with increasing age: While 17 percent of the fourth graders used the library "yearly" or "never," this figure rises to 43 percent among the eighth graders and 61 percent among twelfth graders.

The relationship between library use and reading ability is most likely bidirectional. More reading makes one a better reader, but it is probably also true that better readers take more advantage of the library.

Lance, Welborn, and Hamilton–Pennell (1993): The Colorado Study

Lance et al. gathered data on reading achievement and school libraries from 221 schools in Colorado. This study is impressive because so many factors were considered.

Students in grades 1, 2, 4, 5 and 7 were tested using the Reading Comprehension subtest of the Iowa Test of Basic Skills (ITBS), and tenth graders were tested with the Test of Achievement and Proficiency (TAP).

The results of the Colorado project are best presented in the form

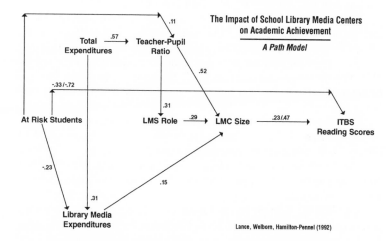

Lance et al. present them, as a path analysis (figure 1). Path analysis is a very useful statistical technique that allows the researcher to determine the effects of variables on each other in a precise way. How this is done will become clear as we work through figure 1.

We begin in the middle with the arrow from LMC (Library Media Center) SIZE to ITBS reading scores. LMC size was made up of the following measures: books per pupil, serials per pupil, videos per pupil, and total library staff hours in a typical week. The existence of this arrow means that Lance et al. found that a significant relationship exists between these two variables: The size of the library media center is positively related to performance on the reading test. The number on the arrow indicates the size of the relationship (when two numbers are given, they indicate the

smallest and largest effects among the grade levels studied).
Note that an arrow exists between AT–RISK STUDENT and ITBS
scores. The AT–RISK factor consisted of the following measures:
percentage of residents in the district over age 25 who had graduated from
high school, the percentage of students in a school who were members of
a minority group, and the percentage of students who qualified for the
National School Lunch program. The existence of this arrow confirms that
socio–economic status is related to reading achievement.

Path analysis allows us to see the impact of different factors on
reading performance independently. In figure 1, library size and SES
(At–Risk Students) both impact reading, but each makes a unique,
separate contribution: In other words, the effect of library size on
reading test performance is not a function of SES.

Note the arrow on the bottom of figure 1 from Library Media
Expenditures to LMC Size. This indicates that money spent in the
library results in larger libraries (which in turn result in better reading).

Total Expenditures refers to the total money allotted to the school.
Note that there is no arrow from Total Expenditures to ITBS. This can
be interpreted to mean that money impacts reading achievement only
when it is put in the school library.

LMS Role (Library Media Specialist Role) was a factor made up of
hours per week put in by media–endorsed staff and hours spent by
library staff "identifying materials for teacher–planned instructional
units and collaborating with teachers in planning such units" (p. 60).
According to figure 1, a larger LMS Role was related to larger libraries,
and in turn to better reading.

A LMCUSE (Library Media Center Use) factor was also identified,
and consisted of measures of book circulation, non–print circulation,
and library/ information skills instruction. Surprisingly, this factor was
not a significant predictor of reading scores at any grade level.

The factor showing the largest impact on reading in figure 1 is SES.
The impact of the school library, however, is formidable, and has the
largest effect on reading of all the school variables studied in the project.

Krashen (1995): The States Study

Krashen (1995) examined the impact of school libraries, SES,
software, public library use, and overall school expenditures on fourth
grade scores on the 1992 NAEP reading comprehension test for 41
states in the United States. Data on books in school libraries per pupil
for each state, software in school libraries, and "library services" were
taken from White (1990). ("Library services" included the extent to

which librarians provided services such as library skills instruction for students, inservices, reference assistance and technical assistance for teacher and interlibrary loans.) Data on per capita public library use was taken from Chute (1992). Finally, the total amount of money each state spent on education was included.

The descriptive statistics presented in table 1–6 are of some interest. They indicate that the average school library in the sample provided about 17 books per child, and that the average use of public libraries was about six books taken out per year per person.

Table 1–6. Descriptive Statistics from the States Study

variable	mean	standard deviation
RC: NAEP score	216.51	8.52
SL: Books	17.15	5.12
SL: Software	29.78	18.89
SL: Service	22.78	3.04
Public Library	5.84	1.89
Expenditures	4903.01	1476.50

RC = Scores on NAEP Reading Comprehension test, fourth graders
SL: Books = school library: number of books per child
SL: Software = school library: software available
SL: Service = school library services available
Public Library = annual circulation per capita
Expenditures = expenditures per pupil

Table 1–7 presents correlations for each of these variables with NAEP reading scores.

Table 1-7. Correlations with Fourth Grade Reading Achievement

	NAEP Score
Books per student in school library	.495a
Software in school library	.377b
Library Services	-.513c
Public Library Use	.559a
Expenditures	.058

n = 41
a: $p < .01$, one tail
b: $p < .02$, 2 tails

(Source: Krashen, 1995)

As indicated in table 1–7, the relationship between books per student and reading was positive and strong. Software was a significant predictor of reading, but was weaker than books. Library services, surprisingly, was negatively associated with reading ability. This result is inconsistent with the results of the Colorado study, which found no direct relationship between Library Media Specialist Role and reading, but found an indirect one, mediated through library size. Public library use was an excellent predictor of children's reading scores. Overall expenditures for schools was not a significant predictor.

In table 1–8, a multiple regression analysis of the data is presented. Multiple regression is, in effect, a simpler version of path analysis. The effect of each of the predictors is determined, with all other predictors held constant.

In table 1–8, the "b," the regression coefficient, is interpreted as follows: Each additional book in the library (per student) is associated with an NAEP reading test gain of .4459 points. The "betas" in table 1–8 are similar to the regression coefficient, except that they are "standardized," which means they can be used to compare the effects of different predictors, as we did in discussing the Colorado study. Thus, books in the school library is seen to be a stronger predictor of reading than software is (.2680 is larger than .1929).

The results of this analysis are quite similar to the correlational analysis presented in table 1–7. Books in the school library and use of public libraries were clearly positively related to NAEP scores, the effect of software was weaker, library services were strongly negatively related to reading, and money spent on schools did not impact reading scores.

Table 1–8. Multiple Regression Analysis of States Data
dependent variable = scores on NAEP Reading test

predictor	b	beta	t	p
SL: books	.4459	.2680	2.07	.046
SL: software	.08659	.1929	1.59	.120
SL: service	−1.2819	−.4566	−4.17	.001
public library	1.3196	.2928	2.37	.024
expenditures	−.000046	.0264	−0.07	.942

r2 = .602

adjusted r2 = .545
F = 10.59, p < .001   (Source: Krashen, 1995)

In total, the predictors accounted for 60 percent of the variation in reading scores (this is the r2 figure in the table), which is a very high amount.

Krashen and O'Brian (1996): The Los Angeles Study

The most recent addition to this literature is the Los Angeles study, which examined the impact of libraries in 53 middle schools and 33 high schools in the Los Angeles Unified School District. Measures included reading comprehension (CTBS), library size, voluntary library use, overall library use, library software and socio-economic status (based on the percentage of pupils receiving Aid to Families with Dependent Children and free lunches).

In table 1–9, correlations between the predictor variables and CTBS scores are listed.

Table 1–9. Correlations with CTBS Reading Scores Predictors

	middle school	high school
SES	.82	.76
total books in library	.2	.21
books per student	.07	.2
voluntary use of library	.49	.01
circulation	.13	.17
software	.02	−.26

a: p< .01
Source: Krashen and O'Brian (forthcoming)

Socio-economic class was a powerful predictor of reading achievement, but books in the library, as measured both by books per student, did not do well. Voluntary use of the library was a good predictor of reading scores for middle school students, but not for high school students. Circulation correlated only very weakly with reading achievement, and the effect of software was practically zero for middle school students and negative for high schoolers.

Multiple regression analyses produced similar results. For both middle and high school samples, SES was again, by far, the strongest predictor. For the middle school, only voluntary use came close to statistical significance ($p = .138$), while for high schoolers, total books showed some signs of promise ($p = .15$). In both analyses, the effect of software was close to zero.

Krashen and O'Brian note that the conditions in the LA libraries help explain why the correlations between books and reading scores were so low: students in some cases have little access to the libraries, collections are badly outdated, and information about libraries is lacking. Clearly, if students don't use the library, there will be little or no relationship between the number of books and reading achievement. We return to this issue below.

Summary of the Research

1. In all studies, a positive relationship was found between a measure of the number of books in the school library and reading achievement. In the Los Angeles study, however, the relationship was very weak. For the Rural study, the sample as a whole had better than average reading scores and better than average collections, when considered as number of books per child, but schools with greater than average books per student did not have better reading scores. (A ceiling effect may be in operation here; because the students in this sample were, in general, good readers, adding more books did not make an additional impact on their reading ability; they may have already had enough access to books. A problem with this interpretation, however, is the finding that in terms of total books, the sample was below the national average.)

2. Total circulation was not a significant predictor of reading performance in the Colorado study or the LA study, but was a significant predictor in the Rural study.

3. Voluntary use of the library was a promising predictor of reading achievement in the middle school Los Angeles group, but not in the high school group, and it appeared to relate to reading ability in the NAEP study.

4. Socio-economic class was a strong predictor of reading achievement in each study in which it was measured, with higher SES corresponding to higher reading achievement (Colorado, World, LA).

5. Computer-related variables were a significant predictor in only one study (States) but the impact was modest. In other studies, the

effect was absent (Colorado, Los Angeles).

6. Library services were positively related to reading in one study (Colorado) and negatively in another (States). In the former study, however, a variable that included teaching students library skills was not positively related to reading ability.

7. Total expenditures for schools was not a predictor of reading in two studies (Colorado, States) but was in one (World). In the Colorado study, money put into the school library resulted in better collections, which in turn resulted in better reading.

Discussion

Libraries and reading: The results of the series of studies reviewed here are certainly encouraging. There is good reason to hypothesize, however, that the potential effects of the school library are much larger than these results indicate. Libraries show a relationship to reading despite findings revealing that in some cases, access to libraries is limited, information on libraries is lacking, and collections are outdated.

Pucci (1994) investigated school libraries in certain schools in Los Angeles, and found that in some cases, access to the library was severely limited, and that students were restricted to taking out only one or two books per week. Constantino (1994, 1995a) reported that knowledge of library functions and services was very low among limited English proficient students, and nearly nonexistent among their parents. Griffen (1990) examined collection recency in science holdings in school libraries in the Los Angeles Unified School District and found that most of the holdings were old, with 21 percent published in the 1950s, and 44 percent published in the 1960s. While it is likely that these factors exist in many places, Pucci's, Constantino's and Griffen's research was all done in the Los Angeles area, which helps to explain why the correlations between books in the library and reading achievement were so low in the Los Angeles study. Steps are now being taken to improve library conditions and access to books in Los Angeles.

If access to collections were consistently easy, if information about school libraries, their collections and policies, were more widespread, and if collections were up-to-date, we would see more of the true potential of school libraries.

An unresolved issue is what the best measure of library size is. Total books was successfully used as a measure in the World and Colorado studies, while the States and Rural studies used the ratio of books per student. It is tempting to conclude that either measure will do. I re-analyzed the States data using total books: The relationship between total books in school libraries and reading achievement was, surprisingly, close to zero (r = -.03), even though the two measures of library size were modestly positively correlated (r = .35).

One could argue that total books available to students, not the ratio of books per student, should be a better predictor of reading behavior, as well as reading ability. It is, after all, better to have one million books available for one million people than 100 books for ten people. My re-analysis of the States study, however, does not support this common-sense argument.

Circulation and use: As noted earlier, causality for circulation and library use is not clear. More library use should result in better reading, but better readers probably use the library more.

Table 1-10 summarizes the results for the different measures of library size, circulation and use.

Table 1-10: Summary of Book Size Predictors

predictor:	books/ student	total books	circulation	voluntary use study
New Jersey		yes		
Rural	no	no	yes	
World		yes		
States	yes (r=.495)	no (r=-.03)		
Colorado		yes	no	
LA: middle	.07	.19	.13	.49
LA: hs	.20	.21	.17	.01
NAEP			yes	

yes: clear impact on reading achievement
no: no impact on reading achievement

Socio-economic class: A likely interpretation of the consistent finding of a strong relationship between SES and reading achievement is that more affluent homes have more books, more models of reading, and provide more leisure time for reading. This view is consistent with observations that lower SES children have fewer books in the home (Constantino, 1994), studies showing a clear relationship between the number of books in the home and reading ability (Elley, 1992; Krashen, 1993), and findings showing a relationship between social class and

literacy development (Kirsch, Jungeblut, Jenkins, and Kolstad, 1993).
Computers: The weak results for software and computers strongly suggest that the current trend of focussing on technology in school libraries, as reported by Miller and Schontz (1993), is not justified. Clearly, books come first.

Library Services: A preliminary hypothesis consistent with the data is that direct teaching of library skills has no effect on reading scores, but time devoted by the librarian to interacting with teachers does.

Money: The results reported in the studies suggest that literacy is a problem we should throw money at. We need to aim carefully, however: The money needs to be invested in the school library, and it is reasonable to hypothesize, based on the consistent finding that books do impact reading and that computers do not have a consistent effect, that this money should be spent on good reading material that students are genuinely interested in reading.

Of course, the school library is not the only possible source of reading material. It is, however, a source that educators can influence directly. Elley's finding that library size in low CDI countries showed a strong relationship to reading achievement suggests that the greatest potential impact of school libraries occurs when other sources of books are not available, in low SES circumstances. Unfortunately, these children often have access to fewer books in school (Kozol, 1991). The solution is obvious.

References

Anderson, R., P. Wilson, and L. Fielding. 1988. Growth in reading and how children spend their time outside of school. *Reading Research Quarterly* 23: 285–309.

Chute, A. 1992. *Public Libraries in the U.S.: 1990.* Washington, D.C.: U.S. Department of Education.

Constantino, R. 1994. Immigrant ESL high school students; understanding and use of libraries: Check this out! *SCOPE* 93: 6–16.

Constantino, R. 1995a. Minority use of the library. *California Reader* 28: 10–12.

Constantino, R. 1995b. Two small girls, one large disparity. *The Reading Teacher* 48: 504.

Elley, W. 1992. *How in the World do Students Read?* Hamburg:

International Association for the Evaluation of Educational Achievement.

Farris, P. and M. Hancock. 1991. The role of literature in reading achievement. *The Clearing House* 65: 114–117.

Foertsch, M. 1992. *Reading In and Out of School*. Washington, D.C.: Office of Educational Research and Improvement, U.S. Department of Education.

Gaver, M. 1963. *Effectiveness of Centralized Library Service in Elementary Schools*. New Brunswick, N.J.: Rutgers University Press.

Griffen, E. 1990. *The Children Can No Longer Wait: Multimedia Libraries*. Publication #589, Los Angeles Unified School District.

Houle, E. and C. Montmarquette. 1984. An empirical analysis of loans by school libraries. *Alberta Journal of Educational Research* 30: 104–114.

Ingram, J. 1981. *Books and Reading Development: The Bradford Book Flood Experiment*. London: Heinemann Educational Books.

Kirsch, I., A. Jungeblut, L. Jenkins, and A. Kolstad. 1993. *Adult Literacy in America*. Washington, D.C.: U.S. Department of Education.

Kozol, J. 1991. *Savage Inequalities*. New York: Crown.

Krashen, S. 1993. *The Power of Reading*. Englewood, Colo.: Libraries Unlimited.

Krashen, S. 1994. The input hypothesis and its rivals. In N. Ellis, ed. *Implicit and Explicit Learning of Languages*. London: Academic Press.

Krashen, S. 1995. School libraries, public libraries, and NAEP reading scores. *School Library Media Quarterly*, Summer, 1995.

Krashen, S., & O'Brian, B. 1996. School library collections and reading achievement in Length of stay Angeles and Beyond. *Indiana Media Journal 18 (3)*: 71–72.

Lance, K., L. Welborn, C. Hamilton-Pennell. 1993. *The Impact of School Library Media Centers on Academic Achievement*. Englewood, Colo.: Libraries Unlimited.

Miller, M. and M. Schontz. 1993. Expenditures for resources in school library media centers, FY 1991–1992. *School Library Journal* 39: 26–36.

Pucci, S. 1994. Supporting Spanish language literacy: Latino children and free reading resources in schools. *Bilingual Research Journal* 18: 67–82.

White, H. 1990. School library collections and services: Ranking the states. *School Library Media Quarterly* 19: 13–26.

Chapter 1

Supporting Spanish Language Literacy: Latino Children and School and Community Libraries

Sandra L. Pucci

Introduction

There is much discussion today, particularly in urban areas of the country, regarding the education of language minority students. A growing number of children in our schools have been classified as "limited English proficient" (LEP), "a student whose native language is other than English and whose skills in listening to, speaking, reading, or writing English are such that he/she derives little benefit from regular school instruction" (Hopstock, et al., 1984). Just in the late 1980s the number of LEP students in the United States increased by 36.2% (Roger & Olsen, 1991). These students, enrolled in various educational programs throughout the country, will require more than traditional English-only instruction to allow them equal access to schooling.

The United States Office of Education (1971) defines bilingual education as

> the use of two languages, one of which is English, as mediums of instruction for the same pupil population in a well organized program which

encompasses all or part of the curriculum and includes the study of the history and culture associated with the mother tongue. A complete program develops and maintains the child's self-esteem and a legitimate pride in both cultures. (Ovando and Collier, 1985, p. 2)

While there is much debate over the various types of bilingual education, research has shown that effective bilingual programs have the following characteristics: subject matter instruction in the native language, first language literacy development and comprehensible input in English (Krashen and Biber, 1988). It is a point of agreement among bilingual education experts that literacy instruction in L1 builds an underlying and conceptual proficiency strongly related to L2 development (Cummins, 1981). This interdependence principle postulates that instruction effective in promoting proficiency in L1 will result in its transfer to L2 provided that there is adequate exposure and motivation to learn L2 (*ibid.*).

While there is abundant documentation in the literature supporting the notion that students transfer their L1 literacy ability to the L2 (Thonis, 1981, Snow, 1990), and that premature transition to English may significantly hinder cognitive and literacy development (Crawford, 1995), the majority of bilingual education programs tend to emphasize a rapid road to English, often denying the students necessary time to develop a real cognitive and linguistic base in their primary language. Children are "transitioned" as quickly and expediently as possible, generally after two to three years, while research has shown that it may in reality take as long as seven years to reach a "threshold" level of literacy in their L1 (Cummins, 1989, Krashen, 1988).

Free Reading and Language and Literacy Development

Free-reading offers the student an important means of obtaining the necessary exposure to written language needed to develop this essential foundation in the primary language. Indeed, free-reading may be the main source of not only the actual "skill" of reading, but also of vocabulary growth, writing style, and grammar (Krashen, 1988).

Several studies have examined the relationship between amount of reported pleasure reading and children's reading achievement. Sheldon and Cutts (1953) surveyed pupils in eight elementary schools who were considered by their teachers to be either in the top or bottom 5 percent of readers and found that "despite an expressed dislike for language arts and much of the reading done in school, almost half of the above-average and the superior readers have reading as an out-of-school interest or hobby" (p. 519). Lamme (1976) investigated the long-term reading habits of sixty-five elementary students over a period of three years. She found a statistically significant correlation between the number of books read and the children's standardized test scores. Similarly, Long and Henderson (1973) found that "time spent reading was positively related to . . . all four measures of the Gates-MacGinitie test . . . and was also related to self-concept scores" (p. 197).

In a study conducted by Anderson et al. (1988), 155 fifth-grade students kept a detailed log of their out-of-school activities for periods ranging from eight to twenty-six weeks. Not surprisingly, book reading was the activity which proved to have the strongest correlation with reading proficiency. In addition, researchers found that "time spent reading books was the best predictor of a child's growth as a reader from the second to the fifth grade" (p. 297). In a similar study, Greany (1980) sought to investigate the relationship between selected personal, social and school variables with the amount of time devoted to leisure reading. Nine hundred twenty 5th-graders in thirty-one Irish primary schools kept a log of their out-of-school activities on three specified days during a period of one week. He found that "two variables which emerged as strong predictors of leisure reading in virtually all of the analyses were gender and reading attainment" (p. 353), which indicates that those individuals who were better readers consistently read more. He also points out that "conversely, the correlations between types of leisure reading and reading attainment suggest that those who obtain low scores on reading attainment tend to devote relatively little time to book reading or comic reading" (p. 354).

Walberg and Tsai (1983, 1984, 1985) have conducted several studies on the relationship between reading achievement and school and out-of-school variables. In their 1983 study, they studied 2,300 seventeen-year-old students and found that 51% of the adjusted variance in reading achievement can be accounted for by motivation, frequency of spare time reading, radio listening, socioeconomic status, home environment, the use of English at home, race, and public school attendance. Researchers reported that the correlation between achieve-

ment and frequency of spare time reading to be a modest .23 (p. 47).
A strong relationship with self-concept was also found as "those with
a good self-concept of themselves as readers tended to be able readers,
support the freedom to read, believe reading is important, enjoy reading,
read more often in their spare time, and rely on newspapers as news
sources. Thus, achievement, attitudes, and opportunities in reading
appear to naturally reinforce one another among students who do well
in reading tests" (p. 49).

More recently, Applebee et al. (1990) reported on a survey of the
nation's high school students' leisure reading habits. They found that "at
both grades 8 and 12, those students who reported reading fiction—alone
or in combination with non–fiction—had higher average reading proficiency
than those students who reported reading only non–fiction. The nearly one–
fifth of the students who reported little or no reading as a leisure activity
had the lowest average reading proficiency" (p. 26).

Vocabulary Acquisition

Extensive research in vocabulary acquisition through reading has
been done by Nagy, Anderson, and Herman (1985, 1987) who
distinguish between "incidental" and "instructional" approaches to
vocabulary acquisition. They refer to the first as the "picking up" of
lexical items from contextual clues both in oral and written language,
and the second as those learnt as a result of direct instruction, in the
form of memorized word lists or any other "school–based" technique
which purposefully tries to teach the meanings of words (Nagy and
Herman, 1985). Studies done on direct instruction of vocabulary reveal
the relative ineffectiveness of such an approach. Whereas children may
add as many as 3,000 items to their reading vocabulary yearly (Nagy et
al., 1987), direct instruction cannot be held accountable for more than
200–300 of these acquired words (Durkin, 1979; Jenkins and Dixon,
1983). Thus "trying to expand children's vocabulary by teaching them
words one by one, ten by ten, or even hundred by hundred would
appear to be an exercise in futility" (Nagy and Anderson, 1984, p. 328).

Given the amount of exposure to vocabulary words in school and at
home "many believe that incidental learning of words from context
while reading is, or at least can be, the major mode of vocabulary
growth once children have really begun to read" (Nagy and Herman,

1987, p. 24). They continue by stating that "because the bulk of children's vocabulary growth occurs incidentally, that is, outside of situations specifically devoted to word learning, the single most important goal of vocabulary instruction should be to increase the amount of incidental word learning by students" (p. 26), including a focus on metacognitive strategies and, most importantly, increasing the actual amount of time spent reading.

Several studies have been conducted explicitly with the intention of measuring vocabulary growth through reading. Krashen (1987) has termed these "incidental read and test studies." In these studies, subjects are asked simply to read a short passage for meaning, apparently unaware that they will be tested on vocabulary, and given a posttest afterwards. Several such studies have been undertaken by Nagy et al. (1985, 1987), and Herman et al. (1987). In the Nagy et al. (1987) study on reading and incidental vocabulary acquisition, researchers looked at a group of 352 children distributed across the third, fifth, and seventh grades. Children were randomly given various narrative and expository texts judged to be of relative appropriate grade level, yet difficult enough to guarantee the occurrence of unfamiliar words. To control for the possible effect of short-term memory, researchers let a week pass before testing students on the targeted lexical items. Their results yielded a .05 chance of a child learning a word from context, in this case a single exposure. Looking at both what would be an average fifth grade child's yearly reading, estimated at a minimum of a million words (Nagy et al. 1987) and the frequency of words occurring in children's books, it would be fair to say that a child meets from 16,000 to 24,000 unfamiliar words yearly. With a .05 chance of acquiring a word, not taking into account repeated exposures to the same item, a child could be expected to learn roughly 800–1200 words per year, which is an amount far exceeding that of any direct instructional program (Nagy et al., 1987). It would seem rational to conclude that regular, wide reading is a major source of vocabulary acquisition.

Other cases of incidental vocabulary learning have been reported in the literature. Miller (1941) observed a class of junior high school students during the course of a thematic unit on conservation. Much of the instruction included extensive independent reading in a certain area of conservation as selected by the student, culminating in an essay. At the conclusion of the unit, Miller remarked on her students' acquisition of scientific terms: ". . . for one thing, in the study of and writing of these subjects, our junior high school pupils were using a technical vocabulary away and above that ordinarily employed by pupils at this level. . . the faculty was impressed. At no time in the study of the unit had we so much as mentioned vocabulary. We had been concerned with content. Yet now we were sure that in the extensive reading done on the subject, our pupils had *incidentally accumulated* an unusual store of conservation terms" (p. 665, emphasis added).

Pfau (1967) conducted a two-year exploratory investigation of the effects of recreational reading with 170 first-grade children randomly selected and assigned to control and experimental groups in five different communities. Although the primary purpose of the study was to investigate students' interest in reading, researchers also investigated proficiency in spelling, reading, and "written and oral fluency" (p. 36). Students were compared using a standardized measure of reading, finding "significant differences in gain scores on sight vocabulary and vocabulary in context," favoring the experimental group at the .001 level (p. 37). Similarly, studies which investigated the relationship between amount of reading and reading ability also support the notion that more exposure to reading will result in increased vocabulary acquisition. As previously cited, Anderson et al. (1988) and Greany (1980) have found that children who do better on measures of reading achievement, including vocabulary knowledge, report more out of school pleasure reading. It would seem then that attempts to increase children's vocabulary knowledge must, as Nagy and Herman (1985) point out, "include an increase in the opportunity to learn new words, and this will occur primarily through regular, sustained reading" (p. 20).

Children, Libraries, and Access to Reading Materials

Krashen (1987) cites the research supporting the view that children will read more when provided with increased access to print material. He asserts that "a reasonable interpretation of these data is that access to books is necessary, but not sufficient, for the development of literacy. Certainly, without reading material, little progress will be made" (p. 3). Research into access and availability of print materials has generally fallen into two categories, that which deals with access to books in the home, and that which looks at the school's print environment. There is ample evidence that confirms moderate but consistent correlations between availability of books in the home and both amount of free-reading and reading achievement (Feitelson and Goldstein, 1986; Morrow, 1983; Neuman, 1986; Pucci and Ulanoff, 1991), but for the purposes of this review, studies which specifically examine the school and/or library environment will be examined.

Several studies have shown that children who are given more access to books will read more, and that immediacy of access is an important factor. Powell (1966) compared elementary students' use of classroom libraries and found that those children in classrooms with a well-stocked classroom library in fact did more recreational reading, finding that "the pupils with the classroom library outread the pupils using the central library at a ratio of approximately two to one" (p. 396). In addition, he found that pupils who tended to use the public library the most were those who had the greatest physical proximity to the facility, i.e. those whose school was next door and regularly visited it as a part of their instruction. He concluded that "the more immediate the access to library material, the greater amount of pupil recreatory reading" (p. 396).

Morrow and Weinstein (1986) installed classroom libraries in kindergarten classrooms to investigate whether an attractive, comfortable, well-stocked library corner would significantly influence the choices these children made during free play. They found statistically significant differences in children's use of literature during play time, in the form of story-telling through use of puppets or felt-boards, roll movies, story-cassettes, manipulation of books, and role-playing between experimental and control groups (p. 136). In a similar study with second graders conducted by the same researchers (Morrow and Weinstein, 1986), outcomes showed that the use of the library corner during "free-choice" time significantly increased, and that this use reflected an actual increase in the amount of free-reading, and a decrease in other literacy-related activities such as those previously mentioned (p. 340).

There is evidence that children obtain a significant proportion of their free-reading books from a library. Krashen (1987) cites three studies which support this claim (Lamme, 1976, Ingram, 1981, Swanton, 1984). In all three studies, children aged 9, 10, 11, and 12 obtained from 70.2 to 99.6% of their books from some sort of library. Swanton (1984), for example, reported that 71% of gifted children and 70% of "regular" children obtained their free-reading books from either public or school libraries, with the "regular" children showing a greater preference for school as opposed to public libraries. No data as to proximity of public libraries is given in her study, but she does imply that the gifted child is possibly more prompted by parents to frequent the public library than the "regular" one (p. 100). Ingram (1981) found some variations between her "outer" and "inner" city samples. Children in the outer sample strongly preferred the classroom library, followed by the school library, with the public library a distant third (p. 110). Those students in the "inner" sample, in addition to the classroom library, also made extensive use of the school library as well as regular use of the public facilities (p.118). Krashen (1987) calculated by age overall general use of libraries for Ingham's groups at between 70.5% and 99.6% (p. 4). Lamme (1976) calculated that from 68.3 to 78.7% of children's (in grades 4-6) books in her study were obtained from the school library, with overall library percentages (combined school, classroom and public facilities) ranging from 81 to 89%.

Use of libraries has also been investigated by Heyns (1978), who looked at the impact of public libraries on summertime learning of children in Atlanta. She found that children who lived nearer to the public library read more, and that the impact of the library was greater in lower socio-economic groups. She states that "as might be expected, the number of blocks to the nearest library influences reading primarily because increasing the accessibility of books and materials heightens the probability that a child will read" (p. 175).

Houle and Montmarquette (1984) conducted an empirical study on loans in school libraries. The purpose of the study was to explore what roles "the quantity and quality of books in the library, the size and composition of personnel, the organizational methods, the physical facilities, and the users' characteristics play in determining whether or not a school library makes loans" (p. 105). Results indicated that the actual number of books per pupil is one of the most important determinants of library use, and that this effect is stronger when library personnel are present (p. 110). In addition, the "number of operating hours is a key element in explaining both the probability that a library makes loans, and the number of loans made" (p. 111). Findings indicated that a 20% increase in the number of books would yield an approximate increase of 10% in loans. These results confirm previous findings that when children are given access to a wide variety of books they will indeed make use of them.

Libraries and Latino Children

There exists a diverse body of literature which addresses the question of library services and Spanish speakers. However, the area of providing Spanish language reading materials to children appears under-developed, both in terms of analysis within a theoretical framework of bilingual education and language development, as well as socio-political analysis from a language planning perspective.

Although an extensive review of the literature was undertaken, very few articles were located which dealt with Spanish-speaking children and their library needs. In general, library science publications tend to have a very different focus, one which oddly enough, does not discuss books. One need only glance at such "special issues devoted to libraries and the Spanish-speaking" of journals such as the *Wilson Library Bulletin* (Vol. 44, No. 7, and Vol. 53, No. 7) to discover that the availability and acquisition of Spanish materials is given only peripheral attention, and school libraries are rarely discussed at all. Instead, one finds articles dealing with diverse issues such as that of Mexican-American attitudes to public libraries, training Latinos to be librarians, information as to the cultural background of Latinos in the U.S., or the advantages of teaching "library skills" to children. Issues of access are often viewed in terms of librarians' ability to communicate with Spanish-speaking patrons, and resolved, as in the Chávez et al. (1978) publication, with a sort of "Spanish phrase book" for Anglo librarians.

Although most of the literature on library services for Latinos does not center around issues of access and availability of reading materials in Spanish, all articles seem to agree that libraries are not serving the Spanish-speaking community adequately. Haro's (1981) book on the development of library and information services for Latinos is typical of this literature. Although much of the book is dedicated to giving the background of different Latino groups in the U.S. as well as their attitudes toward libraries, he does devote one chapter to the issue of Latino children and libraries. The bulk of this chapter, however, focuses on teaching children how to use the library, emphasizing that "effective library instruction can be very important in improving the academic skills of the child of limited English-speaking ability" (p. 105). Also discussed are the intricacies of running the library, as well as book selection, in which he recommends that librarians pay careful attention to issues of bias in their selection of English–language materials for Latino children. When he arrives at the question of Spanish language materials, he does not so much discuss selection and access, but rather his views on why "Hispanic homes" do not provide literate environments. He blames Spanish–language television, asserting that "the quality of TV programming to which the Hispanic child is exposed is not the best, and may actually generate other subtle and cumulative learning impediments. One negative effect of this process is a reading deficiency in the child of Hispanic origin" (p. 115–116). Thus he appears to view the use of Spanish reading materials as compensatory or remedial, saying that they may "encourage reading and correct or diminish reading problems" (p. 116). The issues of access and availability are thus not dealt with in an analytical manner; Haro instead chooses to focus on the implications of Spanish "dialectical differences" in the remainder of the chapter.

The García–Ayvens book (1984) deals with a variety of issues pertaining to Chicanos and library service. Much of the book centers around Chicano collections (in English) in public libraries, the Chicano press, and Chicano librarianship. Two chapters touch directly upon library services to the Spanish–speaking; one is a bibliographic essay citing the (then) most recent literature in this area (Milo, 1984), and the other is a report of public "library user/non–user" surveys conducted in communities with a large proportion of Latinos and Spanish–speakers (Pisano and Skidmore, 1977; Bareño, 1977; Guareña, 1981). Results from these studies indicated that the majority of Latinos fell into the "non–user" category and that services of all types, including the addition of more Spanish and bilingual materials, needed to be upgraded. They also recommended that bilingual librarians should be employed, and community outreach programs should be initiated. Although these studies are not by any means unimportant, they seem to underscore the actual dearth of material in Spanish in the libraries. A study conducted only a few years earlier found that "if one doubled the figure for holdings reported by respondents, there would be in public libraries less than one–tenth of a book in Spanish for each Spanish speaker in the United States" (Eddison, 1972, cited in Dale, p. 29). Given the considerable growth of the Latino community in the last twenty years, it seems doubtful that this statistic has changed. No chapter in the book refers to library services for Spanish–speaking children.

Two studies that sought to examine practices and attitudes regarding library acquisition of Spanish books for children and young adults were conducted by Schon et al. (1988), and Glass and Schon (1988). In the Schon et al. (1988) study, personnel in 77 city libraries, 26 county libraries, and 317 school libraries in Arizona replied to a questionnaire probing budget, circulation, demand and attitude issues regarding Spanish books for young adults and children. More than half of the respondents reported that they do purchase books in Spanish, but 77% also said that less than 1% of their budget goes towards these purchases. Although the majority of librarians viewed the availability of these books as desirable, a surprising 40% did not believe that they served an important educational purpose (p. 25). A finding particularly relevant to the present review concerns elementary school libraries, among which 71% of librarians reported that books in Spanish were rarely used even when purchased (pp. 26–27). Thirty–eight percent of all librarians felt that books in Spanish were "too expensive," and a startling 36% felt that they were "a luxury this library can't afford" (p. 24). A similar study by Glass and Schon examined the impact of Proposition 63, the California English Language Amendment on the policies, practices and attitudes towards books in Spanish, once again for children and young adults. Two separate surveys were conducted with questionnaires being sent out to public libraries, one during August of 1986, the "pre– Proposition 63 era," and another after exactly one year had passed. No significant differences were found on any of the issues investigated. In addition, "no changes in the policies and practices of California public librarians toward books in Spanish for children and young adults were observed which were not also taking place simultaneously in the libraries of a half–dozen comparison states that had no English–only laws" (p. 422).

Literature proving more informative to this review is the area of children's literature, rather than library science. Concern for the identification of both children's and adult's literature in Spanish is not new. Schon has throughout the years provided bibliographic information as to books for children and young adults in her various journal articles (1983a, 1983b, 1984, 1985a, 1985b, 1985c, 1987, 1988a, 1988b, 1989; Restrepo et al., 1986). Typically, she references the book in question, provides a brief summary of its content, and gives it a judicious recommendation. Her emphasis is on original works written in the Spanish language; translations and textbooks are generally not included in her reviews. She states: "I have identified books for children and young adults that highlight the lifestyle, folklore, heroes, history, fiction, poetry, theater, and classical literature of Hispanic cultures as expressed by Hispanic authors" (1978, p. v). Similarly, in other publications, she emphasizes the need for children to "be exposed to attractive, well-written books that they can read for recreational, informational, or educational purposes" (p. 83, 1988a), and references "books published in Spain, Mexico, and Argentina that are likely to delight young Spanish-speaking children (*ibid.*).

Others have as well taken up the cause in identifying works of interest for young Spanish-speaking readers. Proyecto LEER was started in October of 1967 and consisted of two programs, one bibliographical and the other pertaining to screening and selection. The mission of the organization was stated as such by its founder Tomé (1968) in the first issue of its bulletin: "the plan of Proyecto LEER is to identify elementary books and other reading and instructional materials for children and adults appropriate for school and public libraries, to obtain copies from the publishers for review by expert selectors, and to compile and publish annotated lists of selected titles for library procurement" (p. 1). Identification of both Spanish and English language materials appropriate for the education of Latino children in bilingual programs was sought. Subsequent issues presented cumulative bibliographies of both titles and subjects. Criteria for selection was stated as:

> 1. Reading difficulty not to exceed the tenth grade reading level. 2. Subjects appropriate to the needs of the Spanish-American community; i.e., aiding in their cultural identification as well as in their need to adapt to their environment. 3. Writing of a high caliber. 4. Pleasing format and quality of books production. (1970)

The organization continued for several years afterwards, producing bulletins listing reading resources in Spanish. In 1973 the selection criteria were broadened to include print materials other than books; a list of comics and popular magazines for children and adults was also included (Tomé, 1973). Proyecto LEER bulletins dating through 1983 were located in the research library of one major university; a subsequent search at two other institutions did not locate issues published after this date.

Summary

The research reviewed here strongly supports the merits of extensive self-selected reading both in and out of school. Numerous studies have documented that when children read for pleasure, reading development is promoted, and the development of writing proficiency is also influenced. In addition, it has been shown that vocabulary acquisition is also heightened by engaging in free-reading, and that reading itself is undoubtedly a major source of vocabulary acquisition for children. As Krashen (1985) has stated, "the evidence strongly suggests that reading exposure may be the primary means of developing reading comprehension, writing style, and more sophisticated vocabulary and grammar" (p. 90).

However, even with "progressive" literature-based language arts frameworks such as that adopted by California in 1987, emphasis on learning to read through mastery of a hierarchical sequence of skills still predominates in our schools today. Morrow (1986) investigated the attitudes of teachers, principals and parents toward promoting voluntary reading in the elementary school by requesting that they rank four activities: word recognition instruction, comprehension instruction, study skill instruction and voluntary reading. Not surprisingly, with regard to improvement of standardized test scores, all groups ranked voluntary reading last. However, in another ranking, one of "overall importance to reading," they again ranked it last. Although they did not say voluntary reading was unimportant, all groups granted privileged status to skills training in reading development, thus demonstrating the pervasiveness of such beliefs.

Many argue that it is the entrenchment of standardized testing in our schools which skews priorities and subverts the implementation of more holistic meaning-based instruction. Criticism of standardized testing is not new, and educators and researchers have long argued that such instruments cannot adequately measure reading. Johnson (1984), in a review of reading assessments, stated, "The dynamic interactive nature of the reading process does not lend itself well to specification in terms of discrete objectives with simple criteria. Such specification has tended to decontextualize and trivialize the process" (p. 160). Yet, no matter how much we express dissatisfaction with standardized instruments, they still exert tremendous influence in our schools, and no sweeping change seems immediately on the horizon. Although many people find it objectionable as well as atheoretical that these instruments are still used, we must remember that students who participate in reading programs implementing self-selected reading as either part or all of the language arts curriculum tend to do at least as well as the "skills" students on these tests. As a point of fact, nearly all studies done on the effects of free-reading have ironically used these tests as outcome measures. That standardized testing has played an enormous role in determining the curriculum cannot be denied; but we must remember that we do not have to let it drive our instruction, and that children's reading development can be effectively promoted through engaging in the process of reading itself.

Implications

Yap (1977) stated the importance of his results with Hawaiian second graders as follows: "the second finding appears to be particularly significant in that of all the environmental variables, the amount of reading activity is probably one that is most amenable to manipulation. It is within the control of educators to increase the amount of reading activity. . . " (p. 28). It is a conclusion of strong intuitive appeal. If we conceive of reading activity as Yap does, i.e. reading real books, then it would seem obvious that providing more time to read and more reading materials in the form of books, magazines and other sources is a logical step in improving the reading abilities of children. Although this may seem the common sense answer, remediating reading problems or developing reading proficiency is usually not addressed in this way, but in the form of new programs designed to train children in either "skills" or "strategies." It is as Joshua Fishman also put it, in reference to another question but equally as applicable to this one, with every new instructional package or computer program designed to somehow improve literacy that we buy, we seem to be "overlooking the elephant at the zoo."

Access to reading materials is an issue which educators need to be concerned about. If research suggests that children read more when more reading resources abound, then educators and administrators must make sure that school is a "print-rich environment" that affords children both the resources they want and need, as well as the time to explore them both independently and interactively. This involves the building of satisfying classroom collections as well as strong, well-

stocked school libraries, where children are encouraged to both browse
and read. It also entails the reprioritizing of expenditures at the school
site. In light of the research suggesting the importance of extensive
reading, as well as that which shows that children obtain a high
percentage of their books from some sort of library, the importance of
allocating sufficient funds for the purchase of a variety of reading
materials both English and the primary language of language minority
students seems evident.

Purpose of the Study

The primary purpose of this study was to better describe and
understand the availability of free-reading materials in languages other
than English in elementary school libraries. Attention was given to
documenting the processes and chains of events that result in the actual
library collections in selected elementary and middle schools in the Los
Angeles area. School libraries were investigated to examine
implementation of district policies. Teachers, administrators, librarians,
and students were interviewed to determine attitudes towards free-
reading in the primary language and English. Secondarily, community
resources of books in non-English languages were examined in order
to determine their role in providing language minority children with
free-reading materials. Conclusions are drawn as to the effectiveness of
the school library in providing language minority children with access
to reading materials in their primary language, and whether school
libraries are in fact meeting the need.

Importance of the Study

Although much effort has been spent on bilingual education
programs and research as to their effectiveness, surprisingly little
attention has been devoted to the issue of availability of free-reading
materials in languages other than English in school and public libraries.
Schon (1983a, 1983b, 1984, 1985a, 1985b, 1985c, 1987, 1988a, 1988b,
1989) has published numerous articles recommending and commenting
on selected Spanish language publications for children and adolescents,
but literature specifically dealing with availability and access is
exceedingly scarce. Dyer and Robertson-Kozan (1983), in their article
dealing with library services for Spanish speakers, call for greater

attention to the issue of library availability, yet do not address either school district library policy or market availability of such materials. However, they do make the important point that, due to the comparative lesser availability of publications in languages other than English outside the schools, the school library takes on a more important role, as access to primary language reading material for many language minority children "may be limited to what the [school] library has on hand" (p.29).

Given the support for free–reading from the fields of literacy and psycholinguistics (Krashen, 1985, 1987, 1988; Smith, 1986, 1988; Goodman, 1986), in addition to the support for primary language literacy development in bilingual education (Cummins, 1981, 1989), the importance of providing children with access to books in their native language seems evident. Moreover, reading in the primary language may have positive effects on the reading attitudes of language minority students (Cummins, 1979; Schon, Hopkins, and Davis, 1982).

Methodology

The chosen method is a naturalistic "case study" analysis of the reading resources available to Latino children in nine elementary and middle schools in the Greater Los Angeles area. Data collection involved interviewing library aides, teachers, bilingual coordinators, administrators, and children in the schools. Furthermore, documents produced by the school districts and State of California specifically dealing with school libraries were analyzed. Finally, public libraries in the immediate vicinity of the schools were visited and their collections of children's books in Spanish were examined. Thus, data from multiple sources were collected with a view to determining the forces and policies that shape the availability of Spanish language books for children in Los Angeles school and public libraries.

Setting

Southern California is certainly one of the most culturally diverse places in the United States, if not in the world. Historically, California has always been a land of cultural diversity; however, it is currently becoming more so, largely due to immigration and the increasing popularity of Los Angeles as a "first port of entry" to the United States. The 1990 census reported that six million Californians had been born outside of the United States, nearly 20% of the population (Berman et al., 1992). Cultural diversity is easily visible both on the street and in the workplace; but nowhere is it more visible than in our classrooms. This study is situated in Greater Los Angeles, a large urban area with a population of approximately eight million. The large metropolitan school district involved in the study is one of the largest in the country; it has a student population of about 640,000 and employs over 36,000 teachers, counselors, librarians, nurses and psychologists (*Los Angeles Times*, April 5, 1992). The district has 430 elementary schools: 433,681 students in Los Angeles County are reported as limited–English–proficient; 304,444 of these are at the elementary (K–6) level (California Department of Education, 1991). The comparison districts are also in Greater Los Angeles area, but in smaller communities, one in close proximity to Los Angeles International Airport, and the other in a small seaside community. Both districts are appreciably smaller than our large metropolitan district.

Results

State and district policies were examined to determine the chain of responsibility in providing LEP students with library materials. Through an examination of the California Educational Code (1977) as well as in consultation with library services personnel in Sacramento (Haclett, S., 1992), it was found that the State provides very few guidelines for elementary library services, and none specifically dealing with LEP children. Rather, most of the decision–making power in this realm is left in the hands of the individual school districts. An examination of three districts in the study revealed that while the two smaller districts have no policy, our large metropolitan district has extensively delineated guidelines, and recommends that the number of books in non–English languages be equal in proportion to the number of children receiving reading instruction in that language (O'Brian et al., 1989). This district also provides resource guides and book lists; schools are obligated to buy their reading resources from this list and may not buy non–approved materials with funding targeted for libraries (Los Angeles County Office of Education, 1991). Table 1 shows the number of books in languages other than English which are approved for purchase by the district during the 1992–93 school year.

Table 1. Approved number of books in large metropolitan district

Language	Fiction	Non-Fiction	Total
Korean	2	17	19
Spanish	370	864	1,234
Vietnamese	1	18	19
Chinese	38	68	103

The School Library Collections

Nine school libraries were examined. Seven of these libraries were part of the large metropolitan district, which has an office of library and media services, while the others were located in the two smaller districts, which provides no such services. All schools have significant Latino populations, ranging from 30–98%, with LEP levels in the range of 35–88%. Table 2 reports enrollment of Latino and LEP children.

Table 2. School enrollment.

School	# students	Spanish L1	#Asian L1	%LEP
Loma	2,350	95%	50	80%
Estrella	1237	98%	10	82%
Alvarado	2,300	90%	217	82%
Lilly Ave.	430	30%	45	35%
86th St.	1,500	30%	––	65%
Homer	2,600	85%	200	70%
Arapaho	2,800	92%	120	70%
Harbor	375	55%	5	50%
Cedar	1,280	88%	15	69%

Library collections for the nine schools were examined. Results show that there is a limited number of Spanish books in all nine school libraries. Table 3 reports the holdings of the nine school libraries.

Table 3. School library holdings.

School	# Books	Bks English	Bks Spanish	% Spanish
Loma	5,343	4,030	1,300	24%
Estrella	4,418	3,449	969	22%
Alvarado	5,000	3,875	1,000	20%
Lilly Ave.	2,000	1,906	82	4%
86th St.				
Homer				
Arapaho				
Harbor				
Cedar				

In order to give a clearer picture of the number of books per child, and the number of Spanish language books per L1 Spanish speaker, a breakdown of these numbers was done. First, the number of books was divided by the number of children attending the school. Second, the number of books in Spanish was divided by the exact number of L1 Spanish speakers at each site. Table 4 reports the results of these calculations.

Table 4. Breakdown of books per child in the nine schools.

School	# bks per child	# Spanish bks per Spanish L1 speaker
Loma	2.3	0.6
Estrella	3.6	0.8
Alvarado	2.2	0.5
Lilly Ave.	4.7	0.6
86th St.	3.3	1.0
Homer Middle	3.9	0.04
Arapaho Middle	3.2	0.12
Harbor	25.4	5.5
Cedar	5.3	1.0

As can be noted from the table, the majority of the school library collections in the large metropolitan district, as well as Cedar's collection, do not even arrive at one Spanish language title per L1

Spanish student. Furthermore, it should be noted that this calculation is based on the entire Spanish collection, which includes reference books and encyclopedias. Harbor School in our comparison seaside district has the largest number of Spanish books per L1 Spanish speaker. However, several different factors must be considered here. First, the total number of Spanish books included in this library inventory include class sets of basals and core literature. Second, this library had the highest number of "readers" such as *Biblioteca Básica*. Last, being a "two-way" immersion school, these books are also used by L2 Spanish speakers, something unlikely to happen at any of the other schools in this study.

Patterns of Library Use

Patterns of whole-class use during school hours in the libraries are remarkably similar. In all nine libraries, teachers sign their classes up for a block of time, ranging from a half-hour to forty-five minutes. The frequency of sign-up times among teachers who regularly bring their students to the library range from once a week to once a month, with twice monthly being the most frequent. Of course, there are some teachers in each school who never bring their students to the library. Most of these teachers at the elementary level were from the upper (5-6) grades. The librarian at Arapaho Middle School reported that very few teachers bring their classes in regularly, and of those who do, most are ESL teachers. The only elementary teacher who was available for comment on this issue was a fifth-grade teacher at Estrella School, who claimed his children went to the public library, although not as a class, and that the collection in the school library was at best "uninspiring." At Arapaho Middle School the teacher who taught "LAPL," i.e. language arts in the primary language, given only to children who score at a second grade reading level on the CTBS Español, does not take the children to the library because "they do not speak English and there is nothing there for them."

The half-hour to forty-five minutes of scheduled "library time" is at all elementary schools a rather frantic scene. This is the designated period in which children are allowed to browse and check out books for free-reading. At Cedar, students are expected to assemble quietly for the first ten minutes as the instructional aide calls out the children's names, takes back their books and allows them to start browsing for new books. There is a similar procedure at the other elementary schools, although it is primarily the teacher who oversees this process. After this is completed, the room erupts into a flurry of activity, as children actively browse around the library trying to make good choices in the remaining time.

A variety of classes and grade levels were observed during their half-hour checking-out period. Spanish books were mainly checked out by the primary grade children who were in Spanish reading. As the children got older, they tended to check out fewer and fewer Spanish books. Due to the segregation of the Spanish collections at most of the schools, the activity in that section of the library was easily observable. For example, it was observed that not one child checked out or even examined any of Cedar's or Harbor's *Biblioteca Básica* books, but they clamored eagerly around the collection of newer books. It was also noticed that a class of third-grade Latino children who were in an English-only program at Loma did not check out any Spanish books, although two of them lingered in the section for a few minutes browsing and chatting to each other in Spanish. Comments such as "why don't they have any new books" were heard several times, particularly at Loma and Alvarado, the schools with the largest populations. Very few upper grades came in as a class; of those who did, few children checked out books in Spanish.

Libraries at all schools have limits on the number of books children are allowed to check out. Only two books at any one time may be checked out by an individual at any of the elementary schools. Alvarado's limit is one per child. The limit at both middle schools was three books per child every two weeks. All schools have this type of rule, although the degree of enforcement varies. At Cedar and Alvarado it is strictly enforced. The aides feel that if the children were allowed to check out as many as they wanted, the number of Spanish books available at any one time in the library would be very low, and that the tendency for children to lose books would increase. As one teacher at the school put it, "if my kids could come in here and check out as much as they wanted whenever they wanted, they'd decimate the collection within a week." Neither of the Spanish collections in these schools arrive at one book per native Spanish-speaking child, and the number of English books is not much larger. In addition, it was observed at five of seven elementary schools that when children came to the library without having returned borrowed books they were not permitted to check out any others.

At Alvarado the atmosphere about checking out books was particularly tense, and the children's activity was noticeably regimented. Children browse the bookshelves holding a ruler, which they use to mark the place where they remove a book in order to examine it. They are not allowed to walk back to their table with the book. Rather, they must stand near the shelf and look at it there, deciding if they wish to check it out. Once children have chosen their books, they go immediately to check them out and then sit quietly at their assigned seats. Many of them start reading and finish their books before the end of the allotted library time is up. When this happens they are *not* allowed to return the book and check out another. In fact, one third grade teacher was overheard strongly advising the children "not to read."

A few children in one class demonstrated *el truco* (the trick) to beating the system. They sat down at their round table and proceeded to pass their books to the right, reading their classmates' choices instead of their own, "saving" their own book for later. Of course, as they pointed out, *el truco* only works if the other children have not already read the books their classmates have checked out. Ironically, the principal at this school reported that boxes containing "hundreds of library books" are being stored because the library, which is quite large, has run out of shelf space. They had been planning to buy more shelving for three years.

At the other elementary schools, in most instances children who already had books out were still allowed to check out more. The aide at Estrella commented that she bent the rules frequently, especially if it was a child she knew well, one who was "a real regular" at the library. There were no restrictions at any school except Alvarado as to the number of books over time that a student was allowed to check out. That is to say, if the child finishes his/her two books the next day, s/he can return them and check out two more--that is, if they have the opportunity to use the library again this soon.

Public Libraries Near the Schools

An inquiry into the availability of children's books in Spanish at the public libraries nearest these schools found that resources in these facilities were also extremely limited. Table 5 reports the results of this inquiry.

Table 5. Children's books in Spanish in public libraries in the communities.

Public library	Number of children's books in Spanish	Comics and Magazines
near Loma	approx. 2500	no
near Estrella	500–700	no
near Alvarado	approx. 2500	no
near Homer	same as Alvarado	no
near Arapaho	250	no
near 86th St.	approx. 900	no
near Lilly, lib #1	225	no
near Lilly, lib #2	approx. 425	no
near Harbor	approx. 375	no
near Cedar	1390	yes
Downtown L.A.	1250	yes

Children's Reported Sources of Free-Reading Materials

The library situation, both school and public, is particularly significant when we analyze where children at these schools obtain their free-reading materials. One hundred fifty-nine children from the nine schools were interviewed regarding reading interests and sources of free-reading materials. Children were interviewed both in groups and individually. Specifically, they were asked to identify their primary source of free-reading materials. Sources of reading materials are reported in Table 6.

Table 6. Primary sources for free-reading materials.

Source	Primary source	# of Children
School library	71.70%	n = 114
Public library	18.87%	n = 30
Teachers	6.29%	n = 10
Parents	3.14%	n = 5

As can be noted from the table, the school library serves as the main source of books for the children. Children who reported the public library as their primary source for books were mainly from Cedar and Alvarado, where the public library is located in fairly close proximity to the school. In the case of Cedar, it is sometimes visited by whole classes. In addition, students who reported their teacher as the primary source are all from one class at Cedar, whose teacher was in a position to receive a large number of sample books from various publishers. Thus it can be concluded that the school library is the primary source of free-reading materials for students interviewed in the schools in the large metropolitan district, as well as for many of the students at Cedar and Harbor.

The Role of the School Library

There is a prevalent belief among school personnel that the school library exists to "support the curriculum." During "formal" visits to the school library, a lot of time was spent highlighting the encyclopedias and other reference books that the libraries had acquired. The majority of administrators and bilingual coordinators feel that books which deal with subject matter being covered in the classroom are the most important acquisitions a school library can make. Persons responsible for ordering materials said that teachers need to be able to come to the library for "back-up" to lessons they are teaching and need to be able to send children to get information for reports and other assignments, and they felt it was particularly important to have up-to-date reference books available.

There was little mention of free-reading materials, whether in English or other languages. When asked to see what they had recently ordered in Spanish, and what they felt were their important purchases, most library staff pointed with pride to recent acquisitions of encyclopedias, science books, and other reference books in Spanish.

Since the "support the curriculum" line was so strong, librarians and library aides were asked how the library supported the reading and writing curriculum of the school. Most answered that they did this by having both class sets of "core literature" as well as class sets of the most recently published basals available to teachers. One librarian responded that since the school was using a particular literature series, which only had excerpts of stories, she made sure that the library had the whole book should a child express interest in reading the entire thing. Others felt that if the library contained "good children's literature," they would be supporting the reading and writing curriculum. Only one library aide responded to this question by saying "providing kids with books they want to read outside of school."

The "support the curriculum" line was strongest among qualified library personnel. The staff person at Lilly Ave., who has a Master's Degree in library science, said that she did not want to buy any books in Korean for Korean-speaking children because these books "have nothing to do with what is being taught here, they're just story books." This same person was horrified when a child came into the library and asked if they had any Garfield comic books. She reported that this is a frequent request, but they quite obviously had no intention of acquiring such materials for the library.

Discussion

This study was limited in scope to nine specific schools in the Los Angeles area and must be viewed in this light. However, if students and resources at these schools are representative of others in Los Angeles and elsewhere, then the condition of school libraries is extremely inadequate. Results from this study indicate that language minority students in these schools are dependent on the school library for most of their reading resources. As reported, 71% of children interviewed cited the school library as their primary source of reading resources, with 91% of all children depending on some sort of library. An examination of Spanish books in the public libraries closest to these schools reveals that collections are extremely limited, in many cases even more limited than those of the schools, again underscoring the importance of the school libraries. Yet an investigation into book availability at the school libraries indicates that collections are woefully inadequate, both in Spanish and English.

The access provided Latino LEP children to free-reading materials is not consistent with articulations in the large metropolitan district that affirm that "all languages and cultures are perceived as valuable and of equal status" (O'Brian et al., 1989). Rather, the policy restrictions imposed upon the acquisition of books in languages other than English in our large metropolitan district, as well as the low priority placed on school libraries at all schools in this study, only seem to maintain existing inequalities in the education of language minority students. Even if all elementary schools in the metropolitan district had books in proportion to the number of "Spanish readers," as guidelines in this district stipulate, there is an implicit assumption that a child who is "transitioning" or "transitioned," as well as one who has been designated "fluent-English proficient," has no desire, need or right to read something interest-appropriate in her/his first language. This policy is unsound in terms of both research in bilingual education and bilingualism (see Cummins, 1989), as well as a clear case of structural inequality within our educational system. In fact, the most recent research in the area of bilingual education (Ramirez et al., 1991a, 1991b) suggests that children in late-exit programs—that is, children who spend a greater amount of time developing literacy in their native languages—perform better academically in the long term. Therefore, greater efforts to provide children with enjoyable materials in their primary language is of extreme importance to both first and second language literacy development.

It was also evident that the children have only limited access to the books in the library. Recall that for the most part they may only come in as a class, and that the activity during this time is extremely structured. The library time activity consisted of students going through the "checking in" process, rapidly selecting one or two books, and then proceeding to the "checking out" process. Most classes had from a half-hour to forty-five minutes, thus not giving students very much time at all to browse. It was not a relaxed atmosphere, but a rather rushed affair in which students tried to find something interesting to check out. Because there are limitations on the number of books the children can check out due to inadequate collection sizes, a lot of children simply checked out the books and sat there not reading them, saving them for later. The most extreme example of this was at Alvarado School, which has a student population of 2300, with 2.2 books per child and 0.5 Spanish books per Spanish speaker. At this school children were actually told not to read while in the library so that they would have something to read later on. If the children found a book and checked it out before the allotted library time was up, they simply sat at their assigned seat and table, or they exchanged books and read their classmates' selections.

This is not an atmosphere conducive to promoting reading. It has been shown that when the atmosphere is comfortable and children are given time to browse, they read more. Morrow and Weinstein (1982,

1986) found that children used the classroom library corner more when it had pillows and was comfortable, quiet, and well-stocked. Children in these studies elected to use the library corner and demonstrated a significant increase in the amount of free reading they did at school. Unfortunately, the library at the nine school sites in this study was not viewed as a place to actually read; rather, it was a cross between a resource center for teachers and a warehouse for the few free reading materials it housed. The only exception to this situation of "limited access" in the data was the library at Estrella, which has a door leading out to the school's playground and lunch area. This door provides easy access to the library and about fifty children a day come in to read and browse, which is quite different from the "library traffic" in the other schools. Thus the claim that when given access to books children read appears to be substantiated by this example.

Conclusions

Although there has been notable effort on the part of scholars such as Schon, as well as on the part of district offices to provide bibliographic references to books in languages other than English, school library holdings are far from adequate. Results of this study show that the school library holdings of Spanish reading materials are far below what even the bare minimum would warrant; the holdings of English language books are not adequate either. Furthermore, in the case of the large metropolitan district, it seems that policy restriction of only allowing book purchases from a limited predetermined list acts as a blockage to the acquisition of adequate reading resources for language minority children. That the school library possesses adequate holdings of books in the primary languages of its students is particularly crucial, as these students depend greatly on the library to provide them with free-reading materials. Eighty-nine percent of Latino students interviewed in this study (n=159) reported either the school (71.7%) or public (18.9%) library as their primary source of free-reading materials.

As has been demonstrated, sources of books in languages other than English in the community are relatively scarce, especially when compared with the out-of-school availability afforded students whose primary language is English. Not only is there an inadequate number of books at the public facilities, but books available for purchase are also few and expensive. A survey of booksellers in the Los Angeles area

(Pucci, 1990) indicated that when children's materials are available in non-English languages, prices are typically 20-200% higher than their English counterparts.

Thus school districts must seek to better understand the role of the school library and acknowledge its responsibility in the reading development of the language minority student, and make a firm commitment to providing adequate resources. In turn, this commitment must evidence itself in terms of tangible resources, as well as thoughtful policies. The importance of free-reading is abundantly supported in the literature, it is up to schools to translate this into a practice which guarantees students access to a variety of reading materials not only in English, but in their primary languages as well.

References

Anderson, R.C., P.T. Wilson, and L.G. Fielding. (1988). Growth in reading and how children spend their time outside of school. *Reading Research Quarterly,* Vol. 23, No. 3, pp. 285-303.

Applebee, A.N. (1978). Teaching high-achieving students: Survey of the winners of the 1977 NCTE achievement awards in writing. *Research in the Teaching of English,* pp. 339-348.

Applebee, A.N., and J.A. Langer. (1983). Instructional scaffolding: Reading and writing as natural language activities. *Language Arts,* Vol. 60, No. 2, pp. 168-175.

Applebee, A.N., J.A. Langer, I. Mullis, and M. Foertsch. (1990). *Learning to read in our nation's schools.* Princeton, N.J.: Educational Testing Services.

Baker, K.A., and A.A. de Kanter. (1981) Effectiveness of bilingual education: A review of the literature. U.S. Department of Education, Office of Planning, Budget, and Evaluation. Washington D.C.

Bareño, L. (1978). Survey of Spanish-speaking users and non-users. Unpublished report. San Diego, Calif.: San Diego County Library.

Berman, P., J. Chambers, P. Gandara, B. McLaughlin, C. Miniucci, B. Nelson, L. Olsen, and T. Parrish. (1992). *Meeting the challenge of language diversity: An evaluation of programs for pupils with limited proficiency in English.* Berkeley, Calif.: BW Associates.

California Department of Education. (1991). *Language census report for California public schools.* Sacramento, Calif.: Educational Demographics Unit, Program and Evaluation Research Division.

California State Department of Education. (1986). *Beyond language: social and cultural factors in schooling language minority children.* Division of Instructional Support and Bilingual and Bicultural Education. Los Angeles, Calif.: Evaluation, Dissemination, and Assessment Center, CSULA.

California State Department of Education. (1977). State Educational Code. Sacramento, Calif.: California State Department of Education.

Chavez, R., W. Clark, D. Edgmon, Y. Flores, V. Martin, S. Orozco, and E. Williams. (1978). *Quiero un libro, I want a book.* Washington, D.C.: U.S. Office of Education, Title II–College library assistance and library training and research.

Collier, V.P. (1992). A synthesis of studies examining long term language minority student data on academic achievement. *Bilingual Research Journal,* Vol. 16, Nos. 1 and 2, pp. 187–212.

Crawford, J. (1995). *Bilingual education: History, politics, theory and practice.* Trenton, N.J.: Crane Publishing Company, Inc.

Cummins, J. (1979). Linguistic interdependence and the educational development of bilingual children. *Review of Educational Research,* 49, 221–251.

Cummins, J. (1981). The role of primary language development in promoting educational success for language minority students. In California State Department of Education (Ed.), *Schooling and language minority students: a theoretical framework.* Los Angeles, Calif.: California State University.

Cummins, J. (1989). *Empowering minority students.* Sacramento, Calif.: CABE.

Durkin, D. (1979). What classroom observations reveal about reading comprehension instruction. *Reading Research Quarterly,* Vol. 14, pp. 481–533.

Dyer, E., and C. Robertson–Kozan. (1983). Hispanics in the U.S. Implications for library service. *School Library Journal,* April, pp. 27–29.

Eddison, E.B. (1972). Limited library service for Spanish–speaking Americans. Paper presented at the twelfth annual Seminar on the Acquisition of Latin American Library Materials. Los Angeles, Calif.

Evans, H., and J. Towner. (1975). Sustained silent reading: does it increase skills? *Reading Teacher,* Vol. 29, pp. 155–156.

Fader, D. (1976). *Hooked on books.* New York: Berkeley Books.

Farrell, E. (1982). SSR as the core of a junior high reading program. *Journal of Reading,* October, pp. 48–51.

Feitelson, D., and Z. Goldstein. (1986). Patterns of ownership and reading to young children in Israeli school–oriented and nonschool-oriented families. *The Reading Teacher,* Vol. 39, No. 9, pp. 924–930.

Feitelson, D., B. Kita, and Z. Goldstein. (1986). *Effects of reading series stories to first graders on their comprehension and use of language.* Haifa, Israel: University of Haifa.

Fishman, J.A. (1989). *Language and ethnicity in minority sociolinguistic perspective.* Philadelphia: Multilingual Matters.

Garcia–Ayvens, F., and R. F. Chabran. (1984). *Biblio–politica, Chicano perspectives on library service in the United States.* Berkeley, Calif.: University of California, Chicano studies library publications unit.

Glass, G.V., and I. Schon. (1988). Effects of an English–only law on public library acquisition policies, practices, and librarians' attitudes toward books in Spanish for children and young adults. *Library Science and Information Research,* Vol. 10, pp. 411–424.

Goodman, K. (1986). *What's whole in whole language?* Portsmouth, N.H.: Heinemann.

Greany, V. (1986). Parental influence on reading. *The Reading Teacher,* April, pp. 813–819.

Greany, V. (1980). Factors relating to amount and type of leisure time reading. *Reading Research Quarterly,* Vol. 15, No. 3, pp. 337–357.

Guareña, S. (1984). Library survey analysis and the Spanish–speaking in California. In Garcia–Ayvens, and R. Chabran (Eds.), *Biblio–politica, Chicano perspectives on library services in the United States.* Berkeley, Calif.: Chicano Studies Publications Units, University of California.

Gundlach, M. (1992). Personal interview. California State Department of Education. Sacramento, Calif.: Office of Library Services.

Haclett, S. (1992). Personal interview. California State Department of Education. Sacramento, Calif.: Office of Curriculum.

Haclett, S. (1992). Interview. Sacramento, Calif.: California State Department of Education, Offices of Bilingual Education.

Hafiz, F.M. and I. Tudor. (1989). Extensive reading and the development of language skills. *English Language Teaching Journal,* Vol. 43, pp. 4–11.

Haro, R.P. (1981) *Developing library and information services for Americans of Hispanic origin.* Metuchen, N.J.: Scarecrow Press.

Haro, R.P. (1970). One–man survey, how Mexican–Americans view libraries. *Wilson Library Bulletin,* March. pp. 736–742.

Healy, A. (1963). Changing children's attitudes toward reading. *Elementary English,* Vol. 40, pp. 255–257, 279.

Herman, P., R. Anderson, P.D. Pearson, and W. Nagy. (1987). Incidental acquisition of word meanings from expositions with varied text features. *Reading Research Quarterly,* Vol. 22, pp. 263–284.

Heyns, B. (1978). *Summer learning and the effects of schooling.* New York: Academic Press.

Heyns, F. (1962). The theme–a–week assumption: A report of an experiment. *English Journal,* Vol. 51, pp. 320–322.

Hopstock, P.J., B.A. Rudes, H.L. Fleischman, A. Zehler, M.F. Shaycoft, M.R. Goldsamt, J.E. Bauman, G.J. Burkheimer, and M. Ratner. (1984). *The national longitudinal evaluation of the effectiveness of services for language–minority limited–English–proficient students.* Arlington, Va.: Development Associates, Inc.

Houle, R., and C. Montmarquette. (1984). An empirical analysis of loans by school libraries. *The Alberta Journal of Educational Research,* Vol. 30, No. 2, pp. 104–114.

Huey, E.B. (1910). *The psychology and pedagogy of reading.* New York: Macmillan.

Hunt, L.C. (1967). Evaluation through teacher–pupil conferences. In Barrett, T.C., *The evaluation of children's reading achievement.* Newark, Del.: International Reading Association.

Ingram, J. (1982). *Books and reading development.* London, U.K.: Heinemann

Jenkins, J.R., M.L. Stein, and K. Wysocki. (1984). Learning vocabulary through reading. *American Educational Research Journal,* Vol. 21, No. 4, pp. 767–787.

Johnson, D. (1984). Assessment in reading. In P.D. Pearson (Ed.), *Handbook of Reading Research,* pp. 147–182, New York: Longman.

Johnson, D., and P.D. Pearson. (1975). Skills management systems: A critique. *The Reading Teacher,* Vol. 28, pp. 757–764.

Krashen, S.D. (1985). *Inquiries and insights: Second language teaching, immersion and bilingual education, literacy.* Hayward, Calif.:

Alemany Press.

Krashen, S. D. (1987). Encouraging free reading. In M. Douglass (Ed.), *Claremont reading conference 51st yearbook.* Claremont, Calif.: Claremont Graduate School.

Krashen, S.D. (1988). Do we learn to read by reading? The relationship between free reading and reading ability. In D. Tannen (Ed.), *Linguistics in context: connecting observation and understanding.* Norwood, N.J.: Ablex.

Krashen, S.D. and D. Biber. (1988). *On course: Bilingual education's success in California.* Sacramento, Calif.: CABE.

Lamme, L.L. (1976). Are reading habits and abilities related? *The Reading Teacher,* Vol. 30, pp. 21–27.

Los Angeles County Office of Education (1991). *Library books resource list, languages other than English.* Los Angeles, Calif.: LAUSD.

Los Angeles Times. (1992). Bernstein reelected to head teachers' union. Los Angeles, Calif.: Los Angeles Times, April 5.

Los Angeles Unified School District. (1991). Guidelines for elementary library media purchases using ESEA, Chapter 2 funds. Los Angeles, Calif.: LAUSD, Office of Instructional Media Library Services.

Miller, G. (1941). Vocabulary building through extensive reading. *The English Journal,* Vol. 30, pp. 664–666.

Milner, E. (1951). A study of the relationship between reading readiness in grade one and patterns of parent–child interaction. *Child Development,* Vol. 22, No. 1, pp. 95–112.

Milo, A.J. (1984). Library service to the Spanish–speaking in the United States: A selective bibliography. In Garcia–Ayvens, and Chabran, R. (Eds.), *Biblio–politica, Chicano perspectives on library services in the United States.* Berkeley, Calif.: Chicano Studies Publications Units, University of California.

Morrow, L. (1986). Attitudes of teachers, principals, and parents towards promoting voluntary reading in the elementary school. *Reading Research and Instruction,* 25, pp. 116–130.

Morrow, L. (1983). Home and school correlates of early interest in literature. *Journal of Educational Research,* Vol. 76, pp. 221–230.

Morrow, L. (1982). Relationships between literature programs, library corner designs, and children's use of literature. *Journal of Educational Research,* Vol. 75, pp. 339–344.

Morrow, L., and C. Weinstein. (1986). Encouraging voluntary reading:

The impact of a literature program on children's use of library centers. *Reading Research Quarterly,* Vol. 21, pp. 330–346.

Morrow, L., and C. Weinstein. (1982). Increasing children's use of literature through use of program and physical changes. *Elementary School Journal,* Vol. 83, pp. 131–137.

Nagy, W.E., and R.C. Anderson. (1984). How many words are there in printed school English? *Reading Research Quarterly,* Vol. 19, No. 3, pp. 304–330.

Nagy, W.E., R.C. Anderson, and P.A. Herman. (1987). Learning word meanings from context during normal reading. *American Educational Research Journal,* Vol. 24, No. 2., pp. 237–270.

Nagy, W.E., and Herman, P. A. (1985). "Incidental vs. instructional approaches to increasing reading vocabulary." in *Educational perspectives,* Vol. 23, No. 1, pp. 16–21.

Nagy, W.E., and P.A. Herman. (1987). "Breadth and depth of vocabulary knowledge: Implications for acquisition and instruction." In M.G. McKeown and M.E. Curtis (Eds.). *The nature of vocabulary acquisition.* Hillsdale, N.J.: Lawrence Erlbaum Associates.

Neuman, S.B. (1986). The home environment and fifth–grade students' leisure reading. *The Elementary School Journal.* Vol. 86, No. 3, pp. 335–343.

O'Brian, B. (1992) Interview with the Supervisor of Library Services, Los Angeles, CA., March.

O'Brian, B., N. Reich, J. Saraci, R. Wilson, J. Cohn, M. Roberston, and S. Weisman. (1989). Collection Mapping. Los Angeles, Calif.: LAUSD, Office of instructional media library services.

Olsen, R.C. 1991. *Report of the 1991 Limited English Proficient (LEP) Student Enrollment Survey.* U.S. Department of Education.

Ovando, C.J. and V.P. Collier. (1985). *Bilingual and ESL classrooms: Teaching in multicultural contexts.* New York, N.Y.: McGraw–Hill, Inc.

Patton, M.Q. (1987). *How to use qualitative methods in evaluation.* Newbury Park, Calif.: Sage.

Pfau, D.W. (1967). Effects of planned recreational reading programs. *The Reading Teacher,* Vol. 21, No. 1, pp. 34–39.

Pisano, V., and M. Skidmore. (1977). A study of library use within a Spanish–speaking community. Unpublished report. Berkeley, Calif.: Berkeley Public Libraries.

Pucci, S. (1990). Free-reading and the limited-English proficient student. Unpublished paper. Los Angeles, Calif.: USC.

Pucci, S., and S. Ulanoff. (1991). Where are the books? Unpublished paper. Los Angeles, Calif.: USC.

Ramirez, D.J., S.D. Yuen, D.R. Ramey, and D.J. Pasta. (1991a). *Final report: Longitudinal study of structured English immersion strategy, early-exit and late-exit transitional bilingual education programs for language-minority children, Volume I.* San Mateo, Calif.: Aguirre International.

Ramirez, D.J., S.D. Yuen, D.R. Ramey, and D.J. Pasta. (1991b). *Final report: Longitudinal study of structured English immersion strategy, early-exit and late-exit transitional bilingual education programs for language-minority children, Volume II.* San Mateo, Calif.: Aguirre International.

Restrepo, F. (1986). *Spanish-language books for public libraries.* Chicago, Ill.: American Library Association.

Roger, E.W., and B. Olsen. (1991). Results of a K-12 and adult ESL enrollment survey-1991. *TESOL Matters*, Vol. 1, No. 5, p. 4.

Sadoski, M.C. (1980). Ten years of uninterrupted sustained silent reading. *Reading Improvement*, Vol. 17, pp. 153-56.

Sartain, H. (1960). The Roseville experiment with individualized reading. *Reading Teacher*, Vol. 13, pp. 277-281.

Schon, I. (1983a). Books in Spanish and bilingual books for young readers: some good, some bad. *School Library Journal*, March 1983.

Schon, I. (1983b). Noteworthy books in Spanish for children and young adults from Spanish-speaking countries. *The Reading Teacher*, Vol. 37, No. 2, pp. 138-42.

Schon, I. (1984). Trends in literature in Spanish for children and adolescents: An annotated bibliography. *Hispania*, Vol. 64, No. 3, p. 422-26.

Schon, I. (1985a). Remarkable books in Spanish for young readers. *The Reading Teacher*, March. 668-670.

Schon, I. (1985b). Poetry for Spanish-speaking adolescents. *Journal of Reading*, Vol. 29, No. 3, pp. 243-45.

Schon, I. (1985c). Notable books in Spanish for children and young adults from Spanish-speaking countries. *Hispania*, Vol. 68, No. 2, pp. 418-20.

Schon, I. (1987). Referencias en Español. *Instructor*, October. pp. 88-89.

Schon, I. (1988a). Hispanic books, libros hispanicos. *Young Children,* May 1988.

Schon, I. (1988b). Recent children's books in Spanish: The best of the best. *Hispania,* Vol. 71, No. 2, pp. 418–22.

Schon, I. (1989). Recent children's books about Hispanics and recent notable books in Spanish for the very young. *Journal of Youth Services in Libraries,* Vol. 2, No. 2, pp. 157–64.

Schon, I., et al. 1988. Spanish–Language books for young readers in public libraries: National survey of practices and attitudes. *Journal of Youth Services in Libraries 1 (4):* 444–450.

Schon, I., K.D. Hopkins, and W.A. Davis. (1982). The effects of books in Spanish and free reading time on Hispanic students: Reading abilities and attitudes. *The Journal of the National Association for Bilingual Education,* 7, 13–20.

Sheldon, W., and W. Cutts. (1953). Relation of parents, home, and certain developmental characteristics to childen's reading ability. *The Elementary School Journal,* Vol. 53, pp. 517–521.

Smith, F. (1986). *Insult to intelligence: the bureaucratic invasion of our classrooms.* Portsmouth, N.H.: Heinemann.

Smith, F. (1988). *Joining the literacy club.* Portsmouth, N.H.: Heinemann.

Smith, F. (1988b). *Understanding reading: A psycholinguistic analysis of reading and learning to read.* Hillsdale, N.J.: Lawrence Erlbaum Associate.

Snow, C.E. (1990). Rationales for native language instruction: Evidence from research. In A.M. Padilla, H.H. Fairchild and C.M. Valadez (Eds.). *Bilingual education: Issues and strategies.* Newbury Park, Calif.: Sage Publications.

Swanton, S. (1984). Minds alive: What and why gifted students read for pleasure. *School Library Journal,* Vol. 30, pp. 99–102.

Tomé, M.V. (1968). Words from the editor. *Proyecto Leer Bulletin,* No. 1, p. 1.

Tomé, M.V. (1970). Words from the editor. *Proyecto Leer Bulletin,* No. 6, p. 1.

Walberg, H.J., and S. Tsai. (1983). Reading achievement and attitude productivity among 17–year olds. *Journal of Reading Behavior,* Vol. 15, No. 3, pp. 41–53.

Walberg, H.J., and S. Tsai. (1984). Reading achievement and diminishing returns to time. *Journal of Educational Psychology,* Vol.

76, No. 3, pp. 442–451.

Walberg, H.J., and S. Tsai. (1985). Correlates of reading achievement and attitude: A national assessment study. *Journal of Educational Research,* Vol. 78, pp. 159–167.

Yap, K.O. (1977). Relationships between amount of reading activity and reading achievement. *Reading World,* Vol. 17, pp. 23–29.

Yin, R.K. (1989). *Case study research: Design and method.* Newbury Park, Calif.: Sage.

Chapter 2

"I did not know you could get such things there!" Secondary ESL Students' Understanding, Use and Beliefs Concerning the School and Public Library

Rebecca Constantino

With the political climates changing in several Eastern European, Asian and Latin American countries, there has been a large increase in the number of linguistic minority students entering the nation's public schools. At the crux of school success is literacy development-- both in the native language and in English. In the last decade, the federal government launched a massive campaign to address the so-called "illiteracy" among our nation's students. Among the possible explanations for low literacy among language minority groups is that these groups have different literacy values and uses from mainstream practices evident in public schools. In response to this, researchers conducted ethnographic studies into the notions of literacy. This reinforced the idea that literacy is much more than the ability to decode letters and words in text. It is a socio-cultural activity tied to group membership (Langer, 1988). This activity originates from a social order transmitted via the home or school from generation to generation (Olsen, 1982). Common in all literacy practices, however, is the notion that children "learn to read by reading" (Smith, 1988).

Literacy, then, implies access to a wide range and abundant supply of reading materials. That is, to become literate, students need access to an array of written texts. When students have reading material easily available to them, they are more likely to engage in free voluntary reading (FVR) (Krashen, 1987). Free voluntary reading is critical because not only does it facilitate first and second language acquisition and writing ability (Constantino, 1994), but it is related to literacy development as well.

An ideal source for an extensive and varying supply of texts and other literacy tools is the library. Libraries are a means for people to have access to multiple sources of written information and stories. Furthermore, libraries can be found in classroom, school, community and public settings. However, because literacy practices and values vary among social groups and the library is a social institution, people's understanding concerning the purpose and function of libraries and their attitudes toward them may also vary in significant ways. For example, immigrant adults may not understand what types of materials are available in the public library or even who can use the library (Constantino, Tai & Fang–Lu, 1992; Constantino, 1994). Difference among or within groups does not, however, negate the universal value and benefits of the library for promoting literacy and academic achievement among different language and cultural groups.

Purpose of the Study

The purpose of this study is to examine the cultural assumptions about and knowledge of library use among secondary ESL students: (1) What meanings and functions do secondary ESL students attribute to the library? (2) What do ESL students know about how libraries work? (3) How do they find out about how libraries work? (4) For what purposes do they use the library? (5) For what purposes do family members use the library?

Review of the Literature

The Need for Reading Materials

While FVR is one aspect of developing literacy, there still remains a concern of access to texts, that is, having books and other written text to read. Elley (1992) found that "access to books is related to reading ability" (p. 42). A home and school environment that is text rich leads to more reading (Morrow, 1983; Gaver, 1963).

One rich source of diverse texts is the library, both school and public; therefore, libraries are an obvious and ideal source of texts for free voluntary reading. For the purpose of this paper a library is any place where books and other information and reading material are organized and stored for individual use, for a set period of time. There are several types of libraries: public library, school library, classroom library and community library. Libraries of all types provide access to a wide variety of sources for pleasure reading and more specific academic information. As Gaver (1963) asserted, the child who does not have access to the library lacks "a wide range of materials essential to fulfill many purposes for reading...and various types of information" (p. 105).

Library Service

Libraries are social institutions that carry social values and understandings which determine their use by the public they serve. A major assumption is that successful library users have at least some knowledge of and are in agreement with the social practices and values of the library. Knowledge and use and benefit may, then, vary among cultural and language groups. As Payne (1992) points out, ". . . cultural traditions may especially affect how well informed he or she is about the potential benefits of a library and how to use a library" (p. 38). To examine a student's learning process in isolation from cultural factors and knowledge leads to inappropriate assumptions and practices. These assumptions may lead to misunderstandings that hamper the "integration, knowledge acquisition and successful participation . . ." (Trueba, 1987, p. 13) of the linguistic minority student.

Libraries in any context are intended to provide a wide range of diverse information and materials that can be read for pleasure. In the framework of literacy development, libraries in several locales— classroom, school, community and public—have been designed to interact significantly with features that promote literacy development and L2 acquisition. For example, the number and variety of books in a school library is an indicator of the extent that schools hope to encourage children to read (Elley, 1992). Morrow (1983) found that children who had access to classroom libraries spent more time reading than those who did not have access. Moreover, the number and availability of books in school libraries "are the most important factors positively affecting the probability of loans and the number of loans made by school libraries" (Houle & Montmarquette, 1984, p. 112). Gaver (1963) also saw school library services as positively affecting the amount children read. Furthermore, in a study involving several countries, Elley (1992) found "a clear link between reading ability and the size of school libraries" (p. 66). Likewise, Lance, Wellborn and Hamilton–Pennel (1992) found a strong link between library media center expenditures and activity in terms of books checked out and reading scores.

The Narrow Audience of Public Libraries

While the overall mission of public libraries is "to provide access to all individuals and identify and eliminate barriers between people and their services" (Payne, 1988, p. 12), there is evidence that public libraries have generally served white, well educated, monolingual members of communities (White, 1985). The main purpose for public library use in this population is "recreation or personal information" (Payne, 1992, p. 33). Moreover, there is a perception among ethnic minority librarians that public and school libraries do not have the interest of language minority groups in mind when ordering materials, performing community outreach or providing access to materials (Tarin, 1988).

Of critical importance is that library use is voluntary. Thus, it is equally important to find out why some do not use it for recreation and information. Ballard (1986) found that many nonusers were either not interested in reading, did not have time to read, or had other sources for reading material (p. 131–132). However, as Payne (1992) claimed, there may be barriers to library use, especially among minority groups. Obstacles preventing library use may be categorized in two areas: service and information. Service obstacles include lack of knowledge of the library's potential and benefits, lack of knowledge about how to use the library, lack of comfort with library use, or lack of access in terms of library location (Payne, 1992). Information obstacles lie in materials that are culturally inappropriate or even nonexistent. A lack of library use may simply be a case of low English proficiency on the part of the user and a lack of guidance and support on the part of the library (Payne, 1992). Also, in terms of minority library use, there may be broader social and political barriers. In the case of Spanish speakers, for example, there may be reluctance to use the library as a result of fear or resentment toward government agencies (Payne, 1992).

To attribute the lack of library use on the part of minority groups to cultural misunderstandings or a lack of language proficiency is, in a sense, blaming the victim. There may be several reasons for a lack of library use among this group. Among them are their lack of ability or skills, their lack of understanding, or apprehension to use a government agency. However, libraries are obligated to provide a service to the community at large and therefore are obliged to include and serve all members. This means the library should take a proactive stance and role in involving minority groups.

While some researchers (Cuesta & Pearson, 1990; Hoffert, 1992) see a need for including more minority materials, they view this need in very simplistic ways, i.e., purchasing home repair books in Spanish or providing more ESL texts. Cuesta and Pearson (1990) recommend that Hispanic patrons demand that libraries offer "material that helps them to learn about American culture and society, etiquette, idioms, our legal system and how they can adjust to daily life in their new country" (p. 27). Yet, minority needs go beyond these simplistic suggestions. They need "cultural reinforcement in literature and library service" (Haro, 1970). Cultural reinforcement is broader than self-help books and English language idioms.

As Tarin (1988) asserted, there is a larger problem of the "lack of a shared culture and value system" (p. 32). She goes on further to posit that libraries essentially "do not feel comfortable with minorities or welcome them as new users" (p. 32). Haro (1970) claims that library materials represent "a Gringo middle class institution" (p. 740) in that few materials deal with the Mexican-American experience, Chicano information, Raza literature, and information by and about minority youth groups.

Haro (1970) found some cases where there was blatant discrimination on the part of the library in terms of not fulfilling orders for specifically requested Chicano publications and denying access to meeting rooms for youth groups.

Through interviews with Mexican-American adults, Haro (1970) found that his consultants had a general mistrust about the library and librarians and saw the public library "as an Anglo institution which has never cared about their needs, which does not hire their people, and which engages in disproportionate distribution of resources to satisfy first the demand of an Anglo institution" (Haro, 1981, p. 86).

Accordingly, Haro (1970) also found that quite often public libraries were quite unaware of the large minority population in the community.

Libraries in the School Context

When looking at school libraries, Haro (1970) found that Mexican-American students had limited access to information and received poor library service. Comparing predominantly Anglo school libraries with predominantly Mexican-American school libraries, Haro (1970) found that Mexican-American services "suffered from outmoded facilities, strict supervision of library use and traditional approaches to the library as a study hall and place of silence" (p. 739). Also, the use of Spanish for conducting library transactions was often discouraged.

Library understanding and use, like literacy, varies among cultural groups. It is essential, then, that librarians and educators take a primary role in encouraging and mediating library use and understanding among cultural and language groups. With cultural knowledge concerning the benefits of the library, the classroom teacher is in a pivotal role in introducing and promoting libraries. In separate empirical studies, Blazek (1975) and Young (1974) found that the classroom teacher has a strong and dominant role in determining library use or non-use. Also, Kirk (1974) recommended that all students should receive instruction in library use in the actual educational program. Like literacy, it should carry meaning and relevancy. In the case of the bilingual learner, "instruction in library and information skills with a bilingual/bicultural program" (Haro, 1981, p. 106) is necessary. Optimally, this bilingual/bicultural program is a joint project between teachers, bilingual specialists, and librarians.

Methodology

Fourteen secondary high school students were interviewed. All were in a level two (intermediate) English as a Second Language Program, though by the last interview one had moved up a level. The students were interviewed on three occasions, each lasting approximately 30 minutes. After initial icebreakers, there was a structured interview which consisted of questions pertaining to three major areas: (1) the students' understanding of the function of libraries, (2) the students' use of libraries, and (3) the students' perceptions of their parents' use of the library. Within these areas, there were questions concerning introduction to the library as well as opinions concerning library materials. The researcher put the results in a matrix model and, following the guidelines set up by Spradley (1979), clustered the responses around domains or categories. For a complete description of the subjects, see the Appendix.

Results

Home Libraries

All the students said they have a library at home. Some have as few as three books, while one has "close to 70." Those with the fewest number of books arrange them by size. Those with around 20 to 30 books arrange them by frequency of use, while those with more than 30 books seem to arrange them by category. For example, Kim, who has around 20 books, arranges them by how often she reads them, while Francesca, with close to 70 books, arranges them according to author and topic.

The School Library

Without exception, all students were introduced to the school library by a teacher or someone already familiar with the school system-- usually a friend or relative who has been in the U.S. for at least two years. Students rarely visit the school library. Tina, Vladimir, Ben, and Paulo have been there only once, for their first introduction. Among the other subjects, the most frequent visitors were Eugene and Kim, who go about once a week. The others reported going no more than once a month.

Function of the School Library

Patrick, Eugene and Kim see the school library as a source of information for school. All the other students see it as a place to meet friends or to study. No one views the library as a source of pleasure reading. "It is books just like in class, nothing that is too good for me," said Pablo. However, most students view the library as a place to go for some sort of punishment. Francesca said the sentiments of many when she noted, "it's like we go there when the teacher has nothing else for us to do or she feels like being mad at us."

Materials in the School Library

While Patrick and Kim find "pretty much all I need for a homework job," to quote Kim, the other students are not familiar with the type of information available in the school library. "I guess I don't know about it because it is just like school stuff so I don't know," said Pedro. With the exception of Patrick, who is familiar with *Newsweek* magazine, the subjects stated that they were not familiar with newspapers or magazines at the school library. "Hey, they have magazines and other stuff there? I did not know about that!," said Pablo in surprise when asked about his feelings toward the periodicals in the school library.

The Public Library

A few students never use the public library. Their reasons were similar in that they all felt they "don't really know about it," as Ben said or they "don't need it," as Antoni responded. Those who do use the public library were introduced to it in a similar manner and have very similar notions concerning the function of the library. All students see the library as "a quiet place to have a desk and study," as Pedro said. They have very limited perception as to what resources and materials they can get from the library. Furthermore, there is a common thread revealed through the interviews concerning the social notions students hold regarding the public library. All the subjects view the library as a social institution that reflects the American culture. For some, this reflection is seen in a strong desire to learn English while for others it is seen as if they were a voiceless immigrant about whom the library has little concern. Without exception, the students hold strong convictions and viewpoints concerning their parents' use of the public library.

Introduction to the Public Library

Vladimir, whose mother was a librarian in Armenia, noticed the library on the way home from school. Perhaps because of his familiarity with libraries, Vladimir went alone to obtain and later use a library card. The remaining subjects were introduced to the library by someone very familiar with American culture. In the case of Maria, Kim and Rosa, a second-generation relative introduced them to the library. The others were introduced to the library by friends who were born in the U.S. No one learned about the public library from a flyer, radio ad, newspaper, or any other type of library outreach. Moreover, no one reported learning anything about the public library from a teacher.

Function of the Public Library

The students see the public library as having three main purposes: (1) a place to study, (2) as source of information to help them complete homework assignments, and (3) a source of materials to help them improve their English skills.

The Public Library as a Study Setting

Although Francesca reported using the typewriters in the library to practice typing, the students see the library as having no other use except as a study site. Eduardo's words reflected the opinion of most of the students: "The library is for the education. If you go there, you can study a lot. It's quiet so you can memorize many things like spelling and vocabulary. If you don't know anything, they have the dictionaries." The students who frequent the library do so at least once a month and as often as three times a week. Those who frequent it at least weekly reported that they did not have a desk or a quiet place to study at home. For example, Francesca expressed that, "a lot of times there are many people at my house and very much noise and I have no place to study. This is when I go to the library."

The Public Library as a Source of Information

The students have a very common impression as to the type of information available to them. All rely on dictionaries and encyclopedias. Few realize that available information for them far exceeds these two sources. As Ben said, "I don't know about too much more than the dictionaries. I guess I never tried to look." Occasionally, Kim, Maria, Rosa and Pablo use or check out books that will help with a homework project. "Sometimes, I will need an extra book and I may get it from the public library. I try not to because I don't know too much. I most usually use what I get from school or borrow from my teacher," said Rosa.

Vladimir is an exception in that he habitually checks out information type books from the public library. He chooses books that deal with science, coin collecting and Armenian history. The fact that his mother is a former librarian could be significant.

The Public Library as a Source of Information to Improve English Skills

A large portion of the students perceive the library as a valuable source of material to improve their English proficiency. Patrick asserted, "I left my country so I need to learn English. I can get grammar and spelling books to practice it." The students see the English dictionary as a key accessible tool essential to improving their English. "The dictionary at the library is very helpful. It gives me lots of words I need and they are important to learning English," asserted Maria.

The Public Library as a Source of Pleasure Reading

The students do not see the library as a source of pleasure or free voluntary reading materials. Though all engage in what they would call pleasure reading, only Pablo was aware that the public library is a source for it. The students get free voluntary reading materials from their teacher, borrow them from friends or siblings, or purchase them from a local bookstore. When asked if they were aware of the variety of pleasure reading sources such as magazines and novels available to them, the students expressed that they "did not know you could get such things there," to quote Pong. For instance, Pedro enjoys reading several magazines such as *Life* and *Reader's Digest,* yet he has never searched for these at the public library, because he "did not know you could get magazines and stuff like that at the library." Francesca, who devours French fashion and social magazines, was completely unaware and shocked to find out she could read them at her local library. She was also pleased to be told that she can get many French novels from the library. Similarly, Vahan, who hopes to be a race car driver, was thrilled to find out that the library probably has a variety of car and racing magazines. When asked about obtaining free reading books at the public library, Kim responded, "...that is not what it is there for. I wish I could get free Korean books." Moreover, of the several students who read comic books, not one was informed of the fact that they can often find comic books at the public library. Summing up many students' surprise, Pong said, "wow, that's America--even my comic books for me for free!"

Parents' Use of the Public Library

None of the students reported that their parents use the public library for any purpose. While some asserted that their parents did not have time, all stated that their parents had no use for the library. In fact some found the idea, "a bit strange," to quote Antoni, while others found it "ridiculous," as did Vladimir. The students proposed two major reasons for lack of library use among parents: (1) no need for the library because parents are not studying and (2) lack of English language proficiency on the part of the parents.

The students believe their parents do not need to use the library because, "they aren't in school and so have no homework and stuff so they don't need the library," as Vahan said. Pong suggested that his parents don't use the library because "it is for studying and my parents don't study!" Antoni found the notion of his parents using the library "funny, because they are all finished with school."

When probed as to whether parents may simply want to use the library for pleasure reading books or information, the students presented some intriguing responses. Without exception, the students see their parents lack of English language proficiency as a deterrent for library use. All believe, as Francesca said, "later they might use the library" but that will not occur until "they can speak English good enough." Even the students who maintain that the library has an obligation to provide non-English language materials see a need on the part of their parents to speak English before patronizing the public library. "Well, my parents, they don't speak English that good so they do not need the library. Maybe when their English gets ok, they will want to use it," said Rosa. Eduardo's mother visited the library once with a neighbor, and he reported, "she wants to go again because when she went she liked it, but, you know, her English is not so good so she will go after she learns more." Even Vladimir's mother, who was a librarian in Armenia, does not frequent the public library. Though he relies on the library as a source of Armenian books, Vladimir proposes that his mother "needs to study English at home so she will feel comfortable, then I will take her."

Language Use at the Public Library

Kim feels at ease speaking Korean in the library and she is unique in her sentiments. Of the remaining students who use the library, not one feels comfortable speaking a language other than English. All expressed feelings of "uncomfortableness and uneasiness." Maria went so far as to say she "felt like someone was watching and not happy," when she spoke Spanish.

Discussion

An analysis of the interview responses revealed two major domains concerning the students' understanding of library use. The first domain has to do with their perceptions of the purpose of the library. The second domain deals with the broader social implications of the role of particular languages and library materials. In addition, the results of the study suggest several culturally based explanations for variable library use.

Social Implications

Language

The broad category of language has several notions: (1) the importance of English language proficiency, (2) English language proficiency as a prerequisite for library use, (3) the role of English in library use, and (4) the value of and role of the native language.

From the interviews some interesting perceptions arose concerning the importance and role of English language proficiency. For varying reasons, but, without exception, all the students want to obtain a high level of English proficiency. English is seen as the segue into success, whether it be as a race car driver or computer operator. English language proficiency is clearly tied with success, yet also, duty. The students see proficiency in English as an obligation for living in the U.S. Several students made a connection between English and "what should be done" in the U.S.

All the students see the English language as having a strong role in library use. This is seen in their assertions that their parents cannot use the library until at least some level of English language proficiency is attained. Clearly, the students see their parents' English language proficiency as a prerequisite to library use. The students are failing to see the connection of the materials and experiences at the library as a means to English language proficiency. Library use, then, is not seen as a means to English language proficiency but almost as an end product of it. Also, with the exception of one student, the students speak English rather than a native language at the library.

Some of the students are interested in maintaining native language proficiency; yet, they see English proficiency as the first and foremost goal. English is seen as a means to social and academic success and the fulfillment of an obligation while native language proficiency seems to act as a gatekeeper to personal goals and ambitions as well as to ethnic solidarity.

Materials at the Library

The students differ in their opinions as to whether non–English materials should be available at the library. Their opinions about this idea hold powerful social implications concerning the homage paid to the English language and to the place some students see themselves holding in society.

A sense of loyalty to English is reaffirmed in the fact that only a few students see the library as a setting where non–English materials should be available to the general public. Even those who would like to have access to more non–English materials in general appeared uncertain as to whether the library is an appropriate source for those materials. Because the library is an institution of the American culture and society, non–English materials may be unsuitable there as many of the students seem to regard learning and using the English language as a symbolic pledge of allegiance to their new life in the U.S..

Those who see the library in the capacity of a source of non–English materials do not hold much faith in their ability to ask for, let alone insist on, diverse materials. It is apparent that the students do not see their voice with respect to the library as being acknowledged or heard by the general English–speaking society. They perceive themselves as being judged by the language they speak and the clothes they wear. Even though these students have not been in the U.S. for an extended period of time, they have clear perspectives about their ability to be acknowledged and heard. Their desire to have non–mainstream materials in the library and their ensuing opinons as to whether this will come about elucidates and illustrates where they see themselves and their voices in society. In short, they perceive themselves as powerless and voiceless and may even believe that this is how it should be for them.

Social and Cultural Implications

All students were introduced in one form or another to the school library by a teacher. Vladimir found the public library on his own. All other students were virtually unfamiliar with the library system. If they knew something about it, they were introduced to the public library by someone well entrenched in American culture. An introduction by someone established in the society rather than a teacher or the library shows a strong need for quality outreach on the part of public libraries. This unfamiliarity with the library system leads to some inaccurate perceptions on the part of the students concerning the function and possible benefits of the library. These inaccurate perceptions further point out the need for the library to clearly define and establish its role and resulting benefits of the library--both school and public.

Conclusion

It is quite apparent that the ESL high school students interviewed do not fully comprehend the value of the library in achieving many objectives. Also, the students clarified the importance of the English language in American society while also presenting feelings of disempowerment and voicelessness.

References

Ballard, T. (1986). *The Failure of Research Sharing in Public Libraries and Alternative Strategies for Service.* Chicago: American Library Association.

Blazek, R. (1975). *Influencing Students Toward Media Center Use.* Chicago: American Library Association.

Clifford, G. (1984). Buch und lesen: Historical perspectives on literacy and schooling. *Review of Educational Research, 54(4),* 472–501.

Constantino, R. (1994). Pleasure reading helps, even if readers don't believe it. *Journal of Reading, 37,* 504–505.

Constantino, R., Y. Tai, & G. Fang-Lu. (1992). Minority use of the

library. *California Association of Bilingual Education Newsletter,*
15(3), 6.

Cuesta, Y., & J. Pearson. (1990). From survival to sophistication:
Hispanic needs equal library needs and sources of Spanish language
materials. *Library Journal, 115(9),* 26–33.

Elley, W. (1991). Acquiring literacy in a second language: The
effect of book based programs. *Language Learning, 41,* 375–411.

Elley, W. (1992). *How in the world do students read?* Hamburg:
The International Association for the Evaluation of Educational
Achievement.

Elley, W. & F. Mangubhai. (1983) The impact of reading on
second language learning. *Reading Research Quarterly, 19,* 53–67.

Gaver, M. (1963). *Effectiveness of centralized library service in*
elementary schools. New Brunswick, N.J.: Rutgers University Press.

Goodman, K., Y. Goodman, & B. Flores. (1979). *Reading in the*
bilingual classroom: Literacy and biliteracy. Rosslyn. Va.: National
Clearinghouse for Bilingual Education.

Goodman, K. (1982). In F. Gollasch (Ed.). *Language and literacy:*
The selected writings of Kenneth S. Goodman. London: Routledge.

Haro, R. P. (1981). *Developing library and information services for*
Americans of Hispanic origin. Metuchen, N.J.: Scarecrow Press.

Haro, R. P. (1970). One-man survey, how Mexican Americans view
libraries. *Wilson Library Bulletin.* March, pp. 736–742.

Haro, R., & E. Smith. (1978). Si se puede! Yes it can be done.
Wilson Library Bulletin. November, pp. 228–231.

Heath, S. (1983) *Ways with words.* New York: Cambridge University
Press.

Heath, S. (1980). What no bedtime story means: Narrative skills
at home and school. *Language and Society. 16(3),* 162–184.

Hoffert, B. (1992). Se lea español aqui! [Spanish is read here!]. *Library*
Journal, 117(12), 34–37.

Houle, R., & C. Montmarquette. (1984) An empirical analysis
of loans by school libraries. *The Alberta Journal of Educational*
Research, 30, 104–120.

Kirk, T. (1974). Problems in library instruction in four year
colleges. In J. Lubans (Ed.), *Educating the Library User,* 83–103.
New York: R.R. Bowker.

Krashen, S. (1987) Encouraging free reading. In M. Douglas,
Claremont Reading Conference, 51 yearbook.

Krashen, S. (1993) *The Power of Reading.* Englewood, Colo.:

Libraries Unlimited.

Lance, K., L. Wellborn, & C. Hamilton–Pennel (1992). The Impact of School Library Media Centers on Academic Achievement. Denver, Colo.: Office of Educational Research and Improvement Library Programs.

Langer, J. (1988). Language and culture in theory and practice. *Research in the teaching of English, 22(4)*, 349–351.

Morrow, L. (1983). Home and school correlates of early interest in literature. *Journal of Educate Research, 76*, 221–230.

Nash, T., & R. Yuan. (1992/93). Extensive reading for learning and enjoyment. *TESOL Journal, 2*, 27–31.

Olsen, D. (1987). Se! Jumping! Some oral antecedents of literacy. In H. Goelman, A. Oberg, & F. Smith (Eds.). *Awakening to literacy*, 185–192. Portsmouth, N.H.: Heinemann.

Payne, J. (1992) *Public Libraries Face California's Ethnic and Racial Diversity*. Santa Monica, Calif.: Rand.

Schieffelin, B., & M. Cochran–Smith. (1984). Learning culturally: Literacy before schooling. In H. Goelman, A. Oberg & F. Smith (Eds.), *Awakening to literacy*, 3–23. Portsmouth: Heinemann.

Smith, F. (1988). *Understanding Reading*. Hillsdale, N.J.: Lawrence Erlbaum Associates.

Smith, F. (1988b). *Joining the Literacy Club*. Portsmouth: Heinemann.

Southgate, V., H. Arnold, & S. Johnson. (1981). *Extending beginning reading*. London: Heinemann Educational Books.

Spradley, J. (1978). *The Ethnographic Interview*. New York: Holt, Rinehart & Winston.

Spradley, J. (1979). *The Ethnographic Interview*. London: Heinemann.

Tarin, P. (1988). Rand misses the point: A minority report. *Library Journal, 113(18)*, 31–38.

Trueba, H. (1987). *Success of failure? Learning and the language minority student*. New York: Harper & Row.

White, H. (1985). The use and misuse of library user studies. *Library Journal, 110* (20), pp. 70–71.

Young, A. (1974). Research on library–user education: A review Essay. In J. Lubans (Ed.), *Educating the Library User*. New York: R.R. Bowker.

Zweizig, D., & B. Dervin. (1977). Public library use, users, uses: Advances in knowledge of the characteristics and needs of adult clientele of American public libraries in advances in librarianship. In M. Voigt & M. Harris (Eds.). *Advances in Librarianship*. New York: Academic Press.

Chapter 3

Urban Libraries Confront Linguistic Minorities: Programs that Work

Stephanie Asch

In these days of spending cuts and dramatic demographic changes in our communities, librarians cannot be content to mind their own business quietly in their sanctuaries of books; they must be community activists. The quality that defines successful library programs that target linguistic minorities is librarians who persistently seek new ways to serve their communities' needs and thereby make their libraries central to their communities rather than peripheral.

While different librarians create diverse programs each suited to their own communities, there are some characteristics successful library programs share.

Grants

Many innovative programs are made possible through grant money. Olivier, Belvin and Manoogian (1994) found in their survey on library services to multicultural populations that many libraries that serve linguistic minority and immigrant communities cannot afford to pay for extended services or special programming. They can just cover basic operational costs. Indeed, many libraries in affluent areas are confronting budget cuts that limit their ability to stay open, much less develop special programs that target linguistic minorities. Those librarians and library administrators who have developed successful programs have all found it necessary to actively and persistently seek grants. Lien Dao, a San Diego librarian who adminstrates a program serving Southeast Asian patrons, says, "We just live on grants."

Bonds to the Community

Libraries play different roles to different demographic groups (D'Elia, Rodger, 1994) and it is important for librarians to identify their patrons' needs and understand how they can best be served. Librarians who create successful programs targeting linguistic minorities are committed to involving their constituents in the development process from its inception. Indeed, Olivier, Belvin and Manoogian (1994) observed that approximately half of the libraries responding to their survey found the use of focus groups the most effective way to learn of community needs and trends. Most of the libraries profiled in this chapter rely heavily on focus groups, surveys, interviews and liaisons to community organizations to properly assess the needs of their patrons. They thus are able to indentify the kinds of materials and programming their communities want. Importantly, through this ongoing dialogue between library and community, the library staff develops more awareness and sensitivity to the specific culture of the community.

This is not all that successful libraries do, however. Most of the libraries profiled here seek to be a visible presence in the communities they serve. For example, they operate information booths at cultural events, such as Cinco de Mayo or Tet celebrations. Some even become the focal point of such community events by hosting them. The rationale for their involvement is to increase awareness of the library and become an integral part of the life of the community.

Librarians have found that minority communities form an important support network for the library if they perceive that it is serving them well. Sylvia Galan Garcia, former senior librarian of the Echo Park Branch of the Los Angeles Public Library, said that, because of the program targeting Latinos and the relationships with the community she was able to develop through a Partnerships for Change grant, the community stands firmly behind the branch whenever the city council threatens it with speding cuts and closures. "Keeping in touch with our coalition partners and maintaining programs for the community has kept us afloat," she says.

Outreach

Successful library users are knowledgeable about its functions and benefits and also in agreement with its values (Constantino, 1994). Payne (1988) found that there are many barriers to successful use of libraries among minority individuals. One of these barriers is lack of knowledge of the services the library provides. Many of the minority communities that libraries try to target are from countries where there is no public library tradition. The concept of a social institution that is free and based on trust between the community supporting it and individual patrons is new to them. They are often more accustomed to regarding public agencies warily, because they were oppressive in their native countries (Constantino, 1994). Therefore, outreach efforts that educate and inform them about the library and how it works are absolutely critical to successful programming.

Librarians who administer successful programs seek out as many venues for publicity and education as they can. For instance, they regularly do presentations at K–12 and adult schools in their communities. They advertise and publish articles in the communities' local native language newspapers, as they are more receptive to publicizing library programs than big city newspapers. They also do advertisements and press releases on minority communities' native language radio and television stations.

Public relations campaigns extend to bilingual posters and fliers distributed around the community and giveaways such as bookmarks and calendars that list special events at the library.

Bilingual, Bicultural Librarians and Staff

Researchers examining library services to Mexican–Americans in the 1960s and 1970s found that a key barrier to this population's use of libraries was linguistic and cultural. Haro (1970) interviewed a number of Mexican–Americans who lived close to libraries but rarely visited them. Eighty–nine percent of those he interviewed said they would use libraries if Spanish were spoken there and if Spanish language materials, espcially those dealing with Hispanic and Mexican culture, were available. Fernandez (1973) found that many outreach programs targeting Latinos were ineffective because of the lack of well-trained, experienced bilingual and bicultural librarians.

Currently, libraries that lead the way in effective programming for linguistic minorities employ bilingual, bicultural librarians and staff. According to Sylvia Galan Garcia, the former senior librarian at the Echo Park library in Los Angleles, bilingual, bicultural staff made all the difference in her program which targeted the Latino community. "If bilingual, bicultural staff is present," she says, "people feel more comfortable asking questions." This comment is echoed by librarians who administer successful programs. People using a public library for the first time need to have its practices, such as borrowing and late fines, explained to them in their own language so they understand them fully. Galan Garcia says that if they do not, they will feel threatened and reluctant to come back.

Bilingual and bicultural staff make the patrons feel comfortable once they are in the library, but significantly, they also provide the link from the library to the community. They go to the schools and present bilingual educational programs about the library, effectively communicate with their constituents' native language media, and they produce bilingual announcements of events and programs for the patrons. They are also in an incomparably better position to make native language and cultural material selections for their communities than monolinguals.

Equally important as these above factors is what bilingual, bicultural staff reflect about the role of the library in the community. Patrons see the library staff as members of their own communities, and thus the library itself as an integral part of the community rather than an intruder from a different society.

Culturally Responsive Environments

Successful library programs targeting linguistic minorities are extremely user-friendly. Bilingual signage helps patrons find the materials they need and bilingual written instructions help them use library equipment, such as computerized cataloging systems. The libraries also provide bilingual library card applications, the essential first step in becoming a library user.

Profiles of Successful and Innovative Library Programs

San Antonio Public Library

Generally, Spanish language materials have been listed under English subject headings. This naturally makes it difficult, if not impossible for many Spanish–speaking patrons to use the library successfully. This has been the case in San Antonio, Texas, where 56% of the population is Latino. In the winter of 1996, however, the San Antonio Public Library will be the first in the nation to inaugurate a Spanish–language catalogue system. The entire collection in both English and Spanish, spread over the Central Library and eighteen branches, will thus be more accessible to the Spanish–speaking population.

"The Spanish–speaking population is underserved," says Linda Payne–Button, coordinator of services for the San Antonio Spanish–speaking population. "We hope to reverse this trend with a commitment to integrating services, materials and programs in the Library's operations." The creation of the new catalogue is just one aspect of this greater commitment to the Spanish–speaking population. Some of the changes are evident in two newly–created positions in the system––Payne-Button's and that of the new Spanish language cataloguer who will create access and proper descriptions of materials in Spanish. It will be a a public access catalogue, just like the current English language one, which will make the library collection more readily available to schools and private individuals. The screen will feature instructions in Spanish about how to use the catalogue in addition to the Spanish headings and descriptions.

The San Antonio Public Library Foundation, the fundraising arm of the system, raised the money to develop the new catalogue. Other improvements in services to the Spanish–speaking population in the city are also made possible through grants. For instance, in 1993 and 1994 the library was the recipient of a $96,800 grant from the Library Services and Construction Act, which was earmarked to enhance the Spanish language collection. According to Payne–Button, circulation doubled after the library received this grant.

The library has also developed several innovative programs for the Latino population to complement the growth of the Spanish collection. One program, Lea Por Vida (Read for Life), is jointly administered by a local health clinic, the WIC (Women, Infants and Children) program, and the Las Palmas branch. It combines health education with an introduction to library services. When the program starts in September 1995, doctors and nurses at a clinic in a Latino neighborhood will give patients a "reading prescription"--a packet of materials that addresses their specific health concerns and directs them to the library to gather further information. Included in the packet of materials is a library card application in Spanish, which will give program participants access to the enhanced collection of health-related materials that can be checked out at the branch.

Other programs feature Latino writers running workshops for adults and youth. In August 1995, for instance, the library hosted a two-day seminar for teenagers on how to use their Latino heritage as a means of creative expression.

Another grant supports a new program at the Cortez branch called "Born to Read." Serving a poor neighborhood, its purpose is to teach mothers how to read to their children and why this practice is important.

Outreach efforts take the library out of its typical scope. Programs are advertised in Spanish-language media, but more importantly, many of the workshops take place in community centers rather than in the library itself. "We're trying to do outreach for people, instead of making them come to us," says Payne-Button.

California Libraries

Olivier, Belvin and Manoogian (1994) found that library systems that had full-time positions dealing exclusively with multicultural services were exceptional. Only one third of the 231 libraries responding to their survey had one or more staff positions responsible for serving minority communities. They also found that one quarter of 78 responding librarians said that libraries they admired for their multicultural services were in California. California's success is largely due to the Partnerships for Change (PFC) program, which is funded by the California State Library in Sacramento. The PFC authorizes grant recipients to target specific communities that have been traditionally neglected by libraries. As a prerequisite for the grant, the libraries must conduct needs analyses of their target communities. They then must develop coalitions with community organizations, which create focus groups, introduce libraries to community public relations and media outlets, and inform them of cultural sensitivities and community needs. The PFC ideal is that when the grants end, the programs the libraries develop will be fully integrated into routine library services. The following profiles feature PFC recipients.

Echo Park Branch, Los Angeles Public Library

The Echo Park Branch of the Los Angeles Public Library is a small, rectangular building located in a major entry community for Latin American immigrants. Serving a population that generally did not experience public libraries in their native countries, the branch had a need to educate it about their uses, purposes and practices.

With a three-year grant from Partnerships for Change, the branch launched *Biblioteca Para Todos* ("Library for Everyone"). The ideal of the program was to involve those people who had been neglected in the past by assessing and responding to their needs, improving the Spanish and ESL collections, and administrating major outreach and educational campaigns.

The results are dramatic. From the program's inception in 1989 until the end of the grant period in 1992, there had been a 78% increase in materials circulation, a 65% increase in the number of library card holders, and a 300-400% increase in in-house branch use. Surveys conducted from 1990 to 1992 indicated that the new Spanish-speaking patrons had become habitual library users.

These figures represent major changes that took place internally, within the library, and externally, in its approach to the community. Sylvia Galan Garcia, senior librarian at Echo Park at the time of the grant, says, "We touched at least the basic needs of the community because we asked." From the community needs assessment, library personnel learned that one of the primary concerns community members had was to learn English. The branch thus initiated an ESL computer center, with two Macintosh computers acquired through PFC funds. Approximately 3,900 people attended the center from the time it was opened in 1990 until 1992. It complemented a Los Angeles Public

Library program that was already in place at the branch before the grant, the Library Adult Reading Project, through which people receive individualized ESL lessons and literacy tutoring.

Changes within the library were also made in Spanish language services. Two full-time bilingual librarians, including a children's librarian, were able to develop a culturally responsive environment. They extended the Spanish book, video, and periodical collection, and created bilingual signage. They also produced bilingual library literature, such as schedules and announcements of special events. One corner of the library was set aside as Rincon Comunitario (Community Corner) which features comfortable seating, ESL and citizenship materials, a copy machine, consumer and literacy materials, and a bulletin board with current announcements. An intensive Spanish course was given to non-Spanish speaking staff so that they could contribute to the creation of this culturally responsive environment.

As part of its more activist approach towards the community, the branch formed coalitions with local elementary schools, Head Start and WIC programs, and local organizations such as the Echo Park Coordinating Council, El Centro Del Pueblo, and the Central City Action Committee, a youth group. Relationships with these groups have lasted beyond the grant period. For instance, the branch is still working with Head Start for joint programming, and the Central City Action Committee helps with graffiti clean-up at the library.

Outreach efforts during the grant included regular visits to elementary and adult schools, where librarians blanketed the schools with fliers and gave bilingual presentations about the library. These visits were critical, as many in the community had believed they would have to be citizens to use the library. This misconception was a major barrier to usage among adults. The outreach presentations, which reached approximately 4,200 people enrolled in adult schools, began to break it down. Teaching about social practices of the library was another important component of the presentations. Many immigrants did not understand that library services are free. Galan Garcia says that many asked how much it cost to rent materials or referred to the library as *libreria*--Spanish for bookstore. People needed to be taught the practices of loaning and returning books. Galan Garcia said that non-understanding of these practices led to loss of books, but the Spanish-speaking staff reminding new patrons in Spanish of the need to return books helped to turn this problem around.

To advertise the program, the library hung colorful banners with the message *Visitanos* (Come visit us) from street lamp poles at major intersections of the community and on both sides of the 101 Freeway that passes nearby the library. They also posted bus bench ads and distributed promotional materials, such as posters, fliers and bookmarks.

The *Biblioteca Para Todos* program still remains intact several years after the PFC grant ended, but the branch can no longer afford to maintain the same levels of outreach and publicity. It remains committed to developing its entire collection, but with only $35,000 in its yearly budget to buy new materials, it must struggle to strike a balance among community members' desires for Spanish, English, and ESL materials. The branch has been able to maintain some of its more successful programming, such as the bilingual "Grandparents and Kids" story hour, in which senior citizens from the community volunteer to read stories to children. The computer center is still intact and is even growing; the Whitecap Foundation has donated three more computers, software, and funds to employ a bilingual assistant to teach learners. The Centro Latino de Educacion Popular (CLEP) has donated five computers in return for use of office space in the library.

Through grants, the branch can also initiate new programming. One such program, funded by the California Arts Council, is a Spanish-language writing workshop for adults. The library hosts an artist-in-residence, a poet and writer originally from El Salvador, who leads the workshop, and he and the students publish the work they create.

Since the branch can no longer afford such extensive collection development or outreach, there has been a decrease in circulation. Still, the *Biblioteca Para Todos* program transformed the library and continues to impact the current efforts of the staff. Ivan Corpeno Cortez, children's librarian and acting senior librarian, says, "We don't see [what we do] as extraordinary. We are just trying to extend library services to the Hispanic population, and this is how it should be."

Logan Heights and Linda Vista Branches, San Diego Public Library, two branches of the San Diego Public Library were Partnerships for Change recipients from 1989 to 1992. The model they created was so successful that it is now being implemented in other branches of the system to serve more sectors of the population. The first two programs, housed at the Logan Heights and Linda Vista branches, targeted the Latino and Southeast Asian communities respectively.

Logan Heights Branch

The Logan Heights Branch is situated in a large Latino community in San Diego. Bilingual, bicultural community members, including the librarian, staff it. The PFC grant money allowed the branch to expand its Spanish language collection, in addition to its ESL and citizenship–related materials. As with all PFC recipients, the branch did an initial needs assessment, but it recommends ongoing needs assessments to keep up with and respond to changes in the community.

To increase awareness of the library among community members, the branch launched a multi–pronged publicity campaign. They advertised in local Spanish–language media, finding them more effective than large English–language sources such as the *San Diego Tribune*. The branch published an in–house bilingual newsletter, bookmarks, fliers, and brochures. It also made available bilingual information sheets on how to get a library card and how to use other library services. These materials were distributed throughout the community. Library personnel also did school presentations to introduce students to the library and teach them about library practices, such as the importance of returning books.

One innovative publicity technique the branch initiated was a video. Library personnel produced and acted in a Spanish–language video called "Heroes," which introduced Latinos to the library. The staff first presented the video at PTA and community group meetings locally, but now the video is distributed nationally.

The branch also developed programming to draw in the community. For instance, it runs bilingual storytelling sessions and a literacy program. The branch also tries to be part of the community's cultural life by participating in Cinco de Mayo celebrations and inviting Latino performing groups to present at the branch.

The expansion of material collections reflecting community needs and the outreach efforts led to increased program attendence and circulation. Indeed, circulation increased up to 40% during the PFC grant period.

Linda Vista Branch

The Linda Vista branch received a PFC grant to develop its services for Southeast Asian communities living in the surrounding area. The largest population among these is the Vietnamese, but there are also populations of Hmong and Lao. With the onset of the grant, the branch hired Lien Dao, a Vietnamese immigrant, to assist in developing the program targeting the Vietnamese community; Chou Fang, a Hmong born in Laos to help serve the Hmong; and his brother Charles Fang to serve the Laotian community. Charles Fang has since left the branch, but Chou Fang has taken over his responsibilities.

The staff expanded the Southeast Asian languages and ESL material from the beginning of the grant, but they circulated so well that they constantly needed to expand and upgrade the collection. The patrons have a need for both native language and English materials. According to Dao, parents encourage their children to read in their native languages so that family members can communicate and understand each other as the children grow and become more English–proficient. Therefore, the library makes available native language children's books and bilingual story hours. For adults, the library provides native language books, periodicals, videos and books–on–tape. Community volunteers service several of its English–oriented programs, such as ESL and literacy tutoring. Students from a local university give college orientations and advice.

As Southeast Asian immigrants themselves, Dao and Fang are in a strong position to make informed selections of materials, assess community needs and act as liaisons between the library and their respective communities. Dao regularly consults with the Vietnamese Federation, which advises her about community needs and trends. She then selects materials from Vietnamese bookstores and catalogues. Likewise, Fang consults with the Lao Family Community Center.

In the first two years of the grant, the branch mounted publicity campaigns in the local native–language newspapers serving the targeted communities. Since then, advertising in outside media sources has slowed down, but the branch still produces fliers announcing events and a monthly newsletter. The branch has maintained cultural programs to forge close ties with the community, such as a yearly Tet (New Year's) celebration at the branch site which attracts 10,000 people, and a Mid–Autumn festival for children.

Targeting several different linguistic minorities presents problems, such as resentment over attention paid to one group over another. The branch has tried to offset this problem from the beginning of the grant by having each of the groups represented in the library aid staff. The

Vietnamese, however, being the largest group, are naturally targeted for more funding. Library aides and volunteers representing the other groups do develop an equivalent amount of programming for their communities. For instance, in one ongoing program, a group of Hmong college students come to the library every day to help Hmong children with their homework.

Despite this problem, the program has successfully marketed the library to the target communities. After just two years of the grant, circulation doubled. The staff has found that the need for new materials did not stop after the PFC, but keeps on growing.

After the PFC

The Logan Heights and Linda Vista Branches have been able to preserve the core of the programs they developed during the PFC grant period, despite the cut-off of those funds. According to Francisco Pinneli, a supervising librarian at the San Diego Public Library, the branches still maintain their community contacts and relations with publicity outlets. "The heart of the programs are maintained," he says. The success of the programs impressed the city manager, and he has been able to direct more funds from the city budget to the library system and encourage the implementation of the models in other branches. Librarians in the system actively pursue new grants to supplement what the city allocates. For instance, the system received a $96,819 grant in 1993 for the expansion of non-English language materials. The system is also bringing the Internet to its patrons. Pinneli says many volunteers have offered to teach others how to use it and he credits the PFC with building community relationships that are the source of volunteers.

Pio Pico Koreatown Branch, Los Angeles Public Library

Jae Min Roh became senior librarian at the Pio Pico branch of the Los Angeles Public Library in 1984. As a Korean immigrant, he could easily understand the needs of the population his branch was serving, residents of the Los Angeles Koreatown community. He started to reinforce the small collection of Korean and ESL materials from the time he started there, and the branch saw a steady increase of Korean patrons. When the branch received a Partnerships for Change grant in 1989 to target the Korean community, the pace quickened. This is reflected in the circulation rates; in 1984, circulation was 89,000 books a year, and currently it is 210,000 books a year. The Pio Pico Koreatown branch ranks tenth in usage out of the sixty-four branches in the Los Angeles Public Library System.

The nearly $200,000 the branch received from PFC allowed it to increase its Korean materials collection to three times what it used to be, launch a major publicity campaign, develop new programming and hire two more Korean-speaking staff members. All these factors combined to introduce the Korean immigrant population to the library and make them feel comfortable using it. According to Roh, there is not a strong public library tradition in Korea, so many immigrants need to be educated about the U.S. system. In fact, many people hearing about the library or visiting it for the first time have asked if they needed to buy membership to use it. The branch thus publicized its services and programs in the major media outlets of the Korean community: newspapers, radio stations, and television stations. During the height of the PFC, the branch had 20-30 notices in these various media every month. Still, people primarily heard about the library through word-of-mouth. In a survey the branch took, 35% said they learned by word-of-mouth, and 20% said they learned through the Korean media. Only a few people out of the 150 surveyed said they learned through the English-language media.

As the grant stipulated, the branch conducted a needs analysis and built a coalition with community organizations. The coalition, consisting of twenty people representing major organizations in Koreatown, met regularly throughout the grant period to discuss programs and materials.

The outgrowth of the needs assessment and coalition discussions was several successful programs. One of these was a program for new immigrant parents. The library staff conducted a series of workshops that introduced parents to the library, the U.S. educational system, and other aspects of American life. The parents in the program liked the workshops so much, they decided it should continue for the benefit of other parents in the Korean community. So they created their own organization, the Korean Parents Association of Los Angeles, which operates the program at the library site. Another successful program is the bilingual story hour, in which Korean-speaking senior citizens read stories to children. The branch also developed a Korean book review contest, which was designed to encourage people to read books and write reviews of them. Good book reviews were rewarded. The first two programs started with the grant have been maintained. The book review contest stopped.

Roh emphasizes the importance of making the Korean population feel comfortable in the public library since they are generally unfamiliar with the concept in their own country. The Korean signage and Korean staff make a significant difference, but Roh has added smaller touches as well. He taught the monolingual staff some basic Korean. He says that when staff members can say "Good morning" or "Hello" in Korean, it puts patrons at ease. The name of the branch was also modified to reflect the new demographics of the neighborhood. Koreatown was added to the name Pio Pico, so the branch could maintain a part of the old identity while affiliating with the new community that surrounds it.

The branch was the only PFC grant recipient to target the Korean population. At the same time, however, it could not ignore the non-Korean population it also serves, including a large Latino population. Roh says that during the grant period, jealousy among non-targeted patrons was a persistent problem. The branch has tried to alleviate it by hiring Spanish bilingual staff and expanding its Spanish material collection. It currently has one part-time Spanish bilingual librarian and a Spanish bilingual clerk. The branch has trilingual signage in addition to trilingual library card applications.

Since the PFC grant ended in 1992, both Korean and Latino patrons are in need of materials. The branch receives $75,000 a year from the city to buy new materials. Roh says that $27,000 of that is used to buy Korean materials, $15,000 to buy Spanish, and the rest is used for English language materials.

The stoppage of PFC funds also created other problems. Naturally the branch could not run publicity campaigns any longer, but they also had to let go of two full-time Korean-speaking staff and decrease programming. Fortunately, volunteers have been able to take over some of the programs, like the Korean American parents' workshops and the story hour.

Roh says that the grant just provided the initial incentive to make the library culturally sensitive to the changing community, and that he learned a great deal from the experience, such as working with local organizations. Community organizations continue to support the library and are donating the money for the new book review program. The branch continues to buzz with activity; patrons of diverse ethnicities regularly visit. Indeed, the branch is so busy that they staff is looking fo a larger site. Roh summed up his efforts by saying, "All that is needed is your enthusiasm and your commitment to success."

Santa Ana Public Library

The Santa Ana Public Library is a small municipal system in Orange County, California. It consists of a main library and two branches. Still, the system has large responsibilities, as it attempts to serve three diverse populations: Spanish–speaking, English–speaking, and Vietnamese–speaking. The library has provided services to Latinos for some time, but until it received a PFC grant in 1989, the Vietnamese population was underserved. The PFC allowed the library to develop a program called "Vietnamese Voices," which lasted until 1992 and has been successfully integrated into routine library services.

The program was housed at the Newhope branch of the library, which is located next to the largest Vietnamese community in the United States. The staff at Newhope focused on building a larger collection of Vietnamese books, the number of which has now grown to more than 10,000. They also worked on making the library more accessible to the Vietnamese community. Signs in Vietnamese pointing the direction to the branch were posted in heavily populated Vietnamese sections of Santa Ana and nearby cities. They hired bilingual clerical staff and tutors as well.

At the time of the grant, the Santa Ana library, including the Newhope branch, did not have any Vietnamese bicultural/bilingual librarians. Thus, the branch heavily relied on its PFC coalition partners within the Vietnamese community to gain more cultural sensitivity and get ideas for program development. Library outreach supervisor Martha Garcia Almarzouk says, "It's very important when you are doing an outreach program to know who are the key informers, the key organizations of the community you are targeting." With the help of an initial needs assessment, coalition ties and outreach efforts, the Newhope branch was able to serve the Vietnamese community better. This can be seen in the circulation figures, which were in the 20–30,000 per year range at the beginning of the grant period in 1989 and shot up to the 40–50,000 per year range in the next two years.

Efforts were also made to make the Vietnamese feel included in the library community. One such effort was an oral history project in which Vietnamese immigrants reflected on their experiences in Orange County. The histories were compiled in a three–volume collection housed at the Newhope branch. Copies of it were also sold to interested organizations, colleges and universities.

The Vietnamese Voices project has been over for several years, but the library still maintains its ideals and continually seeks to improve services to the Vietnamese population. Vietnamese materials are now spread throughout the entire system, as the collection has become too large to house in the small Newhope branch. According to Garcia Almarzouk, it is still a priority to hire Vietnamese bilingual/bicultural staff, and they have been able to improve on their record. The library currently employs a Vietnamese–speaking librarian for its bookmobile services and a Vietnamese library technician, who provides the same services as a librarian but does not have a master's degree in library science. Both have been able to make a significant difference; they conduct bilingual story hours for children and are capable of developing the Vietnamese collection, translating informational material, and doing outreach that only community insiders can do. For instance, the bookmobile librarian, Trinh Jeanette Pham, serves as the library representative to the Asian Pacific Advisory Committee in Orange County. From her interactions with this group, she learns about how the library can improve services to the Vietnamese population.

Many programs that target one particular ethnic community can raise the resentment of others who feel they are being ignored. Garcia Almarzouk maintains that the Spanish–speaking population benefitted from the PFC grant as well, because they were able to use the new language learning lab and computerized homework center that were made possible through PFC funds. The Newhope branch also provides bilingual Spanish tutors along with the Vietnamese tutors. Moreover, the Latino presence is felt throughout the Santa Ana library system; many of the clerical staff, librarians, and administrators are Spanish bilingual and bicultural.

The library thus already had a multicultural outlook and approach; the PFC allowed it to extend this approach to yet another community. Thus, most of the library outreach efforts are now trilingual and tricultural. For instance, the informational brochures are printed in three languages, as are the library card applications. A video the library often uses at educational presentations on its services is available in English, Spanish and Vietnamese. The bookmobile employs Spanish bilingual staff in addition to the Vietnamese librarian. The bookmobile service is very active. It is a result of a community survey the library conducted in which people reported that they did not use the library because of transportation problems. They also said that if the library came to them, they would probably use it. The library already had one bookmobile, but it pursued grant money to initiate a second. According to Garcia Almarzouk, the bookmobile is less threatening to immigrants than the permanent library facilities, because it looks less like a government institution. They thus feel more comfortable going into it. The bookmobile also allows library staff to make more personal contact with people who do not think the library can serve them; "often, parents think that the library is only for their children, but they don't think there are materials for them too," says Garcia Almarzouk. "So when they come to the bookmobile with their children and wait outside, we go out and talk to them and invite them in, and show them the materials we have." Garcia Almarzouk says that once they see the ESL materials and popular literature like telenovelas in the bookmobile, they start using the services.

The two bookmobiles make 32 weekly stops within Santa Ana, including week nights and Saturdays. They also come to schools and the Boys and Girls Club, where they conduct story hours and teach about library services. "The reason for doing this is to instill a love of reading in the children, so they can remember how fun books are, become adult users of the library, and bring their parents in as well," says Garcia Almarzouk.

Another outreach effort the library is making is Knowledge Link, a pilot program initiated in fall of 1994, and administered jointly with ten schools, grades K–12. The schools provide the space and computer equipment, through which the students can access books at the library and have them reserved. The library then delivers the books to the students at the schools. This program alleviates two problems; one is that children often do not have transportation to the library, and two is that the school libraries in Santa Ana, as in many other districts, have few books.

The library also worked in partnership with a local Spanish-language book distributor, Martinez Books and Art, to produce Isabelle Allende Day in April 1995. The day featured the Chilean author, who delivered a bilingual speech, and displays of her works and other Latin American authors. In addition, there were other activities for adults and children that took place on the grounds of the library and nearby civic buildings. Nine hundred people attended. Plans are under way to develop a similar program next year featuring a different author.

Garcia Almarzouk says, "If we have partnerships with businesses or schools, we can work together to enhance the quality of life of students and other people, and that's what we're doing."

Conclusion

A library's location in the heart of a linguistic minority community does not automatically make it relevant and important to that community. As can be seen in the above profiles, libraries must make huge efforts and have strong visions of what they want to accomplish. Haphazard approaches work like "bandaids" over gaping wounds. For example, at one Los Angeles library located in a major Latino section of the city, there is a concerted effort to improve the Spanish book collection. But there is no senior bilingual staff to do outreach or provide comprehensible information, nor are there any formal ties to community groups who could volunteer or provide access to such services. Many flyers announcing library events and schedules lie on the table for patrons to peruse. Only one of these is in Spanish; it announces auditions for a children's television show. As Garcia Almarzouk explained, people often will not come to a library unless they are invited in and formally introduced to the services and materials. The libraries profiled here are successful because they have an overall sense of mission and because they understand the communities they are serving from the inside.

References

Constantino, R. (1994). *Knowledge and uses of libraries among immigrant ESL high school students.* Doctoral dissertation, University of Southern California.

D'Elia, G., and E. J. Rodger. (1994). Public library roles and patron use: Why patrons use the library. *Public Libraries*, 135–144.

Fernandez, N. (1973). Outreach programs for Chicanos. *California Librarian, 44*, 14–17.

Haro, R.P. (1970) One–man survey: How Mexican Americans view libraries. *Wilson Library Bulletin*, 736–742.

Olivier, L., Belvin, R. and S. Manoogian. (1994). Survey on services to multicultural populations. *Public Libraries*, 197–204.

Payne, J. (1988). *Public libraries face California's ethnic and racial diversity.* Santa Monica, Calif.: Rand.

Chapter 4

Impact of School/Library Partnership On a Linguistic Minority Community

Sharon Honig-Bear
Sally Kinsey

> I always tell people that I became a writer not because I
> went to school but because my mother took me to the
> library. . . . I wanted to become a writer so I could have my
> name in the card catalog.
>
> --Sandra Cisneros, poet and novelist

Like most librarians and educators, we like to hear and to tell
stories. If you share that enthusiasm, especially when it's a success
story about getting books into children's hands, then gather 'round. Here
begins the tale of partnership libraries, a cost-effective way of bringing
libraries into communities that might not otherwise have them.

Partnership libraries bring books within reach. They can be a useful
way to introduce books and literacy services to populations having little
previous experience with libraries and what they have to offer. They are
especially effective in reaching minority or ethnic populations, in their
"backyards," acting as resource centers for people who lack personal
resources and are often cut off from, or unfamiliar with, other
community resources. They can assist communities in meeting the first

of the National Education Goals, that by the year 2000, *all American children will start school ready to learn.*

The story in Washoe County, Nevada isn't much different from most communities. The county is experiencing population growth at a time when public funding can't keep pace with the public's demand for services. Libraries, like parks and other "discretionary services," fail to get increased funding. Even in rapidly growing neighborhoods, building new libraries has become a dream.

The challenge in this community has been to provide library and literacy services to previously unserved-- or seriously underserved-- areas in Washoe County. Our solution has been partnership libraries.

The Partnership Concept

Washoe County Library (Reno, Nevada), like several other libraries throughout the United States, has found the partnership concept a practical tool to reach people with new branches in tough budget times. In this community, new library branches have been opened through a partnership with the Washoe County School District. In other communities, libraries have teamed with parks departments or senior centers.

Partnership libraries are not for everyone, and they're certainly not a panacea for all library ills. It takes work and dedication on many people's parts for them to succeed. They are, however, a paradigm, a model, a creative way to share resources and stretch tax dollars. They provide necessary services to the community in an innovative way.

The idea is known by other names, including joint use, cooperative, or community libraries. Whatever it's called, we're referring to public facilities that double as public libraries. They allow public libraries to reach areas not previously served, in a very cost-effective way.

Schools are often the largest institution and gathering spot within neighborhoods, and yet they remain empty for much of the day. Even more, they are completely ignored on weekends and idle at summer vacations. By teaming with the public library, these expensive pieces of real estate are put to greater use.

Partnership facilities in Washoe County are typically open to the general public after the school day ends. The facilities operate during late afternoon, evening and weekend hours. Special provisions are made to keep them operational during summer months, a great bonus to the children who often have few educational opportunities during the long vacation.

Benefits of Partnership Libraries

The benefits of partnership libraries are numerous and exciting. And in this era of political correctness, agency boards and administrators look good when they cooperate and maximize resources!

In *Becoming a Nation of Readers: What Parents Can Do,* parents are called upon to lay the foundation for their children's reading. In addition to this foundation (reading to the children, discussing stories and events, etc.), "parents need to facilitate the growth of their children's reading by *taking them to libraries,* encouraging reading as a free activity and supporting homework." Partnership libraries not only link up two government agencies, but they also partner with parents, regardless of income levels, to bring quality reading and learning materials within their grasp.

The benefits to students, teachers, and the public are enormous. Washoe County's partnership libraries are equipped with on–line databases that allow students and teachers to gain access to information about books in the collection as well as other community information, i.e., public meetings and other factual material. Students gain access to literally thousands of titles in the public library's collection and to up–to–date computer technology. Everyone has the ability to place holds on particular books.

With extensive resources available in their schools, students no longer need to arrange for a ride or make a special trip to the public library, and they achieve an independence that didn't exist before. Teachers will find that the additional resources available in their own school through the partnership arrangement enhance and expedite class assignments.

The expense of collection development is shared in partnership libraries, and the result is a well–rounded collection that offers something to anyone of any age or literacy level. In *Becoming a Nation of Readers: What Parents Can Do,* it is stated that, "The essential point is that students should have easy access to a wide variety of books and that they be given an opportunity to read with a minimum of interruptions."

The collection should interest both children and adults. Washoe County's partnership facilities contain both books and audiovisual items. The public library develops a collection that complements, not duplicates, the school collection. For example, in a facility located in an elementary school, the public library added pre-school materials and items to appeal to junior high school level and above. The school provides the elementary level collection, a collection that reflects the curriculum, one it would need on a day-to-day basis for its students.

Like all branch libraries, it's important to tailor the collections to the ethnicity and other demographics of the community. To select the best materials possible, seek input from experts in the field, be open to requests from the community, consult library journals and book reviews. This will guarantee that the materials will be used and appreciated by the people who will use this facility.

Depending on the physical facilities, many other benefits are possible. The library can act as a community gathering site, providing space for public meetings, clubs and other community events and activities. Staffing and facilities will determine the amount and scope of library programming but these also can be tailored to the surrounding community. The library has a wonderful opportunity to respond to the residents who live near it and play a key role in making the community better.

Washoe County Applies the Concept

Washoe County Library serves a population of approximately 272,420 people, most of whom live in a rapidly growing metropolitan area. However, the county extends more than one hundred desolate miles to the north and to the alpine beauty of Lake Tahoe, thirty miles to the southwest. Within the metropolitan area, the suburbs are steadily expanding to the east, south and west.

In response to population growth, partnership facilities have helped Washoe County Library dramatically. They've allowed Washoe County to open four libraries within the past ten years (three of them within the past three years), serving three outlying regions and one inner-city area. Two additional sites opened in 1995.

As all good real estate people know, location is a critical factor to success. Our experience shows, however, that rural, urban or suburban communities can all benefit from partnership facilities.

The Rural Experience

Washoe County's first partnership facility evolved when bookmobile services were cut to Gerlach, Nevada, a community of approximately 500 people. This town is 108 miles from the metropolitan center in Reno, at the edge of a formidable desert and is isolated from all educational and cultural stimuli.

The public library's concern was to maintain some type of service to this outlying area; the school district's concern was to maintain accreditation for their high school, which required a library. The solution was to combine the public library with the high school library, generating a win-win situation for both institutions. The resulting partnership library brings materials to students of all ages and to the general public. It also provides programming and a much-needed meeting room.

The Suburban Experience

Washoe County's next two partnership sites were located outside the city limits, in rapidly expanding suburban areas. In one case, we teamed with an already existing elementary school, adapting the space for the cooperative needs. In the other case, a new high school was specially designed with the partnership library's needs in mind.

Two additional sites opened recently in two neighborhoods experiencing rapid development. These areas are primarily attracting young families.

In one case, a new middle school was being designed to include a partnership library, assuring that the public has easy access to the facility after school hours. The second site is located in an area with a large enough population base to warrant a permanent branch. However, construction funds are not presently available, and thus the partnership library acts as an interim solution. The partnership library, also housed in a middle school, will operate for approximately two years. At that time, a permanent facility will open nearby, and the library materials, equipment and furnishings purchased through library funding will be transferred there. It is expected that computer connectivity to the public library network, as well as a ready reference collection, will remain in the middle school. Thus, even after leaving the partnership library agreement, students and staff using the middle school library will still be enriched beyond their original resources.

The Inner City Experience

The fourth site, recently opened, is located in an inner-city area, isolated by freeways and major arterial blocks. The residents of this community are primarily low-income. It is well known that many residents in this area find it difficult to get to one of the existing branches of the Washoe County Library. Many residents lack automobiles; many have older vehicles and often find them not in working order. Public transportation is expensive and often doesn't connect easily to library locations. For many families, there is concern about the safety of children leaving the neighborhood.

These problems were overcome by locating the partnership library in the neighborhood middle school. The school shares a city block with an elementary school and a public pool, and this area comes as close to being the "center" of the community as any other location.

The primary focus of this chapter will be on partnership libraries as a solution to the special problems associated with inner-city communities.

How to Create a Model
Partnership Library

Ten years in the partnership business has taught us a lot, particularly how vital careful planning, communication and cooperation are to the ultimate success of a project.

Asking the right questions from the beginning is critical. If the idea of a partnership library sounds good to you, then it's time to sit down and do some serious evaluation. This chapter can help you determine if you're ready.

Planning for the Partnership

Identifying a need for library services in an underserved community can act as a catalyst for the planning process.

The need can be identified in several ways. In some cases, there's a grass roots cry from a community for library service. In other cases, the library may identify the need. Either way, it's important to conduct a survey to make sure the neighborhood welcomes the library and is ready to use it. A survey will tell you how people feel about the project and also if they understand how it will work. The results will alert you to the need to do more community outreach, education and planning.

Like all complex projects, the top administrators and boards of the agencies involved must fully endorse the partnership idea. Administrators can guarantee or thwart success. The more cooperative the administrators, the greater likelihood of success. Smart government agencies understand that networking and resource sharing make them look good. By combining resources of several agencies, your buying power is far greater. In an era where the public is very skeptical about politics, partnership libraries stand out as smart government.

In Washoe County's case, the School District petitioned the Library Board of Trustees with requests to open cooperative sites. With the success of each partnership library, other schools saw the benefits to students and families, thus generating additional requests for partnership libraries in other parts of the school district.

There is one other initial factor that can contribute to the success of a partnership project. School personnel should be involved, as early as is possible, in the planning for the facililty. It is possible for school personnel to have fears about how the library will impact them and their working conditions. Their input is critical to whatever success will be achieved. Many problems can be avoided by getting them involved and providing them with an understanding of the potential benefits for them and their students.

Funding the Partnership

A contract must carefully define the financial and other obligations of all agencies involved.

In Washoe County's case, the contract specifies that the public library provides computer equipment and phone lines, access to the library's catalog via Dynix, a fax machine, a photocopy machine, and InfoTrac. The public library also outfits the branch with an opening day collection and, importantly, a budget for continuing collection development. As Washoe County Library provides Internet services to patrons, users of the partnership libraries will also benefit.

Washoe County Library also provides professional support in other areas. Because the partnership facility must adapt to the County Library's computer system, extensive training by the County Systems Librarian is provided. The Collection Development Librarian oversees cataloging and processing of both the school and public library collections.

Partnership facilities vary in how much programming is conducted, but a Partnership Library Coordinator, who oversees the operation of all partnership libraries, provides training to personnel in storytelling, book talks, collection development, and management issues.

So what does the school provide? Most significantly, they offer the site. They are also responsible for maintaining the facility and providing adequate shelving and security.

Special attention should be paid to determining how the public will gain access to libraries that do not offer entrances directly from the street. The school pays for any remodeling of an existing facility. Other needs include a compatible book detection system, proper lighting, adequate parking, handicapped accessibility, and designated bathrooms.

It is important that the contract include a plan for routing materials to and from the sites. Ideally, there are several deliveries a week between the public and partnership libraries. This is essential for the patrons to gain access to the larger holdings of the public library.

In our situation, signage is a shared responsibility. Plan for adequate signage, placing signs where they can be the most visible. The County Library places them on the streets near the facilities, and the school district is responsible for adequate signs on the buildings. It is best to place the signs close to the entrance to the school building, especially when they state the library's hours of operation.

More than one sign may be necessary. At one of Washoe County's sites, the entrance to the school is a long walk from the parking lot, and it has been necessary to have smaller signs pointing library patrons in the right direction. It has been our experience that you can never have enough signs!

Administering the Partnership

As stated above, top administrators and board members need to endorse the projects. However, the problem is that they are not typically involved in implementing the day–to–day operation.

The solution in Washoe County was to create a Partnership Library Advisory Committee. Members of the Partnership Committee work closely with library coordinators for both agencies.

The Committee's challenge is to integrate the separate policies and procedures followed by each agency into cohesive, shared documents such as a "Materials Selection Policy" and "Operations Manual." Faced with so many details and decisions, working in sub–committees has proven to be the best use of staff time.

After the Partnership Library Advisory Committee drafts policies and procedures, they must be approved by appropriate Boards. When contractual agreements are developed, examination by legal counsel is essential.

Liability is a significant issue that must be addressed and resolved between the agencies involved.

It works best when creating these documents also to involve the classroom teachers, the school principals and the school librarian. Making certain everyone understands and provides input for the procedures they will live with will avoid many problems in the future.

Composition of the Partnership Library Advisory Committee

After three years' experience, Washoe County has slightly altered the original composition of its Committee. With fourteen members, efforts have been made to achieve an equal balance between members representing school, library and community.

The school district sends a board member, a curriculum specialist, a school librarian, a principal, a teacher and a parent selected by the Parent Teacher Organization. The Library sends a board member, a partnership librarian, a representative from Library administration (in our case the Associate Director), a member of the public and a parent from the community at large. The School Library Coordinator and County Partnership Library Coordinator serve as ex–officio committee members, with voting privileges.

While they are not officially members of the Committee, principals and relevant staff in all partnership schools are encouraged to attend meetings. Their comments and input can seriously influence issues being decided by the Committee. Their on-site expertise is valuable when considering items like library hours, security, chain of command, etc. Their involvement in the decision-making process will minimize confusion and misunderstanding at a later time.

Ideally, all members of this committee will endorse the concept of partnership libraries. It is worth careful thought in selecting people who want to make the project succeed and who have experience building consensus. Many issues have the potential to divide the group and a spirit of cooperation among Committee members will make this process run more smoothly.

Responsibilities of the Partnership Committee

The duties of the Committee are to oversee and approve the operation of the sites. Some specifics include:

- Annually review and modify existing partnership library agreements.
- Modify and adapt existing partnership library agreements at new locations.
- Meet with agencies' Risk Managers, Attorneys, plant facilities staff, and central administration to insure interests are protected.
- Communicate site administration and staff concerns.
- Actively promote a positive image regarding partnership libraries.

Making It Work

Obviously, during the school day the librarian (and any support staff) are in charge, and their positions are funded by the school district.

Ideally, the librarian who staffs the public hours should be paid and supervised by the public library. Washoe County has learned this the hard way. Originally, the County Library reimbursed the school district for the salary and benefits associated with the public hours, even though the staff member was considered a school district employee. This led to problems with supervision and chain of command. A shift was recently made to claim all librarians working during the public hours as county library personnel.

Special arrangements must be made to handle times when school is not in session. This includes the long summer months, as well as school holidays, vacations, and teacher conference days. To avoid conflicts, these arrangements should be carefully defined in the contract that governs all policies and responsibilities of the partnership libraries.

If school personnel, such as the principal, janitor, school secretary, etc., are also absent during the summer, special arrangements need to be made to allow for the smooth operation of the public library in the facility. Issues include security for library staff and patrons, emergency procedures, plant management, telephone and mail service, etc.

During the summer, Washoe County's partnership libraries function exclusively as public libraries. Activities common in public libraries, such as Summer Reading Clubs, are conducted by the public library staff. Public library hours are adjusted to meet the needs of the local community.

Experience shows that communication and regular, positive inter-action between the school staff and the public librarian is essential to the smooth operation of the facility. Ideally on a daily basis, they will discuss concerns and keep each other informed about the site's events and activities.

Because public libraries and school libraries often see access to information (as in intellectual freedom issues) differently, it is vital to discuss this at the start. Washoe County Library's policies and contracts reflect the American Library Association's principles and guidelines, upholding unlimited access to information for youth.

Impact of a Partnership Library
on an Inner City Neighborhood

We need to educate young people about what's inside of books. Libraries are doing that. And you'd be surprised at the people in the inner city who are fighting the closing of libraries, such as Terry McMillan, author of the bestselling novel *Waiting to Exhale*.

"Libraries opened up a whole new world for me," explains McMillan. Now a speaker in great demand, she says, "I give a lot of talks at libraries in the inner city, so I know what is happening there. I know libraries are playing a role in the inner city to help young people get off drugs and stop using guns."

Washoe County's inner city partnership library is located in the Traner Middle School Library, and only after two years of operation, there is much anecdotal evidence that it is making a positive contribution to the neighborhood. Through statistics and through "snapshots" or quick portrayals of library use, this section outlines the impact of the Traner Partnership Library. Despite its modest size--less than 2,000 square feet--it supports a large volume of activity.

Partnership libraries can act as a catalyst for positive change in inner cities. *The Roles of the Public Library in Society-the Results of a National Survey* outlined the results of a survey conducted in 1993. Differences emerged in how ethnic communities and lower socio-economic households viewed public libraries. The results were clear: "Most of those surveyed, especially Blacks and Hispanics, regard public libraries as a very important source of support for their community's educational aspirations." It continued, "Also, the lower the education and income level of the public, the higher they rate the educational importance of their public library."

Out of a list of roles that the library can play, households with incomes below $15,000 and those with an eighth grade education or less rated the *educational roles of the library* as "very important" more often than did those with incomes of $60,000 of more or those who completed college.

Another conclusion drawn from this survey was that among all racial-ethnic groups, the highest percentages of "very important" responses occurred for the three educational roles of the public library: as an educational support center for students of all ages; a learning center for independent learners; and a discovery and learning center for preschool children. Most significantly, Blacks and Hispanics systematically evaluated the importance of each of the roles of the public library to the community more highly than did whites.

A View of the Neighborhood

The Traner school occupies part of a large city block. Adjacent to the middle school is Duncan Elementary School. Between them are fields and a seasonal swimming pool.

This complex is located in northeast Reno, in a socio-economically deprived area caught between the prosperity of Reno and Sparks. The area is isolated, cut off from many other public services by a complex criss-crossing of freeways and highways.

This area represents the highest concentration of minority and non-English-speaking students and families in the metropolitan area. More than 30% of the neighborhood is considered minority. Although 5.7% are black, the greater number are immigrant, non-English speaking populations. Hispanics make up 15% of the area's residents, and the 7% Asian/Pacific families represent the fastest growing component. The area served by these schools also encompasses an urban Indian colony.

In a special report in the *Reno Gazette-Journal* entitled "Failing Our Children," Traner was identified as the middle school with the highest risk factors, compared with all ten middle schools in Washoe County. It has the highest percentage of English as a Second Language (ESL) students, the highest percentage (50%) of children on free or reduced lunch and was tied for last place (at 46%) for transiency. Most significantly, Traner is the only middle school that scored below the national average on CTBS scores, a standard achievement test.

Solving a Neighborhood's Problems

The unique socio-economic problems of the neighborhood surrounding Traner Middle School have been identified for some time.

As part of efforts to increase educational opportunities in the Traner neighborhood, the middle school was identified by the Citizens' Blue Ribbon Advisory Committee, a private group that has assisted Washoe County Library in strategic planning for almost a decade. In a 1992 update, the Committee had nine recommendations. One of them stated, "Establish a public/school library at Traner Middle School by December, 1993." This group identified the high-risk population surrounding this school and has made a commitment to redevelopment of this area.

Representatives from Washoe County Library began meeting in 1992 with community leaders to help bring library service to northeast Reno, with the Traner site identified as the most likely location. Schools, government, parents, and minority groups have been involved in the planning of this project.

The Library also worked closely with another unique agency, the Family Focus Center. The Center was established to provide health and human services directly from the Duncan Elementary School. It recognized, as has the public library, that neighborhood residents have trouble getting to various agencies around town for job counseling and training, permits, health check-ups and immunizations, parenting information, etc. Thus, the Center brought these services directly into the neighborhood.

The Family Focus Center saw that a library in the community would complement its work, bringing educational and cultural stimuli. The Center anticipated the contribution the library would make to families, especially in the evening and on weekends. A public meeting space during those hours was especially attractive. The prospects for training, counseling and tutoring were exciting.

As a result, the Family Focus Center worked to involve the families in the neighborhood surrounding Traner Middle School in planning the new library. The families were particularly helpful in providing support during the funding process for the partnership library. Later, as the partnership library opened, the Center helped promote the library and help introduce it to area residents. The library was able to capitalize on the already-established credibility of the Family Focus Center.

Working with the Family Focus Center was important for funding. Since some start-up costs were provided through grants, demonstrating grass roots involvement was a real plus. Working with the Center and the School District also made Washoe County Library eligible for Library Services and Construction Act dollars earmarked for cooperative projects. Depending on the availability of funds, it is possible that multi-agency programs such as partnership libraries may be eligible for federal funding.

Snapshot

It is September, 1994. The school year begins and the new Traner Partnership library opens, with the librarian distributing about 1,000 library card applications. Not knowing what to expect, she certainly wasn't prepared for the flood of completed applications that immediately followed. Despite the huge effort needed to input the data on the applications and produce and distribute cards to all students, she says, "The rewards go beyond statistics to the human element. Having a library card has become the 'in thing' among the children. The pride and joy is visible."

In the first four months of operation, 1,408 people signed up for new library cards. This number leveled off, with only 34 registrations in January 1995. Now that the schools immediately surrounding the partnership libraries have had personal contact with the librarian, she now realizes that her attention can be directed towards outreach to other surrounding elementary schools, day care centers and preschools. With the public hours in the partnership library beginning in the afternoon, morning hours are available to her to make site visits and promote library use in the community.

Numbers tell us something. In the first four months of operation at Traner, there were 21,133 visits to the library. In January 1995 alone, there were 6,320 visits.

Collection use also tells us something. The basic collection has 10,766 items. In its first four months, 10,771 items were checked out in the branch. Interestingly, during this period 13,758 items were returned to this branch, indicating that as neighborhood residents become more aware of the library system overall, they are borrowing items at other branches and returning them to their "home" branch. This is especially true of the faculty of the schools.

Snapshot

The bell rings at Duncan Elementary School. Every day at 3 p.m. the parade of young students begins. They leave Duncan, cross the broad expanse of lawn and head to the adjoining middle school. Their destination? The partnership library within Traner Middle School, where they will comfortably visit with the librarians (whom they have already met while taking tours of the partnership library with their classroom teacher) and take out armloads of new books. This happens almost daily. While there, they will have the opportunity to explore the personal computers and participate in library programs. Interestingly, the students are also bringing along their younger siblings. The older children act as leaders within their own family, promoting literacy and early exposure to books and other language–enriching materials.

Snapshot

It's Saturday morning storytime, and children ranging in age from one year to eleven years may show up to hear the partnership librarian read tales. They may also get involved in activities, such as craft projects relating to the books shared that morning.

On one such occasion, the librarian was using a puppet to relate a story. She suggested that the children could borrow the book and the puppet, learning the story themselves and relating it to people in their own neighborhood or family. A fourth grade boy approached the librarian, saying, "But I can't read. How can I learn this story?" After hearing from the librarian that there are resources available to help him, he asked, "Will you be here tomorrow to help me?"

These types of questions and encounters will confront the partnership library in a linguistic minority community. Programming should ideally address these needs. If staffing is inadequate, working with established literacy projects and using other volunteers become essential.

Programming is having an immediate impact on area families. The children, many of whom were accompanied by their families, had made it quite clear that Saturday mornings started with storytime at the neighborhood library–– and that the family's other activities would need to work around that schedule.

In a circumstance like this, with libraries based so close to home, children are empowered to pursue educational and cultural opportunities. They can even act as literacy leaders within their own families.

Snapshot

The Traner librarian worries about putting on weight, loaded down with "goodies of thanks" from parents and students. Even the treats offered by families reflect the ethnicity of the neighborhood. She is just as likely to receive fresh, hot potstickers as she is homemade cupcakes.

The Traner librarian confirms, "the students and staff at Traner are thrilled that they can get books from other branches and get InfoTrac articles faxed to them."

Snapshot

Kindergartners at Duncan Elementary (as in all elementary schools in Washoe County) were recently given a "personal kit" as a way to introduce them to the public library. Among the contents of the kit were bookmarks, magnets, and a special key. Children were told to bring the key, and an accompanying adult, to any library branch. There the key would open a treasure chest, filled with small prizes and a free book for the child to take home. It was also an opportunity to meet with parents and encourage library card sign-ups.

At Traner, within hours of children receiving their kits, families showed up with keys to redeem their prizes. Often, the older brothers and sisters who supervised the kindergartners were disappointed that they didn't get a prize as well.

In inner-city areas, where it's important to help families develop patterns of literacy, promotions such as these are worth considering. Activities that encourage full family participation can play significant roles in developing lifelong literacy skills and values.

The best thing about a good story is that it can be adapted in the retelling. As the teller, you can make changes in the story to meet your own needs. The story then becomes your own. This is as true of the tale of partnership libraries as any traditional tale.

Overall, the partnership library can be a major player in improving the quality of life for the residents who live nearby. Partnership ventures are succeeding for Washoe County, where use of facilities is doubling every year. Even more dramatic figures are expected for the inner-city library at Traner Middle School. The community is supportive and enthusiastic about this wise use of tax-supported structures and dollars.

Just as Washoe County provided its kindergartners with keys to unlock the treasure chest of books, the model of partnership libraries is a simple key for communities to unlock barriers to literacy services. The ending of the story belongs to you. . . .

References

Binkley, Marilyn R. (1988). *Becoming Readers: What Parents Can Do.* D.C. Heath and Company, in cooperation with U.S. Department of Education, Office of Educational Research and Improvement.

Chepesiuk, Ron. (1994). Writers At Work: How Libraries Shape the Muse. *American Libraries*, 984–987.

Failing Our Children. (Special Report). (December 20, 1992). *Reno Gazette–Journal.* Reno, Nev.

Public Libraries Serving Communities: Education is Job #1. (1994). U.S. Department of Education. Library Programs, Office of Educational Research and Improvement.

Chapter 5

Providing Pleasure Reading Material to Adult Immigrants: The Effects on Reading Behaviors and Second Language Acquisition

Kyung–Sook Cho

Many adult immigrants in the United States are unable to use English as a second language for social or practical purposes beyond basic survival. In particular, many educated adult immigrants, despite formal language study, lack casual conversational proficiency in English. Some people, although they have lived in the United States for a long time, are still reluctant to speak English with native speakers, or are even afraid to receive a telephone call. I interviewed many adult immigrants and some international graduate students at an American university. Many of them reported that they do not feel confident when conversing with native speakers of English. They frequently ask me how conversational proficiency in English can be successfully acquired. As a result of my interest in this common problem and my concern for the adult immigrants, I asked myself the same question: How can a second/foreign language student develop conversational language proficiency in ways other than simple exposure to conversation?

Importance of Pleasure Reading

Light reading (Krashen, 1993) for pleasure was an important missing element in second and foreign language education. Light reading means comic books, detective books, romance books, popular newspapers, magazines, etc., that readers can read comfortably for pleasure. It is completely free voluntary reading because people want to read, and readers have the option of putting the text down and selecting another one. Light reading for pleasure, suggested by Krashen (1993), is the method that second/foreign language students can use to facilitate their reading proficiency and improve their language ability. On the basis of working with other international graduate students and adult immigrants, I have seen that light reading for pleasure can contribute to improvement in English language proficiency for both conversational and academic purposes. Moreover, I have observed that pleasure reading in a second/foreign language can continue to facilitate language development even if native English speakers are not available.

Pleasure Reading and
Second Language Development

During the past few years, I have been eager to find out how successful second-language students acquired conversational English language proficiency with methods other than in interactions with native speakers of English. So I informally interviewed some of these successful English language students.

My interviews provided some evidence that successful language students gained second language competence, especially conversational language proficiency, through extensive free voluntary reading for pleasure or interest. Interestingly, the results of the survey showed that most of subjects who feel very confident in conversation have done more light reading (e.g., science fiction, detective novels, romance books, etc.) than the intermediate level subjects who did not feel confident in their ability to speak English.

Some Case Histories

In addition to the above interviews, I conducted in-depth interviews with proficient English-as-a-second-language speakers. All of them revealed that they had done extensive free voluntary reading for pleasure for many years. I was fascinated by two cases in particular.

The first one was a female student from Japan. Yashiko, a Japanese graduate student, is considered by American students to speak English as well as a native–speaker of English. Yashiko credits her language competence to reading detective novels in English. She has been obsessed by detective stories for ten years: three years in Japan and seven years in the United States. One of her American friends said, "I am amazed at Yashiko's English language proficiency. Her English speaking and writing abilities are extraordinary among international students. She speaks almost as well as a native speaker of English, although she has an accent." Yashiko knows every detail of detective stories and enjoys watching detective movies and video tapes. It is interesting to see that extensive reading of detective stories for pleasure transferred to understanding aural language and developed both speaking and writing competence in English.

The second interesting case was reading romance books and second language competence. H.J., a female graduate student from Lebanon, is a good example of the importance of extensive reading of romance books. She gave credit to reading romance books for her English language competence and reported that her conversational competence improved from reading hundreds of romance novels for many years:

> After I graduated from senior high school in Lebanon, I started reading "Harlequins," a series of romance books that I borrowed from my friend. I wanted to read more. So I located a used book store, where I could buy many Harlequin books. I have read hundreds of romance books for many years. I gained my English language competence from reading Harlequins.

Interestingly, H.J. was still carrying a romance book in her bag, saying, "When I get nervous before a school exam, I read a romance book to relieve the pressure."

Yashiko's and H.J.'s cases show that extensive pleasure reading is an important natural approach for the development of second language proficiency, especially for conversational language improvement.

Problems

As indicated previously, although many immigrants have had formal language education, their conversational language has not developed to a satisfactory level of proficiency. After interviewing with many adult immigrants, I found that they had tried many ways to increase their language ability but had not experienced free reading.

It has been demonstrated in the research literature that reading is an excellent way of improving language development (Day, Omura, & Hiramatsu, 1991; Elley, 1991; Elley & Mangubhai, 1983; Gradman & Hanania, 1991; Pitts, White, & Krashen, 1989).

However, many second language acquirers do not do much free reading in English even though they are very much interested in improving their language ability. I have found this to be a common phenomenon among these people.

They do not read books in their second language because they believe all reading in another language must be difficult and hard work, that it must entail word by word decoding of difficult texts or because they have not found the right texts, texts that are both interesting and comprehensible. How do we get adult second language students to start reading books in English?

Some Solutions

The problems facing the second language acquirers may be overcome through narrow reading using light reading materials. Krashen (1985) has recommended narrow reading for language and literacy development. In narrow reading, readers read the works of one author or a few authors or works in only one genre, such as science fiction or detective novels, and a series. As mentioned earlier in case histories, Yashiko's detective story reading and H.J.'s romance book reading are good examples of narrow reading for pleasure. In narrow reading, background knowledge gained from previously read text helps to make the current text comprehensible, which in turn aids language acquisition, especially both structures and vocabulary from many exposures (Krashen, 1985). Thus, books of one author, one topic and the same genre, e.g., romance books, science fiction, etc., will motivate second language students and support English language acquisition.

In the following section, a series of case studies is reported to reveal whether adult second language acquirers would do more reading when given teen romance books as narrow pleasure reading to increase their second language proficiency.

Sweet Valley Series and Adult ESL Acquisition

One interesting and easy type of reading that can encourage an interest in reading is teen romances. Teen romance books are very popular among high school girls (Moffit & Wartella, 1992) and are also read by many other people.

On the basis of work with other international graduate students, teen romance books were chosen for female adult immigrants because this type of literature is a readily available form of light reading that is both interesting and comprehensible. The original plan for the study was a single–subject case study with Miae; but inspired by Miae's case, five additional case studies were added. Five of the subjects were native speakers of Korean, and one subject was a native speaker of Spanish. They were considered to be typical of many in the immigrant population who have not read any books in English for pleasure but are interested in improving their language ability.

Miae

Miae was a 30–year–old female adult native speaker of Korean who had been living in the United States for five years. She completed high school in Korea and currently works in a small clothing shop in Los Angeles. She enjoys pleasure reading in Korean, both magazines and novels, but she had not read any books in English during the last five years. She reported, in fact, that she found English reading to be painful: "Whenever I see English letters, they give me a headache and make me sleepy." (This quote and all subsequent quotes are translated from Korean.) Miae reported that she had studied English in Korea for six years (grades 7 to 12). Classes had been traditional, with a focus on the grammar of the language and an emphasis on memorizing vocabulary. She had attended ESL classes in the United States for six months, but said that she did not continue because of the overemphasis on speaking in class. On her own, she had tried memorizing English phrases and idioms from the bilingual Korean newspaper but felt that this practice had not helped her much. Miae reported that she had limited interactions with English native speakers, and she watched some English television. She was afraid to speak English with native speakers, and sometimes even avoided them.

Sujin

Sujin, our second subject, was a 23-year-old native speaker of Korean who had lived in the United States for only three months when the study began. She had previously visited the United States for two months. Sujin had studied English as a foreign language in Korea for six years from the 7th grade to 12th grade in a public school and for one year at the university level. Her classes had emphasized the traditional grammar-translation method. Sujin had done no pleasure reading in English and reported that she was reluctant to speak English with native speakers.

Janet

The third subject, Janet, was a 34-year-old native speaker of Korean who had been living in the United States for five years. Janet was a secretary for a Korean company where there was almost no interaction with native speakers of English. She reported that her English was limited. Like Miae, Janet completed high school in Korea. She had studied English for six years from grades 7 to 12. Janet also reported that her English classes were grammar-based. Janet reported that she had attended ESL classes with Miae in the United States for six months to improve her conversational language. Janet did not continue ESL classes, since she felt that ESL classes focused on grammar and had not helped her English language improvement much. Janet reported that she had not read any books in English for the past five years, because it was too difficult to read, so she gave up trying to read in English.

Jinhee

Jinhee, the fourth subject, was a 35-year-old native speaker of Korean who had been living in the United States for 5 years. She had studied English in Korea for six years, but had also majored in English education at the university. She had taught English as a foreign language in a secondary school for three years and had completed a Master's degree in secondary education in the United States. Jinhee reported that she had taught English in Korea with a focus on grammar, translation, and memorization, and had not included reading for pleasure. In addition, Jinhee herself had not done much pleasure reading in English, except for religious books. Jinhee reported that she watched English television and had frequent interactions with native speakers of English but still did not feel very confident in using English.

Alma

The fifth subject, Alma, differed from other subjects in several ways. Alma was 21 years old and a native speaker of Spanish. She came to the United Stated with no knowledge of English at age 13, and attended junior high and high school in the United States, where she was mainstreamed in grade 10. Alma reported that ESL classes in school were grammar–based. She reported that in these classes, "I did work hard. I learned some grammar, but I still get confused about it. I do not know how to use them correctly." In contrast to other subjects, Alma interacted with native speakers of English frequently and with only minimum difficulty.

May

May, the sixth subject, was a 34–year–old native speaker of Korean who had been living in the United States for five years. May studied English in Korea for seven years and had completed a two–year fashion design course at a college in the United States. Like other subjects, May reported that English classes in her school were grammar–based. Unlike other Korean subjects, May used English at home for three years, because she married a native speaker of English. May could converse in English, but she reported that her English was limited in some ways. May enjoyed pleasure reading in Korean. When I visited her clothing shop, I observed that she was reading a book in Korean that she had borrowed from a public library. May had had no experience with pleasure reading in English for the past five years.

Table 1 summarizes the characteristics of our six subjects.

Table 1 Characteristics of Subjects

Name	Sex	Age	L1	Time in US	English study
Miae	female	30	Korean	5 years	6 years
Sujin	female	23	Korean	5 months	7 years
Janet	female	34	Korean	5 years	6 years
Jinhee	female	35	Korean	5 years	10 years
Alma	female	21	Spanish	7 year	3 years
May	female	34	Korean	5 years	7 years

As Table 1 indicates, our subjects differed quite a bit in their exposure to English and in the amount of formal English study they had experienced.

Free Reading

Our six subjects were asked to participate in a free reading program. They were asked to read for pleasure in English in their free time. No specific amount of reading was requested, nor were they asked to read for a certain amount of time each day.

Reading Materials and Procedures

As noted previously, the hypothesis in the study was that if we gave adult second language students reading materials for pleasure, we would see more reading and increased language development. The selected texts were from the Sweet Valley series, published by Bantam. The best known books in the Sweet Valley series are the Sweet Valley High novels, which are designed for junior high school and high school girls and are written at the sixth-grade level. On the basis of earlier work with other adult female second language students, it was felt that these subjects might enjoy these novels as well. Initially, our subjects were asked to read a Sweet Valley High novel. This request proved to be too difficult for Miae and Sujin. Fortunately, easier versions from the series are available: Sweet Valley Twins, a series written at the fourth-grade level, and Sweet Valley Kids, written at the second-grade level, deal with the same characters at an earlier age. Both Miae and Sujin were able to read Sweet Valley Kids. Therefore, all six women were asked to begin with books from this series.

To facilitate comprehension, I gave the subjects some background knowledge about the series, explaining who the main characters were (Elizabeth and Jessica) and describing their very different personalities. In addition, I occasionally discussed the readings with the subjects. These discussions were mostly concerned with the plot of the stories, aspects of American culture, and idiomatic expressions. On a few occasions, subjects were asked about the content that they had not understood; but for the most part, they were able to read on their own with good comprehension.

Enthusiastic Readers

All six women became enthusiastic readers of the books in the Sweet Valley series. Miae reported that she read fifteen Sweet Valley Kids books during a three-month period. Because personal reasons prevented her from reading for about four weeks during this time, this meant she averaged about two books per week and eight Sweet Valley Kids books during a one month period. Sujin read eighteen volumes in two months, Janet read eight in one month, Jinhee read twenty-three in a little less than one month, Alma read ten volumes over a two-week period, and May read seven in a one week period.

Table 2 summarizes how many books were read and subjects' use of the dictionary. In computing the total number of words read, it is estimated that each volume of Sweet Valley Kids contains about 70 pages of text and about 7,000 words.

Table 2. Amount of Reading and Dictionary Use

Subject	Books read	Total number of words	Books per week	Dictionary use
Miae	8	56,000	2	yes
Sujin	18	126,000	2.25	yes
Janet	8	56,000	2	yes
Jinhee	23	161,000	5.75	first 4 only
Alma	10	70,000	5	no
May	7	49,000	7	no

Table 2 shows that all subjects had a substantial amount of exposure to print. By way of comparison, Anderson, Wilson, and Fielding (1988) reported that the average middle–class child in the United States reads about one million words per year in English, both inside and outside of school, approximately 80,000 words to 100,000 words per month, depending on how much reading is done during school vacations. Miae, Sujin and Janet were able to read at least 50–60% of this rate in their spare time, despite being slowed down by use of the dictionary; and Jinhee, Alma and May read at a considerably faster rate, about 161,000, 140,000 and 196,000 words per month respectively.

After reading the first volume, all subjects were clearly hooked on the Sweet Valley Kids series.

Miae

After Miae had read several volumes, I suggested that she try a volume from the next series, Sweet Valley Twins, but she preferred to remain with Sweet Valley Kids. She reported reading them in nearly every free moment and expressed the desire to read the entire series. In her own words: "I never get bored reading the Sweet Valley series. This series of English books is the most interesting and understandable I have ever read. The Sweet Valley series are the only English books I keep reading."

Sujin

Sujin made similar comments: ". . . When I finished reading one volume of Sweet Valley Kids, I was looking forward to reading the next one. This was the first experience in which I wanted to read a book in English continuously. . . ."

Janet

Janet also was clearly involved in the plots while reading: "When I read Sweet Valley Kids, I seemed to interact with the children, wher–ever they were, in the classroom, playground, party, trip, home. . . . " Janet reported that she took Sweet Valley Kids with her on a trip so that she could read them on the airplane. Like Miae and Sujin, Janet reported that reading the Sweet Valley Kids series was her first experience of consistently reading books in English:

> . . . as a matter of fact, since I came to the United States, I bought around 10 novels in English to improve my English. But I would not read them at all. There were nothing but difficult things for me. I got exhausted right away even before finishing one page of the book. Since then I have not touched them. . . . Sweet Valley Kids books are easy and interesting, I am going to read all of them. . . .

Alma

Alma also told me that she would read all the books I could give her. She contrasted them with required reading she did in school: "I read English books that a teacher brought. They were not good for me because they were too difficult to understand, not like the Sweet Valley series . . . I cannot remember what I read . . . not even one title. . . ."

Jinhee

Jinhee, who had had a great deal of English instruction and who initially was not interested in this kind of reading material, found she liked Sweet Valley Kids far better than other things she had attempted to read in English:

> I read the Sweet Valley series with interest and without the headache that I got when reading *Time* magazine in Korea. Most interestingly, I enjoyed reading the psychological description of each character. When I read the second volume of Sweet Valley Twins, I was infatuated by it. I finished reading it without stopping.

May

Like Jinhee, May initially was not interested in reading Sweet Valley Kids. After May read the first five pages of the first volume, she stopped reading and said, "This book is boring. It is for children." But she was asked to finish just one book to see if she liked it or not. After finishing one book of Sweet Valley Kids, May read seven volumes in only one week. May told me that she wanted to read more if other books were available. Like the other subjects, May clearly enjoyed them: "At first, I wondered why you asked me to read children's books. But when I finished one book, I became interested in Sweet Valley Kids. This book was so interesting that I did not read the Korean books that I borrowed . . . ."

Miae's, Sujin's and Janet's enthusiasm and willingness to read these books were especially interesting, because they used the dictionary consistently, which must have been very hard work. Their perseverance is good evidence of the high level of interest aroused by the Sweet Valley series. They also overcame the traditional approach to English language study such as analyzing the grammar in sentences. Janet reported that she forgot about studying English while reading Sweet Valley books, although initially she started reading books with the intention of studying English. Sujin also commented that she was relieved from the hard work of studying English.

Language Acquisition: Vocabulary

To get some indication of the amount of language acquisition that took place, three of our subjects were asked to underline words they did not know the first time they encountered them. They varied in how they carried out this request. While Jinhee underlined in all the books she read, Miae underlined new words only in the first two books; after that, she listed words that were unfamiliar to her in a notebook. As we will see, Sujin did much more. Janet, Alma and May were not asked to underline at all. Miae, Sujin and Janet used the dictionary throughout the study. Along with their lists of new English words, they provided the dictionary definitions in Korean, and Sujin even listed an example sentence from her reading for each word. According to their self-reports, however, neither Miae nor Sujin studied or reviewed their vocabulary lists. In fact, they both told me that they were relieved to be able to read without having to memorize vocabulary.

For Miae, Sujin and Jinhee, a list of words was made from those words they had listed and underlined in the volumes they read, and each of them was asked to define the word in their first language. They were given credit only for providing a synonym or definition that captured the full meaning of the tested word. This was a lengthy procedure and was spread out over several days. Testing was done at times convenient to Miae, Sujin, Jinhee and to this researcher.

On the basis of experience with Miae and the other subjects, a 165–item test was constructed for Alma from the first seven books of the Sweet Valley Kids series. For Janet and May, in order to save testing time and for their convenience, a 100–item multiple test was constructed based on a 165–item test. The same test was given to Alma and May as a pretest and as a posttest. For Janet, only the posttest was given after reading the books. Results of all these assessments are given in Table 3.

Table 3. Vocabulary Growth.

Name	Number of target words	Number correct	% correct	volumes read	words per volume
Miaie	535	299	56%	8	37.4
Sujin	396	316	80%	18	17.5
Jinhee	275	189	69%	23	8.2
Alma	165	71		10	7.1
Janet	100	55		10	5.5
May	100	30		7	4.3

Note. Target words for this testing were the unknown words underlined and listed by Miae, Sujin, and Jinhee during their reading. Alma and May scored 39/165 and 62/100 on the pretest respectively and 110/165 and 92/100 on the posttest, a gain of 71 and 30 words. Janet gained 55 words on the posttest.

Test results indicated that the subjects acquired impressive amounts of vocabulary. Nagy et al. (1985) calculated that native speakers gain about 3,000 words per year from reading one million words. In order to compare our subjects' rate of acquisition of vocabulary to that of native speakers, it was extrapolated what their rate would be if they had read one million words. Miae acquired words at much greater rate than the native speaker rate (over 5,000 words per million), Sujin acquired vocabulary just under the native speaker rate (2,500 words per million), Jinhee and Alma well under the native speaker rate (about 1,200 and

1,000 words per million respectively) and Janet and May at about one fourth of the native speaker rate. For Janet and May, their rates may be higher than this figure because they may have gained other words that were not tested.

It is interesting to note that sometimes all of the subjects referred to the story context that the testing words were used in with an answer. For example, when they were asked what "grumpy" meant, they gave the answer with a smile, "This is the way Jessica was all the time." This showed that they acquired words in the process of reading the story.

Language Acquisition: Speaking and Understanding

While testing was limited to vocabulary, it was clear from subjects' comments and reactions that their ability to speak and understand everyday English improved as well. Particularly, Miae felt that her reading resulted in considerable improvement in her ability to both understand and speak English.

Miae

Miae was interviewed again after she had read 15 volumes of Sweet Valley Kids; she reported:

> Reading helps me understand TV better. I ran across many of the same words and phrases I saw in reading while I was watching TV. I used to be afraid to speak with Americans. But the other day when I went to Disneyland, I enjoyed talking to some American children and their parents who came from Arizona.

Interestingly, after reading thirty-nine books from Sweet Valley Kids and four books from Sweet Valley Twins, Miae provided her own listening comprehension pre and post-testing:

> I had two movie video tapes. I did not understand them at all five years ago, and just looked at the pictures. I did not understand them two years ago, either. Last Tuesday, I watched them again to see if I could understand them. I understood them from the start. I could not catch everything, but I

understood the entire story. I was so happy that I could understand words that I knew from the reading, such as 'envy,' 'avoid,' and 'wet.'

Miae watched more English programs on TV than before reading the Sweet Valley series. The number of her favorite TV programs in English has increased from one to six within a year, including *Full House, 21 Jump Street, In the Heat of the Night, Chips, Home Improvement,* and Disney movies.

There is also informal evidence that Miae's speaking ability in English has improved. She reported that a friend of hers, whose husband is a native speaker of English, commented recently that Miae's English had improved since the last time they had seen each other one year ago. Miae's friends, in fact, asked her if she had been taking English classes. All she had been doing, she responded, was reading Sweet Valley novels.

Sujin

As with Miae, the same findings appear to be true for Sujin, improvement in her ability to both understand and speak English. Like Miae, Sujin felt that she began to understand some English TV programs, since she ran into same words and expressions she read in the books in the Sweet Valley series:

> The more I read the book, the more I got the words and phrases. So I started understanding little by little when I watched English TV program such as *Who's the Boss?* and *The Wonder Years.* Understanding English TV programs little by little made me keep watching them every day. . . . I understood the words that I saw in the book such as 'swallow,' and 'dizzy.'

Miae's and Sujin's cases showed that increased reading experiences resulted in increased listening comprehension. Sujin also reported that she gained much more confidence and competence in everyday situations, such as shopping and in conversation:

> Confidence toward English has been approaching me with interest little by little since I read Sweet Valley books. Although I knew some words I could not use them appropriately before. I learned how the words could be used

right and differently.

Alma

After reading sixteen volumes of Sweet Valley Kids, Alma felt that her grammatical accuracy in speaking improved:

> The other day, my younger brother told me that my English had improved a lot these days. He said he could notice that I spoke right. . . [He] thought my English had improved because of speaking with native speakers. But he was wrong. After I read Sweet Valley Kids, I speak more correctly.

Jinhee

Even Jinhee, the former English teacher, knew her English had improved. After going on to read thirty volumes of Sweet Valley Kids, seven volumes of Sweet Valley Twins, and eight volumes of Sweet Valley High, all in only four months, Jinhee said that her confidence in casual English conversation increased. Jinhee also reported that she acquired some useful discourse structures.

Janet

Janet was asked if her understanding and English conversational language improved after reading. She commented:

> . . . I feel like saying something in English but I do not have good opportunity to speak with a native speaker of English. However, I feel that reading Sweet Valley series is very helpful for my conversational language improvement.

May

May also reported that she acquired many useful words for English conversation from reading, such as nudge, shrug, pout, gulp, frown, nod, etc.

It is interesting to see that subjects felt that reading helped their oral/aural language improvement. Books such as the Sweet Valley series contain a great deal of useful, everyday language that language students with mostly formal language instruction experience have missed. Interestingly, subjects indicated that the Sweet Valley series books are very useful for conversational language development. As they commented:

> Sweet Valley books contain everyday English, that I can use them. I can see many different words from a different topic: western story, fishing, ghost story, hospital, party, etc. (Miae).

> I can use the vocabulary contained in the Sweet Valley Kids books every day. The other books that I read in school had a big word, I mean, more like a literature word, which I could use once in a while or a certain time. Sweet Valley Kids has stories of real life. Each volume has a different topic that happened in real life, so I could get useful new vocabulary in each volume. . . (Alma).

> . . . it was a natural story. Each volume had a different topic in the different places and contained many different words related to different events such as Thanksgiving day, Halloween, Valentine day, Christmas day, western story, picnic on the beach, soccer game, skiing, trip to Grand Canyon, camping, birthday party, slumber party, dancing, field trip to the broadcasting company, etc., so I could get many different words and expressions that I was not familiar with. (Sujin).

> . . . all these expressions in Sweet Valley series are very useful for English conversation, I did not want to pass them by. . . . I saw many easy expressions that I could not use before, which I thought were very difficult. I wondered why I could not use these kinds of easy expressions . . . these were easy expressions but they were new to me . . . I thought I could use them when conversing. I used to try to use them a hard way. . . (Janet).

> . . . this kind of reading is a more natural way to learn English than overemphasized grammar instruction and memorizing vocabulary . . . (Jinhee).

> . . . this was easy to read but there were more unknown words than I thought. Now I realized why you gave me good books. These are good books to learn English . . . these books are very useful for conversational language improvement. . . . (May).

As the subjects mentioned, the Sweet Valley series of books contain a variety of topics in different situations, and the texts of the Sweet

Valley books contain conversation, description and narration to help readers develop conversational language. Thus, subjects may acquire not only useful vocabulary but also grammar and discourse structures necessary for conversational language proficiency.

In conclusion, all six women became enthusiastic readers of the Sweet Valley books, shattering the misconception that reading books in English is hard work and not interesting. They not only gained in vocabulary knowledge from reading novels, but also reported increased competence in understanding and speaking English. They also gained much more self-confidence and positive attitudes toward reading books in English and toward improving their English language ability. In addition, they reported that they acquired a great deal of cultural knowledge from reading and an understanding of American life, especially the life of American children. The women expressed the desire to read all of the Sweet Valley books, and some were still reading the books at the time of this writing. As I expected, some of the subjects gradually expanded their reading in English not only to the more challenging Sweet Valley series and to adult romances, but also to other types of materials such as magazines, a popular newspaper, detective novels, and poems in English. As seen from two case histories, Yashiko and H.J., my expectation is that our subjects will continue to read in English for pleasure and develop their English language ability in a natural way, particularly their conversational language proficiency.

The results of these case studies show that providing narrow pleasure reading was successful in promoting increased reading in English and resulted in increased second language acquisition. A series of books like the Sweet Valley series is very motivating for the improvement and enjoyment of reading. Familiarity with the main characters and the context facilitates interest and comprehension, resulting in the development of English language proficiency. Even though there are some difficulties with unfamiliar words and structures, the interest and background knowledge gained from the previous book appears to support continuous reading and understanding of the subsequent books. Thus, the readers will acquire vocabulary, discourse structures, grammar and other aspects of the new language. As a result of this increased competence, second language students better understand aural language and continue to develop more conversational language proficiency.

Suggestions

Although not all second-language students will be interested in books such as the Sweet Valley Kids and Sweet Valley High, there are many other options for narrow pleasure reading. A reading series and other forms of narrow reading for pleasure for some adult immigrants, ESL and limited English proficient students will provide a conduit to more complex prose reading and make a major contribution to the development of second language proficiency. It is suggested that a major goal of intermediate second language classes should be to expose students to a variety of narrow reading options for pleasure, so that students will find books that appeal to them. The advantage of a series like the Sweet Valley books is that they provide plenty of reading at different levels of difficulty.

References

Anderson, R., P Wilson, & L. Fielding. (1988). Growth in reading and how children spend their time outside of school. *Reading Research Quarterly, 23*, 285–303.

Day, R., C. Omura, & M. Hiramatsu. (1991). Incidental vocabulary learning and reading. *Reading in a Foreign Language, 7*, 541–551.

Elley, W. (1991). Acquiring literacy in a second language: The effect of book-based programs. *Language Learning, 41*, 375–411.

Elley, W., & F. Mangubhai. (1983). The impact of reading on second language learning. *Reading Research Quarterly, 19*, 53–67.

Gradman, H., and E. Hanania. (1991). Language learning background factors and ESL proficiency. *Modern Language Journal, 75*, 39–51.

Krashen, S. (1985). *The input hypothesis: Issues and implications.* Torrance, Calif.: Laredo.

Krashen, S. (1993). *The power of reading.* Englewood, Colo.: Libraries Unlimited.

Moffit, M., & E. Wartella. (1992). Youth and reading: A survey of leisure reading pursuits of female and male adolescents. *Reading Research and Instruction, 31*, 1–17.

Nagy, W., P. Herman, & R. Anderson. (1985). Learning words from context. *Reading Research Quarterly, 20,* 233–53.

Pitts, M., H. White, & S. Krashen. (1989). Acquiring second language vocabulary through reading. *Reading in a Foreign Language, 5,* 271–275.

Chapter 6

Using SSR in the Secondary ESL Classroom: A Powerful Way to Increase Comprehension and Develop Positive Attitudes Toward Reading

Janice Pilgreen
Barry Gribbons

SSR has been around for as long as people have been reading. Whenever a person selects something to read for his/her own purpose, spends more than a few minutes reading it and comprehending whatever (s)he wants, SSR is occurring (Manning–Dowd, 1985, p. 1).

The Search for an Affirmation of Faith

Having been a secondary school teacher for almost twenty years, I confess that I have been having my students do SSR since my very first year; but I made this decision based solely on intuitive evidence: I simply gave in to what I felt was a common–sense notion——that students get better at reading by reading. Perhaps equally important, I noticed that when given the opportunity to select materials that they wanted to read and the time to read them, students generally enjoyed their reading experiences.

It was only as I became a more "seasoned" teacher that I began to search for a stronger rationale to support SSR. I wanted to be able to establish a clear theoretical premise, based on current research, for providing students with fifteen minutes of instructional "free reading" time each day of the week, five days a week. (Of course, in my heart I continued to adhere to the premise that people learn to read by reading––and I still consistently noticed how much my students enjoyed their SSR time each day.) My first step was to find out about the origins of SSR programs, including the identification of their initial proponents and descriptions of the early programs.

SSR Programs: Their Roots

In-school free reading programs are not a new idea. In fact, they have been in existence since the advent of "Individualized Reading" in the 1950s and 1960s and have been labeled in a wide variety of ways: Sustained Silent Reading (SSR), Uninterrupted Sustained Silent Reading (USSR), Free Voluntary Reading (FVR), Self-Selected Reading, High Intensity Practice (HIP), Drop Everything and Read (DEAR), Sustained Quiet Reading Time (SQUIRT), Free Reading, and numerous other titles.

While some of the components of these programs vary, what they all have in common is either a "pure" or "modified" element of Sustained Silent Reading. Hunt (1967) is credited with the idea of SSR, and McCracken (1971) with its application (Petrimoulx, 1988). The objective of SSR is "to develop each student's ability to read silently without interruption for a relatively long period of time" (McCracken, 1971). There are six rules for SSR, and they include the following: (1) the students read self-selected materials silently; (2) the teacher models by reading silently at the same time; (3) one book, magazine, or newspaper is selected by each student for the time period; (4) a timer is set for a prescribed, uninterrupted time period; (5) no reports or records are kept; and (6) the whole class, department, or school participates.

Free Voluntary Reading refers to any in-school program where part of the school day is set aside for reading (Krashen, 1993). Two types of FVR are SSR and Self-Selected Reading. The difference between these programs is that Self-Selected Reading may incorporate some accountability measures such as having student/teacher conferences during which the students do "retells" or other sharing activities. The conferences can be devoted to skill building, record–keeping of books read, and discussion of their content. Often, the purpose of the conference is for the teacher to assess whether or not the student is comprehending the materials that are being read. With SSR there is no accountability. Book reports, quizzes, and comprehension checks are avoided in favor of simply allowing students to enjoy what they read.

Some Self–Selected Reading programs today are reminiscent of the "Individualized Reading" (sometimes called "Personalized Reading") programs in elementary schools in the 1950s and 1960s. In "Individualized Reading," quiet reading time is first provided, and then reading conferences occur between the teacher and the students. Groups are then organized to discuss common interests or to tackle shared reading problems identified by the teacher during the reading conference. Finally, a record is kept of each student's problems, interests, and scores on standardized tests (Greaney, 1970). In this kind of program, SSR rules two, four, and five are violated: first, there is an emphasis on accountability; also, it is sometimes necessary for the teacher to conference with one student while the others are reading, so the "modeling" and "silent, uninterrupted" aspects of the program are lost, as well.

HIP, or High Intensity Practice, is a term unique to studies done by Oliver (1970, 1973, 1976) in the 1970s. HIP programs include SSR, SSW (Sustained Silent Writing) and SSA (Self–Selected Activities). SSR incorporates the usual components identified by McCracken (1971), while SSW requires that students write whatever they wish for a given length of time and do not have to show their work to the teacher. The SSA period permits the students to engage in "any activity that involves active response to words--reading, writing, studying, or doing content area classwork" (Oliver, 1970, p. 70).

Finally, DEAR (Drop Everything and Read) and SQUIRT (Sustained Quiet Reading Time) are simply other terms for SSR (Clary, 1991). SSR can be implemented on any scale: in single classrooms, in one school, or throughout an entire district, where everyone--teachers, administrators, and classified staff members--stop what they are doing and read at a particular time for a specified length of time (Moore, Jones, and Miller, 1980).

Whatever term is used for free reading programs, they have gained renewed attention as a promising instructional component in school programs. In some cases, they form part of the regular language arts program, and in others they represent the entire program or are supplementary to the regular program.

SSR: The Current Research Base

A second step that I took in my quest to find a clear rationale for implementing SSR was to see how the concept of SSR has been described and developed in the literature and to identify the advantages associated with it.

What I discovered is that there are two primary reasons why schools have been interested in developing free reading programs at various levels of involvement: one is that they have hoped to see an increase in students' reading achievement (and concomitantly, reading test scores), and the other is that there has been a perceived lack of student motivation to read.

In terms of reading achievement, the circular question has been whether readers are more proficient because they read so much or whether they read so much because they are better readers (Mork, 1972). Originally, when free reading was incorporated into "Individualized Reading" programs, the emphasis was upon allowing students the opportunity to have the "drill" or practice necessary in learning to read, a time during which the student could apply and transfer the isolated skills learned during the regular instructional reading period (Jenkins, 1957; Lawson, 1968). However, with the movement toward a constructivist philosophy in the 1980s and 1990s, the notion that the more one reads, the better a reader one becomes, has gained appeal. As Sadoski (1980) summarizes it, "Students who read tend to become better readers, and the best way to develop reading ability is not through assessment or isolated skills drill, but by reading" (p. 154). This view of reading, with its highly personalized, "meaning–making" emphasis, has been stressed by Smith (1988a): "The purposeful nature of reading is central, not simply because one normally reads for a reason . . . but because the understanding which a reader must bring to reading can only be manifested through the reader's own intentions" (p. 3). The role of the reading teacher, then, is to make sure that students have adequate demonstrations of reading being used for evident meaningful purposes and to help students to fulfill such purposes themselves.

Based on a similar theoretical position, Krashen's (1988) research indicates that in-school free reading programs show outstanding results in promoting the development of reading comprehension. His hypothesis, that genuine reading for meaning is far more valuable than workbook exercises, echoes Smith (1976) and Goodman's (1982) belief that people learn to read by reading. Arguing that Free Voluntary Reading is the "missing ingredient in first language language arts, as well as in intermediate second and foreign language instruction," Krashen (1993) highlights the value of in-school free reading programs for students from any language backgrounds (p. 1). Maintaining that while FVR may not produce the highest levels of competence, he asserts that it will provide a foundation so that higher levels of proficiency may be reached. Without FVR, these advanced levels are very difficult to attain.

The academic results of free reading programs are impressive. Both in-school free reading studies and out-of-school self-reported free voluntary reading studies show that more reading results in better reading comprehension (Krashen, 1993). This finding is given further support by Elley's (1992) study of twenty-seven countries, in which a steady trend upward in achievement was seen in the populations which engaged in the greatest amount of voluntary reading.

A second impetus for the implementation of free reading programs has been the perceived lack of student motivation to read. Despite teacher encouragement, many teachers, parents, and administrators are concerned that students do not read much outside of school. (Moore, Jones, and Miller, 1980; Pfau, 1967; Watkins and Edwards, 1992). Young people may not have a quiet place to read or have adult role models to help them foster a desire to read. Junior high and high school students often have additional demands made upon them due to organized sports, peer group activities, homework, part-time employment, and dating; these activities all tend to decrease the amount of leisure time the students have in which to pursue their own reading. Therefore, they "need to be guided into a situation where reading is respected, quiet is expected, and the students see each other and their teachers in a productive and enjoyable reading environment" (Cline and

Kretke, 1980, p. 504). Free reading programs provide just such a situation.

As Barbe and Abbott (1975) explain it, school programs must "produce not only readers but also children who will grow into adulthood loving books and constantly enriching their lives and the lives of others by what they have found on the printed page" (p. 20). Because reading is "intrinsically rewarding," and as such functions as its own best motivational device (Everett, 1987, p. 2), free reading allows for the opportunity of developing the book reading habit, which is a positive, long-term effect. Research has shown that children who participate in such programs do more outside free reading than children in comparable programs (Krashen, 1993). In fact, Greaney and Clark's (1975) longitudinal study indicates that as much as six years later, students who had participated in a free reading program were reading more books than the participants from the non-SSR, "skills-based" comparison school.

Numerous studies have dealt with the question of how much free reading programs actually contribute to the fostering of positive attitudes toward reading. In general, findings reported in free reading studies indicate that positive attitudes towards reading and growth in a variety of reading interests occur as a result of these programs (Sadoski, 1980).

A Closer Look at the Potential of SSR Programs for Increasing Comprehension and Developing Positive Attitudes Towards Reading: 32 Studies

As a way of more powerfully validating the assertions that SSR programs do have the potential to increase reading comprehension and develop positive attitudes toward reading, I reviewed 32 SSR studies in which the goals were (1) to increase reading comprehension, (2) to develop positive attitudes toward reading, or (3) both. (All together, there were 41 separate groups, as some of the studies included more than one group.) In these studies, the experimental SSR groups were compared with the more traditional, "skills-oriented" reading groups.

The results of the 32 studies indicated that, of the 29 groups whose goals were to increase reading comprehension, 10 of the SSR groups outperformed the regular groups; and of the 31 groups whose goals were to develop more positive attitudes toward reading, 22 of the SSR groups outperformed the regular groups. However, in the cases where the experimental groups did not do "significantly better" than the regular groups, the experimental groups did just as well as the conventional groups, with the exception of two groups. (And in these groups, where various combinations of SSR and skills were used, the amount of actual SSR time was difficult to identify.) In short, the conclusion was that SSR provides at least the same benefits for students in terms of increased comprehension and the development of motivation as traditional classes offer, and in many cases, greater ones. This is an astounding finding, particularly when one considers which alternative is more enjoyable for students; clearly, free reading is less "work" and a good deal more fun.

Some Remaining Questions

Armed with my newly found research data (which only served to reinforce my original intuitions), I realized that I had all the information that I needed to continue my SSR procedures with confidence. Yet, there were two issues which still plagued me. First of all, my students are all ESL students, yet only eight of the thirty-two studies which I surveyed dealt with ESL populations (totaling eleven experimental groups). I was reluctant about generalizing the results of these studies to samples of ESL acquirers, even though the results of the few ESL studies that were included in the survey were extremely encouraging: of the ten groups which sought improved reading comprehension, eight were more successful than the traditional groups; and of the five groups that sought the development of positive attitudes toward reading, all five were successful. (There was some overlap among groups that aimed to achieve both goals.)

Second, none of the studies that I reviewed specifically discussed the steps that a teacher should take to develop an effective SSR program. In other words, though the theory was there, the practical guidelines for implementation weren't. In fact, I wondered how a new teacher would know how to begin to implement SSR in her/his own classes.

Given these two concerns, I decided to investigate the appropriateness of using SSR for language minority students. Further, I wished to take another look at the survey of thirty-two studies to determine the elements that had made the SSR experimental groups successful. In this way, I thought perhaps I could isolate the components of an "effective" SSR program so that those who wish to implement strong, optimal programs can have specifically the information they need.

A New Role for Reading:
Advantages of SSR for ESL Students

As I pointed out previously, one of the gaps in the SSR research has been the failure to include a large percentage of ESL samples. Yet, the number of language minority students in our schools has been steadily growing over the past decade. A major concern is how to contribute to the literacy development of these students who are classified as Limited English Proficient (LEP). Certainly, they must learn to read and write if they are to participate fully and effectively in society.

Interestingly, it has been pointed out that "while reading is widely encouraged in first language learning for a variety of reasons, its role has been repeatedly played down in ESL" (Mangubhai and Elley, 1982, p. 151). This is because reading has seldom been regarded as a means of extending children's grasp of the language; exposure to unfamiliar words and structures has been thought to confuse the students, to cause errors in interpretation, and to distort the pronunciation of new words. Mangubhai and Elley (1982) assert that this perspective is quite narrow and that reading has a positive, constructive role to play in second language (L2) acquisition. They note that, unlike the oral-first approach, which restricts second language acquirers' language growth "without justification," extensive reading allows students to progress naturally and quickly (p. 152).

Also, Krashen (1993) reports that when second language acquirers read for pleasure, they develop the competence they need to move from the beginning "ordinary conversational" level to higher levels of literacy. He remarks that for all of its virtues, the Natural Approach that is used in beginning ESL instruction has its limits; Natural Approach students are not able to use their second language for more demanding purposes such as reading the classics, engaging in the serious study of literature, using the language for international business, or for advanced scholarship. Free reading is one way of extending the principles underlying the Natural Approach to the intermediate level. It can help to bridge the gap between easier and more difficult reading materials. By combining free reading with the usual kinds of assigned reading in a literature–based language arts class, students have the ideal opportunity to develop second–language literacy.

The type of input that is received through free reading is qualitatively different, then, from what an L2 acquirer receives through usual daily contact with the language. This may result from "the possibility that through the reading materials provided, learners can explore a wider range of topics and situations, with the accompanying linguistic elements, than was available to them in their everyday interaction" (Hafiz and Tudor, 1989, p. 9).

In addition to providing opportunities for L2 acquirers to read better, free reading is also a facilitator of overall language development. In fact, Krashen (1985) asserts that the evidence strongly suggests that "reading exposure may be the primary means of developing reading comprehension, writing style, and more sophisticated vocabulary and grammar" (p. 90). In a two–year study on Fijian primary schools, Elley and Mangubhai (1983) found that by the end of the first year, the free reading experimental group had made substantial improvement in receptive skills; by the end of the second year, however, this improvement had extended to all aspects of the subjects' L2 abilities, including both oral and written production. As Elley (1991) asserts, this kind of spread of effect from reading competence to other language skills is a "most striking finding" (p. 404).

Aside from the development of related language competencies through reading, there is also evidence that transfer of language ability takes place between or among languages. This transfer effect occurred in the Fiji studies just described and was also found in an experiment in Tempe, Arizona, in which gains in English and Spanish reading abilities were positively correlated in the experimental group, suggesting that there was also a transfer in reading skills across the two languages

(Schon et al., 1985).

Finally, free reading has the potential to change second language acquirers' conceptions about the reading process, as a whole. As Cho and Krashen (1994) point out, many L2 acquirers do not believe that reading will help them. They believe, instead, that language acquisition is the result of the conscious learning of rules and output practice with error correction, rather than the result of comprehensible input. Based on this view, they come to see reading as "hard work" which entails word–by–word decoding of different texts.

Another problem has been that it is sometimes difficult for second language acquirers to find the right texts (Cho and Krashen, 1994). In many ESL classes, the input may well be comprehensible but not very interesting. An optimal free reading program could expose students to a variety of light reading options which would satisfy their craving for material that they can understand and enjoy. By engaging in free reading, it is possible that second language acquirers will come to view reading not as a task, but rather as a pleasant activity that leads to language acquisition.

How to Put the Theory into Practice

Having established that SSR offers numerous benefits for ESL acquirers, the next logical step was to determine the best way in which to implement it as a program. As I indicated earlier, this is somewhat harder than it would at first seem. "Doing SSR" has sometimes been translated into "letting kids read for a short time each day." While this is certainly part of the SSR package, there is a great deal more that goes into it. I know this because I have floundered at times myself; and I know it because teachers constantly ask me questions about SSR implementation. Typical questions include the following: Where do SSR books come from? Does the teacher supply them, or should students bring their own? Should I give students comprehension checks to be sure that they are understanding what they are reading? For how long should students read when they first start SSR? After they've been doing SSR for awhile? What if a student chooses a book that is too easy for him/her? Too hard? What do I do if students do not read during SSR but continuously fidget during the reading period? (Or worse, they think of ways to distract those who are reading!)

It is true that the early 1970s rules for SSR may serve as a starting place for determining the components of an SSR program. As you may recall from the beginning of this chapter, these six rules included the reading of self-selected materials; teacher modeling of the reading process; the selection of only one book, magazine or newspaper during an SSR period; continuous, uninterrupted reading for a prescribed period of time; no reports or records; and whole class (or department or school) participation. However, I wanted to have a more systematic method for identifying the entire range of SSR components. Therefore, I went back to the 32-study survey of SSR programs.

A Book Makes a "Safe Date"

I have found that it is difficult enough to teach high school level students without compounding the problem by being too serious with them. In looking at the characteristics of the successful SSR programs in the survey, I began to cull out several common components; appropriately, the acronym that could be formed from it was "Safe Date." Given the physical and emotional concerns that adolescents have these days about getting heavily involved in the dating scene, I often tease my students by telling them that if they don't have plans for the evening, a book represents a Safe Date. Knowing that the "book habit" rarely replaces opportunities for social interaction, I usually hear giggles and guffaws in response to my suggestion that they spend a quiet evening reading, but I'm also certain that once I have put the idea into their heads, some actually do it.

What, then, is a "Safe Date"? The acronym of Safe Date represents the eight SSR components that were common to the most successful programs in the 32-study survey: staff training, appeal of books, follow-up activities, environment, direct access to books, accountability (NON), time to read, and encouragement. Five of these components mirror the original McCracken (1971) six, the only exception being the rule that students choose one book or article to read. In the section on "access" to follow, I will emphasize the notion that students should be free to change reading materials if they find what they have decided upon is not interesting or appropriate for their purposes, just as they have the opportunity to make their own selection(s) in the first place.

What is significant about the identification of these eight components is that they provide specific information that has not been known previously: that is, precisely what factors should be included in an SSR program in order for it to be maximally effective. These factors, once understood, can easily be translated into specific implementational strategies and can serve to answer often-asked questions about SSR procedures. Therefore, in the two sections that follow, I will provide a brief summary of each factor and then describe how they came to be incorporated into what I consider to be an optimal, or "stacked for success," SSR program for high school ESL students.

Definitions of the Eight Factors

The first factor, "staff training" (which begins the acronym SAFE) refers primarily to acquainting teachers, administrators, and instructional aides with the philosophy underlying the theoretical underpinnings of SSR and the practical steps that need to be taken to implement it. Ganz and Theofield (1974) observe that those who wish to develop SSR programs should find faculty members who "feel as strongly as they do that SSR should be started and are willing to take their lumps to make it happen" (p. 614). If possible, the entire staff should be involved, particularly if the free reading program is being developed on a school-wide basis, and ideally, even if it is not. The larger the number of supporters that exist in any one school, the stronger the message is that free reading is important and the greater the number of students there will be who actively participate in the SSR program.

The second factor, "appeal of books," relates to having materials that large numbers of students find engaging. This includes providing a wide variety of sources and types of materials (paperbacks, tradebooks, periodicals, picture books, and comic books), different levels of readability and length, and an array of inviting cover illustrations. A crucial element of appeal is self-selection, or the opportunity to choose what is read. If a chosen material does not prove to be compelling enough, the student may exchange it for something else during the SSR period. Of utmost importance is that teachers find books that match learners' perceived preferences, perhaps by utilizing interest inventories, conference questionnaires, or interviews, rather than relying upon what the teachers imagine the students want to read. As

Van Jura (1984) claims, "The key point is to accept the students' reading choices" (p. 541). Potentially awkward behavior problems will often disappear when good "matches" can be made between students and what they read.

The third factor which the successful studies included was "follow–up activities," which must be carefully distinguished from accountability measures. There is much agreement that interactive, or sharing activities, which may follow the SSR period, can be positive contributions to reading programs. McCracken (1971) maintains that once students have become accustomed to independent reading, the teacher should then encourage responses from them--without making any effort to evaluate the responses. He notes that if the teachers talk about what they themselves have read and "share their delight" with students, students begin to do the same thing (p. 407). It has been suggested that books produce intellectual constructs in the minds of readers which can be better understood and appreciated by the readers if they are externalized by talking with others. For this reason, students have a "need to talk about their reading" (Carlsen and Sherrill, 1988, p. 88). Aside from opportunities to read and to share, creative activities can help to foster enthusiasm for reading. Such activities can include the development of student–produced newspapers with book recommenda–tion sections, book and author luncheons, student–produced stories and plays, and various other projects. Special activities in which the students engage after free reading can be motivating and challenging because they offer students chances to interact with others and to extend the ideas that were developed during reading. As long as these activities represent positive experiences for the students (and not thinly–disguised methods of assessment for the teacher), they can be effectively incorporated into the program.

Factor four, "encouragement," combines the influences of staff members, parents, and peers. Certainly, encouragement to read comes from having a staff that is committed to the value of reading and to the idea of SSR programs. Those who provide time for free reading "are likely to be instrumental in motivating children to seek enjoyment from recreational reading (Everett, 1987, p. 3). Staff members can portray their enthusiam for reading in a number of ways. Simply telling children to read may have an impact on the amount of reading done, argues Krashen (1993). A key element which is an effective tool for encouraging children to read is modeling. When students see that adults are reading, they sense that reading is being valued and receive the message that it is a worthwhile activity in which to participate (Gambrell, 1978; Mork, 1972; Cardanelli, 1992; and Clary, 1991). Similarly, parents can support in-school free reading programs by encouraging their children to select and obtain materials of interest for the program--and by making reading a natural and ordinary activity which occurs regularly at home. Finally, peer encouragement is particularly motivating. When students see their peers reading, the communication is that the activity is a socially-acceptable one. This kind of "peer group imitation" can be very influential in getting students to learn to read for pleasure (Sadoski, 1980, p. 154). The key is to make SSR a comfortable and enjoyable time so that students will decide that the "Reading Club" is one which they all want to join. (Smith, 1988b).

Factor five, which begins the acronym DATE, is "direct access" to books. McCracken and McCracken (1978) concluded over fifteen years ago that "a major obstacle to the successful implementation of SSR is the lack of adequate reading materials for students" (p. 78). Providing a "book flood," or what Fader (1976) terms "saturation," is the key to the beginning of an effective free reading program (p. 57). School and public libraries, classroom libraries, and students' personal book collections provide crucial means of access to reading materials. The greater the number of books available, the larger number of opportunities to use book sources, and the longer the number of hours that students have to browse and select books will determine just how good that access will be. Other important sources include donations from parents and community service clubs, peer-produced works, and materials from book clubs, book stores, and book fairs. Clary (1991) notes that it is important for reading materials to be "physically close" to students. When students are simply told to "bring something to read for SSR," it is likely that this lack of access will lead to their not bringing books at all or, at best, to their bringing materials that are not chosen for interest's sake.

The sixth factor, "accountability (NON)," refers to the absence of any required performance level and therefore the lack of any type of assessment or accountability (to be distinguished from "follow-up activities," discussed earlier). Just as students cannot acquire a language if they are anxious or afraid because their "affective filter" is too high

(Krashen, 1985), students cannot concentrate simply on the pleasure of reading when they are held accountable for what they read. Gallo (1968) points out that young people have many reasons for reading, and the chief reason is for pleasure: "Without a doubt, most students read primarily for enjoyment, and a book ceases to be worth reading as soon as it ceases to be enjoyable" (p. 535). In agreement with this position, Oliver (1976) reports that when there is no performance criteria, it reduces the frustration of the attempts of students to read more difficult books. They cannot be embarrassed, shamed or ridiculed for failing to demonstrate "competence." In general, then, measures that make students accountable are not recommended as components of SSR programs. This does not mean, however, that students should not participate in "follow–up activities" which serve as extensions to students' reading experiences and allow readers to share their expanding interests with classmates (e.g., creating ads, making art projects, doing dramatic presentations).

The seventh factor that successful programs included is "time to read." This may at first appear to be an obvious statement, yet in some ways it is not. The "sustained" and "silent" aspects of SSR must be stressed so that students are truly engaged in the reading process, rather than simply passing time or viewing SSR as an opportunity to socialize. Also, students must be offered frequent and routine opportunities to do free reading in order to ensure that students develop the "habit" of reading (Sadoski, 1980). In order for reading to become a routinely established activity, an SSR program should offer students a "distributed" time approach, in which they read on a regular basis at least twice or several times a week, as opposed to a "massed" time approach, where they read for longer periods of time on a less frequent basis (e.g., weekly or bi–monthly). It is generally recommended that teachers begin their free reading programs by starting with a "realistic" amount of time (Mork, 1972). Many SSR proponents advocate starting with small increments of time, as low as 3–10 minutes for very young children, and moving toward a planned, gradual increase in the length of the period, as high as 40–60 minutes for older students (Allington, 1975; McCracken, 1971; Botel, 1977; Gambrell, 1978; Manning–Dowd, 1985; and Moore, Jones, and Miller, 1980).

The eighth and final factor which the successful SSR programs included was "environment." A good deal of attention has been paid to the idea of providing an environment that is conducive to free reading. It is logical that when readers are in comfortable, quiet surroundings, they will be more motivated to start reading and to sustain it. In terms of comfort, the student must feel physically, as well as emotionally, at ease. Certainly, pillows, easy chairs, and carpeting can contribute to the "homey" atmosphere, as well as the presence of students' art work, colorful posters, and mobiles (Gambrell, 1978; Clary, 1991). However, part of making students relax comes from creating a structure for reading so that they know what to expect during free reading periods. Students should be allowed to self-pace, which means that they can read at rates that are appropriate for them without feeling the necessity to compete with others. In addition, they deserve reading time that is free from interruptions such as phone calls and other distractions and during which they can forget about the passing of time (since the teacher will note the ending time of the SSR period for them). With both elements of comfort and quiet in place, the SSR period can offer students a valuable "20-minute vacation" (Jones, 1978, p. 102).

Implementing an SSR Program with All Eight Factors: "Stacking It for Success"

Having determined what components should go into the development of an optimal SSR program, I set out to implement what I termed a "stacked for success" SSR program with my own sample of 131 intermediate level ESL students. I decided to contrast a one-semester time period of progress for my students with the same period of progress for 117 intermediate ESL students from a neighboring high school, whose staff members were not familiar wih the eight components of SSR. In this way, I hoped that I could determine as objectively as possible that any difference in results that I attained would be due to a difference in reading programs. The group from my school was called Group A, and the group from the comparison school was called Group B.

The background of the students in both high schools was similar. Both samples came from a wide variety of language groups and were approximately from the same socioeconomic scale levels. All of the students had been placed in intermediate ESL classes based on their performance on a district placement test and their earlier records of placement in ESL classes, if available.

The goals of the experiment were to determine whether the students in a "stacked for success" SSR program (one containing the eight identified SSR components) would make greater progress in the areas of reading comprehension and the development of positive attitudes toward reading than the students who were in an SSR program that did not contain all of the eight components.

I administered the Stanford Diagnostic Reading Test (Brown, Form G) to both groups in early September and then gave the posttest (Brown, Form H) again at the end of the semester, in January. In addition, the students answered questions related to their reading habits and preferences on a revised form of the Estes Attitude Survey, in order to determine the degree to which the students felt positively toward reading at the beginning of the semester and again at the end. They were also invited to respond to a pre and post Student Questionnaire which focused on frequency of outside reading habits and the range of reading sources students used to find books for SSR.

Group A participated in a four-month "stacked for success" SSR program, in which the eight components were included in the following ways: (1) *Access to books* was provided by purchasing an additional 250 books for the in-class collection (which already included 230 books), though students could select books from any other sources they wished, including the school library, the public library, their homes, stores, and book clubs. (It must be noted, however, that the school library was only open three periods a day and rarely at snack or lunch times.) Funds were provided through Chapter I resources allocated specifically for the SSR program. (2) *Book appeal* was incorporated by surveying students about their reading interests before the new books were purchased and by helping students to locate books by favorite authors or on special topics as the semester progressed. As students became interested in specific series or genres, additional books were purchased, giving students a measure of "personalized" attention and maintaining their interest levels. All reading materials were self-selected. (3) *A conducive environment* was established by providing a physically comfortable area for reading. All of the SSR rules for quiet and uninterrupted periods of time to read were observed. Office personnel and other staff members were requested not to call or send messengers during the SSR period. (4) *Encouragement to read* was offered by (a) informing students of the theoretical reasons why free reading was important to their literacy development; (b) asking them to read when they were not reading; (c) modeling the reading process as the students read; and (d) personally helping students to find books when they could not initially get "hooked." In some cases, the teacher loaned students books from her personal library or made calls to public libraries in order to locate particular titles. (5) *Staff training* was already undertaken since SSR procedures represented a primary interest of the teacher. (6) There were no accountability measures following the SSR period. (7) *Follow-up activities* were developed on a weekly or bi-weekly basis, where students could extend their involvement with the individual books they had been reading through sharing activities with other students. Favorite projects included the designing of book covers and "advertisements" and the formation of literature groups, in which students could discuss what they had read with others who had read the same books. (8) *Time* to read silently was offered daily for 15-20 minutes (representing a "distributed time to read" approach).

Group B also participated in a four-month SSR program, but because all eight components were not present, it could not be classified as a "stacked for success" program. Two factors, follow-up activities and staff training, were entirely missing. Additionally, two others that were included, access and encouragement, were implemented in a limited fashion and are discussed in their respective sections to follow: (1) *Access to books* was provided by allowing students to utilize materials from existing classroom collections and to visit the school library, which was open five periods a day and had just purchased a large number of "easy reading" books though Chapter I funds. However, this factor was limited because many teachers in the Group B school did not allow students to take home the classroom materials that they had begun reading during SSR; therefore, these students lost access to their current reading books for outside pleasure reading purposes. (2) *Book appeal* was incorporated by allowing students to read any kinds of materials (magazines, newspapers, books, etc.) and to self-select these materials. (3) A *conducive environment* was established by providing a physically comfortable area for reading. All of the SSR rules for quiet and uninterrupted periods of time to read were observed, with the exception of a few telephone conversations. (4) *Encouragement to read* was offered by asking students to read when they were not reading and telling them that reading was important. However, encouragement was restricted in two ways: Though teachers verbally encouraged students to read, they often did not model the reading process, engaging in tasks such as lesson planning and paper correction and occasionally making phone calls during SSR. In addition, though the teachers urged students to read, they did not share with them the philosophy underlying the benefits of SSR, as the Group A teacher did. (5) There were no accountability measures following the SSR period. (6) *Time to read* silently was offered daily for 15–20 minutes (representing a "distributed time to read" approach).

Results of the standardized test, the attitude survey, and the student questionnaire in late January indicated that the students in Group A had outperformed the students in Group B in a number of ways, all of which were statistically significant: (1) Though Group A's average reading comprehension pretest scores were below Group B's (Stanford Diagnostic Test), their average posttest scores were 1.67 raw score points higher, given a scale of 1–60; (2) similarly, on questions related to the development of positive attitudes towards reading (Estes Attitude Survey), Group A's average scores were below Group B's on the pretest but higher by an average of 2.01 raw score points on the posttest, given a scale of 1–40; (3) as determined by the student questionnaire, (a) Group A students did less outside reading than Group B students at the outset of the program but more outside reading at the end of the program (an average posttest difference of 0.41 raw score points, given a scale of 1–4), and (b) Group A students sought a smaller variety of sources (e.g., school library, public library, friends' books/magazines, book club, book store, classroom collection) for their in–school and home free reading activities than Group B students at the beginning of the program but a wider range of sources at the end of the program (an average posttest difference of 0.64 raw score points, given a scale of 1–7).

What These Results Really Tell Us

First, the students in both groups did very well. They increased their reading comprehension levels in only four months by a little over one full year. The reason that the difference in raw score points between the two groups does not translate into a difference in grade equivalency is related to the fact that the Group B students started higher than the Group A students. An average increase of 1.67 raw score points on the lower end of the norms booklet range is reflected in a higher grade equivalency gain than that same increase toward the middle of the norms booklet range. Both groups also developed more positive attitudes toward reading and looked to a wider variety of sources from which to find their reading materials. The only area in which Group B did not make any gains (and, in fact, sustained a slight loss) was in frequency of outside reading. One explanation for this is that the students were already doing a good deal of outside reading at the beginning of the semester (an average of "sometimes to often") and didn't have much room to "grow"; another possibility is that they may not have received enough encouragement or been provided sufficient access to "take-home" materials to continue their free reading outside of school. As discussed before, both encouragement and access were limited factors in the Group B program.

What is clear is that Group A, which experienced an optimal SSR program, did better than the students in Group B, which engaged in what can be called a limited version of SSR. Because all eight components were not present, the program could not be identified as "stacked for success." With this information in hand, it seems obvious that teachers who wish to offer the most powerful program possible should make every effort to include all eight factors. Though no definitive data exists at the present time to identify if some components are more important than others, it is significant that the most successful programs in the original survey included an average of 6.5 of the eight factors, while the unsuccessful groups included a lower average of 4.5 factors. Notably, six factors were present most often in the successful groups: Included most frequently were access, environment, and distributed time to read; and (2) included next most frequently were appeal, encouragement, and non-accountability. Follow-up activities and staff training were included least often. It is not possible to ascertain precisely which factors made the greatest contributions in the four-month study without conducting a multiple regression analysis, but there is a similar pattern within the successful groups which should be acknowledged, at the very least. Perhaps the six most frequently included factors will eventually be determined to be the most important.

Intuition Plays a Large Role; But It's Reassuring When Our Premises Are Supported by the Research

All those years that I asked my students to participate in SSR, I felt that the theoretical concept of free reading was right, and it was. I believe that most teachers have a very good handle on what "works" with students, and those involved in helping students to develop literacy can see fairly early, positive results with SSR, even when all eight factors have not been implemented. However, by becoming familiar with the eight factors, it is now possible for staff members to start SSR programs that have the greatest potential for helping students to read better and to enjoy reading more. The hope is that, once having become engaged in the reading "habit," students continue to read more frequently outside of class and turn to a wider variety of sources to find their reading materials, as the students in Group A did in the four-month study.

The Bottom Line: What Students Think About SSR

As a short testament to the SSR experiences of a few of the students who participated in the Group A program, I include some of their end-of-semester journal entries, in which they were asked to write a thank-you letter (to be sent eventually, or not) to someone who has influenced their lives. I was the lucky recipient of these:

You were great in teaching us. You brought me joy of reading, and I made my spelling better in your class. I never liked to read, but when I got your class and we had to read, I thought it was boring, but when I did it, I really enjoyed reading. I just want to say thank you from my heart.

Thanks a lot. I loved to have this class. You taught us a lot, and now I read better. And I'm very proud to speak with other guys without shame.

Thank you for teaching me how to read. Because I'm not used to reading. In fact, I used to hate reading a book. But now I like to read what I used to NOT read last year, and I'm getting better. I write better too.

These comments show that students can learn to enjoy reading; and more important, that they understand the benefits they receive from reading. Even in these few letters (and there were many more like them), students refer to other areas of language (spelling, speaking, writing) that developed along with their reading ability, enjoyment, and confidence.

Though Manning–Dowd (1985) has said that "whenever a person selects something to read for his/her own purpose, spends more than a few minutes reading it and comprehending whatever (s)he wants, SSR is occurring" (p. 1), it is important to recognize that making this happen for all students is not always so spontaneous. Effective SSR programs must be planned, developed, and modified, in accordance with the needs of specific groups of students. (One teacher whom I know found that SSR worked better for her students when she played soft music; another found that she needed to post "Quiet" signs around the room and on her door in order to avoid interruptions.) Good free reading programs do not simply happen.

I am heartened by the opportunities that lie ahead for teachers and students. It is encouraging to know that there are specific steps to take that can inspire learners to become lifetime readers; for once they have been "hooked" by the reading habit, the likelihood is that students will continue to read when their teachers are no longer a part of their lives. As Allington (1975) has pointed out, the case for free reading is a good one if the major goal of schools is to "develop children who do read, as well as children who can read" (p.813).

References

Allington, R. (1975). Sustained approaches to reading and writing. *Language Arts, 52(6)*, 813–815.

Barbe, W., and J. Abbott. (1975). *Personalized reading instruction: New techniques that increase reading skills and comprehension.* West Nyack, New York: Parker Publishing Company, Inc.

Botel, M. (1977). *A comprehensive reading communication arts plan.* Harrisburg, Pennsylvania: Pennsylvania Department of Education.

Cardanelli, A. (1992). Teachers under cover: Promoting the personal reading of teachers. *The Reading Teacher, 45(9)*, 664–668.

Carlsen, G., and A. Sherrill. (1988). *Voices of readers: How we come to love books.* Urbana, Illinois: National Council of Teachers of English.

Cho, K. S., and S. Krashen. (1994). Acquisition of vocabulary from the Sweet Valley Kids series; Adult ESL acquisition. *Journal of Reading, 37(8)*, 662–667.

Clary, L. (1991). Getting adolescents to read. *Journal of Reading, 34 (5)*, 340–345.

Cline, R., and G. Kretke. (1980). An evaluation of long–term SSR in the junior high school. *Journal of Reading, 23(6)*, 503–506.

Elley, W. (1991). Acquiring literacy in a second language: The effect of book–based programs. *Language Learning, 41(3)*, 375–411.

Elley, W. (1992). *How in the world do students read?* Hamburg, Germany: The International Association for the Evaluation of Educational Achievement.

Elley, W., and F. Mangubhai. (1983). The impact of reading on second language learning. *Reading Research Quarterly, 19(1)*, 53–67.

Estes, T., J. Johnstone, and H. Richards. (1975). *The Estes Attitude Scales.* Charlottesville, Virginia: Virginia Research Associates, Ltd.

Everett, I. (1987). *Recreational reading effects on reading comprehension achievement.* M.A. thesis. New Jersey: Kean College of New Jersey. (ERIC Document Reproduction Service No. ED 283 123)

Fader, D. (1976) *The new hooked on books*. New York: Berkeley Medallion Book, Berkeley Publishing Company.

Gallo, D. (1968). Free reading and book reports: An informal survey of grade eleven. *Journal of Reading, 11(7)*, 532–538.

Gambrell, L. (1978). Getting started with sustained silent reading and keeping it going. The *Reading Teacher, 32(3)*, 328–331.

Ganz, P., and M. Theofield. (1974). Suggestions for starting SSR. *Journal of Reading, 17(8)*, 614–616.

Goodman, K. (1982). *Language and literacy: The selected writings of Kenneth S. Goodman*, (Vols. 1–2). Edited by F. Gollasch. London: Routledge and Kegan Paul.

Greaney, V. (1970). A comparison of individualized and basal reader approaches to reading instruction. *The Irish Journal of Education, 4(1)*, 19–29.

Greaney, V., and M. Clarke. (1975). A longitudinal study of the effects of two reading methods on leisure–time reading habits. In D. Moyle (Ed.), *Reading: What of the future?* (pp. 107–114). London: United Kingdom Reading Association.

Hafiz, F., and I. Tudor. (1989). Extensive reading and the development of language skills. *English Language Teaching Journal, 43(1)* ,4–13.

Hunt, L. (1967). Evaluation through teacher–pupil conferences. In T.C. Barrett (Ed.), *The evaluation of children's reading achievement* (pp. 111–126). Newark, Delaware: International Reading Association.

Jenkins, M. (1957). Self–selection in reading. *The Reading Teacher, 11 (2)*, 84–90.

Jones, C. (1978). 20 minute vacations. *Journal of Reading, 22(2)*, 102.

Krashen, S. (1985.) *Inquiries and Insights*. Menlo Park, California: Alemany Press.

Krashen, S. (1988). Do we learn to read by reading? The relationship between free reading and reading ability. In D. Tannen (Ed.), *Linguistics in context: Connecting observation and understanding* (pp. 269–298). Norwood, New Jersey: Ablex.

Krashen, S. (1993). *The power of reading*. Englewood, Colorado: Libraries Unlimited.

Lawson, H. (1968). Effects of free reading on the reading achievement of sixth–grade pupils. In J. A. Figurel (Ed.), *Forging ahead in reading* (pp. 501–504). Newark, Delaware: International Reading Association.

Mangubhai, F., and W. Elley. (1982). The role of reading in promoting ESL. *Language, Learning, and Communication, 1(2),* 151–160.

Manning–Dowd, A. (1985). The effectiveness of SSR: A review of the research. Information Analysis (Report No. CS 008 607). (ERIC Document Reproduction Service No. ED 276 970)

McCracken, R. (1971). Initiating sustained silent reading. *Journal of Reading, 14(8),* 521–524, 582–583.

McCracken, R., and M. McCracken. (1978). Modeling is the key to sustained silent reading. *The Reading Teacher, 31(4),* 406–408.

Moore, C., C. Jones, and D. Miller. (1980). What we know after a decade of sustained silent reading. *The Reading Teacher, 33(4),* 445–450.

Mork, T. (1972). Sustained silent reading in the classroom. *The Reading Teacher, 25(5),* 438–441.

Oliver, M. (1970). High intensity practice: The right to enjoy reading. *Education, 91(1),* 69–71.

Oliver, M. (1973). The effect of high intensity practice on reading comprehension. *Reading Improvement, 10(2),* 16–18.

Oliver, M. (1976). The effect of high intensity practice on reading achievement. *Reading Improvement, 13(4),* 226–228.

Petrimoulx, J. (1988). Sustained silent reading in an ESL class: A study. Paper presented at the 22nd Annual Meeting of the Teachers of English to Speakers of Other Languages, Chicago, Illinois. (ERIC Document Reproduction Service No. ED 301 068)

Pfau, D. (1967). Effects of planned recreational reading programs. *The Reading Teacher, 21(1),* 34–39.

Sadoski, M. (1980). Ten years of uninterrupted sustained silent reading. *Reading Improvement, 17(2),* 153–156.

Schon, I., K. Hopkins, and C. Vojir. (1985). The effects of special reading time in Spanish on the reading abilities and attitudes of Hispanic junior high school students. *Journal of Psycholinguistic Research, 14(1),* 57–65.

Smith, F. (1976). Learning to read by reading. *Language Arts, 53,* 297–299, 322. Reprinted in Smith, F. (1983). *Essays into literacy.* Exeter: Heinemann Educational Books.

Smith, F. (1988a). *Understanding reading.* Hillsdale, New Jersey: Lawrence Erlbaum Associates, Inc.

Smith, F. (1988b). *Joining the literacy club: Further essays into
education.* Portsmouth, New Hampshire: Heinemann Educational
Books.

Van Jura, S. (1984). Secondary students at risk: Two giant steps toward
independence in reading. *Journal of Reading, 27(6),* 540–543.

Watkins, M., and V. Edwards. (1992). Extracurricular reading and
reading achievement: The rich stay rich and the poor don't read.
Reading Improvement, 29, 236–242.

Studies Used in the Survey of SSR Studies

Aranha, M. (1985). Sustained silent reading goes East. *The Reading
Teacher, 39(2),* 214–217.

Cline, R., and G. Kretke. (1980). An evaluation of long–term SSR in
the junior high school. *Journal of Reading, 23(6),* 503–506.

Collins, C. (1980). Sustained silent reading periods: Effect on teachers'
behaviors and students' achievement. *The Elementary School
Journal, 81(2),* 109–114.

Davis, F., and J. Lucas. (1971). An experiment in individualized
reading. *The Reading Teacher, 24(8),* 737–743, 747.

Elley, W. (1991). Acquiring literacy in a second language: The
effect of book–based programs. *Language Learning, 41(3),* 375–
411.

Elley, W., and F. Mangubhai. (1983). The impact of reading on second
language learning. *Reading Research Quarterly, 19(1),* 53–67.

Evans, H., and J. Towner. (1975). Sustained silent reading: Does it
increase skills? *The Reading Teacher, 29(2),* 155–156.

Everett, I. (1987). *Recreational reading effects on reading comprehen
sion achievement.* M.A. thesis. New Jersey: Kean College of New
Jersey. (ERIC Document Reproduction Service No. ED 283 123)

Fader, D. (1976) *The new hooked on books.* New York: Berkeley
Medallion Book, Berkeley Publishing Company.

Farrell, E. (1982). SSR as the core of a junior high school reading
program. *Journal of Reading, 1(26),* 48–51.

Greaney, V. (1970). A comparison of individualized and basal reader
approaches to reading instruction. *The Irish Journal of Education,
4(1),* 19–29.

Hafiz, F., and I. Tudor. (1989). Extensive reading and the development of language skills. *English Language Teaching Journal, 43* (1), 4–13.

Holt, S., and O'Tuel, F. (1989). The effect of sustained silent reading and writing on achievement and attitudes of seventh and eighth grade students reading two years below grade level. *Reading Improvement, 26(4)*, 290–297.

Jenkins, M. (1957). Self–selection in reading. *The Reading Teacher, 11 (2)*, 84–90.

Kaminsky, D. (1992). *Improving intermediate grade level ESL students' attitudes toward recreational reading.* Ed.D. Practicum. Florida: Nova University. (ERIC Document Reproduction Service No. ED 47 509)

Lai, F. (1993). The effect of a summer reader course on reading and writing skills. *System, 21(1)*, 87–100.

Lawson, H. (1968). Effects of free reading on the reading achievement of sixth–grade pupils. In J. A. Figurel (Ed.), *Forging ahead in reading* (pp. 501–504). Newark, Delaware: International Reading Association.

Manning, G., and M. Manning. (1984). What models of recreational reading make a difference? *Reading World, 23(4)*, 375–380.

Maynes, F. (1981). Uninterrupted sustained silent reading. *Reading Research Quarterly, 17(1)*, 159–160.

Minton, M. (1980). The effect of sustained silent reading upon comprehension and attitudes among ninth graders. *Journal of Reading, 23(6)*, 498–502.

Oliver, M. (1973). The effect of high intensity practice on reading comprehension. *Reading Improvement, 10(2)*, 16–18.

Oliver, M. (1976). The effect of high intensity practice on reading achievement. *Reading Improvement, 13(4)*, 226–228.

Petrimoulx, J. (1988). *Sustained silent reading in an ESL class: A study.* Paper presented at the 22nd Annual Meeting of the Teachers of English to Speakers of Other Languages, Chicago, Illinois. (ERIC Document Reproduction Service No. ED 301 068)

Pfau, D. (1967). Effects of planned recreational reading programs. *The Reading Teacher, 21(1)*, 34–39.

Schon, I., K. Hopkins, and C. Vojir. (1984). The effects of Spanish reading emphasis on the English and Spanish reading abilities of Hispanic high school students. *Bilingual Review, 11(1)*, 33–39.

Schon, I., K. Hopkins, and C. Vojir. (1985). The effects of special reading time in Spanish on the reading abilities and attitudes of Hispanic junior high school students. *Journal of Psycholinguistic Research, 14(1)*, 57–65.

Sperzel, E. (1948). The effect of comic books on vocabulary growth and reading comprehension. *Elementary English, 25(2)*, 109–113.

Summers, E., and V. McClelland. (1982). A field–based evaluation of sustained silent reading in intermediate grades. *The Alberta Journal of Educational Research, 28(2)*, 100–112.

Wiscont, J. (1990). *A study of the sustained silent reading program for intermediate grade students in the Pulaski, Wisconsin School District.* M.S. Thesis. Oshkosh, Wisconsin: University of Wisconsin. (ERIC Document Reproduction Service No. ED 323 520)

Chapter 7

Maestro, Can We Go to the Library Today?
The Role of the School Library in the Improvement of Reading Attitudes and Achievement Among Bilingual Elementary Students

Daniel T. Brassell

The Problem

How do children learn how to read? How long does it take them to learn? What motivates them? These three questions have been engraved in my thoughts since I began teaching four months ago. These questions, in my opinion, concern all teachers, librarians and parents.

As a first year teacher, *maestro*, in Springfield, California, I had absolutely no idea how to teach my second grade students, many of whom are non-English proficient (NEPs), how to read. The only materials provided to me (which were limited) encouraged drilling of consonants and vowels. The majority of teaching strategies I have utilized have been concepts learned in my graduate classes this past semester, such as Krashen's notion (1987) of free, voluntary reading (FVR).

Drawing on this notion, I have reworked several of my classroom activities so that there is a promotion of this concept. I agree with

Krashen that students who are allowed to read whatever they want will become more interested in reading and, therefore, become better readers. I take my students to the school library every day and allow them to read whatever they want, wherever they want, with whomever they want, as long as they read. In my classroom I supply a variety of books in English and Spanish. Finally, I use free reading time as a positive incentive for students to finish their work early. For the purposes of this study, I will focus solely on taking my students to the school library daily.

Of my thirty-two second graders, only one knew how to read at the beginning of the school year. Four students knew the alphabet, and eight students knew how to write their first and last names. Many students copied words from right to left rather than left to right, and most could not follow words in books with their index fingers. None of the students knew their addresses or telephone numbers.

Appalled by what I perceived as my students' illiteracy and determined to teach them basic skills, I taught them things I thought they needed to know, such as phonics, the alphabet, etc. My preoccupation with language skills blinded me from seeing how students really learn: through meaningful experiences.

Students must want to read in order to become good and, more importantly, habitual readers. As their teacher, I found it my responsibility to provide them with positive reading experiences, allowing them to read whatever and how much they wanted. I asked students about their various reading experiences and was startled to find that close to none of my students had ever been to a library before, certainly never on a regular basis.

Faced with this issue, I set out to see what role the school library could play in improving my students' reading attitudes and comprehension.

The Purpose

In investigations conducted by Morrow and Weinstein (1982, 1986), literature use increased dramatically when teachers incorporated enjoyable literature activities into their daily programs and when library centers were created in the classrooms. The purpose of this study was

The Role of the School Library in the Improvement   157
of Reading Attitudes and Achievement
Among Bilingual Elementary Students

to determine whether bilingual children's increased visitations to the school library positively affected their attitudes and competency in reading. This study is composed primarily of anecdotal records and personal observations of my second grade bilingual class kept during an eight-week period from October 25–December 23, 1994. These observations were used to assess students' attitudes and behavior at the beginning and end of the study. While increased reading achievement was not observed, I found significant increases in student interest in the school library and in books. This result has prompted me to continue this reading program throughout the school year, continuing to focus on the goals of improved reader interest and capabilities.

The Research

Krashen (1987) found that students who do more free voluntary reading (FVR) show superior levels of competence in reading, vocabulary, writing style and grammatical development. Empowering students to read voluntarily seems to teach children to connect reading with pleasure. Morrow (1991) points out that "if youngsters enjoy looking at books, then eventually reading them, they will tend to read more, which in turn can lead to improved reading ability" (p. 681).

However beneficial FVR may be to students, the problem for educators seems to be motivating students to read. Two motivations seem to be most important in explaining reasons for reading: reading for knowledge and reading for pleasure (McEvoy & Vincent, 1980).

In their 1978 study on reading among adults in the United States that included 1,450 in-depth personal interviews, McEvoy and Vincent (1980) found that although a majority of all readers mentioned general knowledge as among the reasons they read, pleasure appeared to be the key motivating factor for book readers. Those reading only newspapers and magazines, they found, were chiefly motivated by general knowledge. In either instance it can be said that motivation is created by interest (Irving, 1980), and an element of personal motivation (interest) in voluntary reading leads to greater skill development.

The competition of other media for the leisure time of children and youth raises the question of interest in reading, compared to interest in other activities (Robinson & Weintraub, 1973). Based on the research available, it seems that children use other media far more frequently than they use reading.

This leads to an interesting comparison between the concepts of reading given by children defined as "good" readers and those given by "poor" readers. Perhaps there is a significant relationship between children's concepts of reading and their reading achievement. The meaningful definitions of reading are given by students who are identified as good readers rather than those identified as poor readers.

Furthermore, a number of studies have reported significant relationships between amount of reading for pleasure and level of reading competency (Connor, 1954; Long & Henderson, 1973; Whitehead, Capey & Maddren, 1975; and Maxwell, 1977). Put simply, students who demonstrate voluntary interest in books are rated higher by teachers on school performance than are children with low interest in books (Morrow, 1986).

The crisis that American society faces today is that large numbers of students do not care to read. Few schools (Morrow, 1986) encourage those activities and attitudes that will lead to development of voluntary reading, and many tend to support and implement programs that may actually impede development of voluntary reading by emphasizing reading skills. Morrow (1991) argues that "if success in reading is influenced by children's attitudes toward reading, by their association of reading with pleasure, by the opportunity to practice skills through actual reading and by exposure to a rich literary environment, then the development of voluntary reading must be a key component of efforts to foster literacy" (p. 684). Teachers do not seem to be doing an adequate job of promoting voluntary reading habits.

Irving (1980) reports that the teacher can play an important role in stimulating voluntary reading in children. It would appear that the most critical way a teacher can stimulate voluntary reading would be to provide students time to read for pleasure.

In her study on the effect of individualized reading on children's reading test scores, Aranow (1961) found that New York City children in the fourth and fifth grades who were involved in individualized, free reading programs tended to make gains on standardized reading tests that were larger than the gains other comparable children made with more usual reading programs. Once again, students will not become lifetime readers unless they frequently experience reading as a

The Role of the School Library in the Improvement   159
of Reading Attitudes and Achievement
Among Bilingual Elementary Students

pleasurable activity, and teachers play an important role in facilitating this activity.

McDermott (1977), in a study of a single classroom, found poor readers spent less time than good readers and differential interaction patterns between the teacher and the different groups--differences that seemed to favor the good readers. By providing class time (Sanacore, 1990) for reading self-selected resources, the teacher increases the potential for generating habitual reading among both poor and good readers. Teachers may utilize all kinds of different strategies to foster positive reading habits among students.

Morrow and Weinstein (1982) found that despite widespread agreement among educators that early exposure to literature is beneficial, it would appear that many kindergartens do not have a regular literature program or a well-designed library corner. They found that providing a suitable library corner enhanced the level of voluntary literature in kindergartens by 25% in the classes they studied. The results of their investigation further support the relationship between early exposure to literature and success in beginning reading.

In addition, Forester (1975) points out that "children learn to speak by speaking, but when a child opens a book, it suddenly seems that the only 'right way' to learn is to begin with the ABCs and rules of reading." In the first grade class Forester observed in Victoria, Canada, children listened to stories and read familiar nursery rhymes from large wall charts. The teacher constantly modeled good reading habits while the children read. Students hear and say the sentences and stories they themselves dictated and listen to tape recordings of books while following along page by page. They read to each other and put on plays. Most importantly, they develop a highly positive attitude toward learning and reading. These techniques may prove especially essential in the bilingual student's development of reading skills.

When considering other cultures in reading comprehension, it is important to realize that in many instances more attention is given to oral language skills and more demands are placed on the ability to memorize (Field & Aebersold, 1990). Cohen (1968) suggests that "the importance of reading to children as a precursor to success in learning to read has been shown to be vital in the case of socially disadvantaged children who do not have experiences with books at home" (p. 213). This leads to the question of strategies that may be developed to teach these children how to read.

Of particular concern in my study were reading strategies used for bilingual students, unable to read in either their native language (in this case, Spanish) or in English. Janopoulos (1985) says that if FVR proves to be as effective in second language acquisition (L2) as it seems to be in first language acquisition (L1), it could become an integral part of English as a Second Language (ESL) classes. Again, free reading seems to benefit all students.

One study in particular by Greaney and Neuman (1990) shows how cross-cultural research may be critical to building a broader conceptualization of why people read. The findings of this investigation suggest that, for 10- and 13-year-olds, reading may serve educational and moral needs as well as offering a source of pleasure and a means of escape. By identifying whether certain aspects of reading are unique to particular cultures or are universal, we can begin to develop a better theoretical understanding of the nature of reading (Greaney & Neuman, 1990).

It should be noted that students learning to read English are less proficient in using both textual and contextual clues (Carrell, 1983). The way to increase this proficiency, as in first language acquisition, seems to be by encouraging students with limited English to read more (White, Graves & Slater, 1990). A hypothesis that spelling and vocabulary are developed in second languages as they are in the first language--by reading--is, then, at least reasonable (Krashen, 1989).

In a study on the effect of book-based school programs, Elley (1991) found that bilingual children exposed to, and encouraged to read and share, a lot of illustrated story books are consistently found to learn the target language more quickly. In this way--through books-- children appear to learn the language incidentally and to develop a positive attitude toward books. Again, the importance of books is stressed, supporting the notion (Bilingual Education, 1988) that "a print-rich environment is essential for successful language acquisition and literacy development" (p. 119).

The school library is perhaps the most "print-rich environment" students may encounter. Cleary (1939) found that one of the most significant factors influencing children's reading interest is accessibility of reading material. A study by Lamme (1976) showed that the school library was the overwhelming primary source of books among

The Role of the School Library in the Improvement   161
of Reading Attitudes and Achievement
Among Bilingual Elementary Students

elementary students. Swanton (1984) found that 71% of the "gifted" students and 70% of "regular" students in her study mentioned the public library or school library as their primary source of recreational reading material.

Constantino (1994) writes that "an essential aspect in the encouragement and development of literacy and FVR is access to abundant supplies of printed materials. The library, therefore, becomes an extremely helpful tool in developing literacy" (p. 87). By promoting library use, school and public libraries may provide a good atmosphere for encouraging children's early interests and habits in reading (Swanton, 1984). This study seeks to examine if increased accessibility to the school library enhanced the reading abilities and attitudes of my second grade bilingual students.

The Setting

Harry S. Truman Elementary School in north-central Springfield includes grades K–5 as well as a preschool. Approximately 750 students go to Truman, the majority of which--around 85%--are Latino. Last year (1993) Truman students ranked twenty-third out of twenty-four Springfield elementary schools in their reading and writing test scores.

All schools in the Springfield Unified School District are classified as Chapter One--low income--by the federal government, and they receive additional funds from the federal government. The District was taken over this past February by the California State Administrator, making it the first school district run by the state.

In an effort to revamp Springfield's schools, the District has hired new principals for virtually every school, including Truman. Of the twenty-three teachers on staff at Truman, seven of them are first year teachers on emergency credentials, including myself and two other Teach for America corps members.

There are four second grade classes, with average class sizes of thirty-three students. The other three second grade teachers are African-American women with between three and thirty-two years of teaching experience.

While each teacher has a homeroom class (and my homeroom class will be the focus of this study), students switch classrooms in the morning for Language Arts and Social Studies instruction, according to their language proficiency. Mrs. Turner teaches high level English–only students (E.O.s), Mrs. Gatling teaches low level E.O.s, Mrs. Hopkins teaches Limited–English Proficient students (L.E.P.s) and I teach Non–English Proficient students (N.E.P.s). In the afternoon students return to their homerooms to receive English instruction in Mathematics and Science.

From October 25–December 23, 1994 (eight weeks), I took my homeroom class of thirty–two students (twenty–seven Latino and five African–American) to the school library daily from 12:30–1:00 p.m., barring interruptions or special school events (which both seem to happen too frequently). Students line up according to quietest group at their seats with their heads on their desks. The six groups––The Power, Yellow Rangers, Black Rangers, Green Rangers, Pink Rangers and Red Rangers––line up between the week's line leaders and line monitors. When the line leaders and line monitors give the "thumbs up" that the lines are straight and quiet, we leave the room.

The students enjoy the walk to the library because I allow them to run around and pick up garbage. Each group is anxious to clean and work in front of me so that their group may earn "Table of the Day," for which they receive a bathroom pass. Once we reach the library (about a minute's walk away), students again line up between the line leaders and line monitors and wait for the thumbs up. Since they want as much library time as possible, they usually quiet each other down as soon as possible.

We use the side entrance to the library, which creates problems if it has been left locked. On a few occasions I have had to walk through other teachers' classrooms to unlock the library for my class. Once I had to ask a janitor to turn on the lights since there are no light switches that can be turned on without a special key.

The school library provides a wide array of services, several of which may be more appropriate in another area. On rainy days it often serves as a playground for students. On Friday afternoons some teachers show their students movies on a school TV/VCR in the library. It serves as an "overflow" room on days when teachers are absent and there are no substitute teachers to take over their classes. One day my class could not go to the library because a District nurse was conducting student eye exams, and on another day the library was where student pictures were being taken.

The Role of the School Library in the Improvement   163
of Reading Attitudes and Achievement
Among Bilingual Elementary Students

The library itself is about the size of four classrooms, and it has two classrooms on each of its north and south sides. One of the teachers insists on keeping her door open, which often causes a distraction to my students who are trying to read. Along the east and west sides of the library are book carts with various unshelved books to choose from. Bookshelves line the north and south walls in between the doors to the adjacent classrooms. There are a couple of tables along the walls where students may read quietly. In the center of the room are seven circular tables which can seat up to six students each.

There is a school resource specialist who takes care of the library, but her responsibilities are not specifically related to library order and maintenance. The card catalog is virtually useless, since books are just placed on the shelves. There are also very few books here in Spanish. Still, every day my students nudge at my pant leg and ask, "Maestro, can we go to the library today?"

The Method

Thirty–two students, my entire second grade homeroom class, were observed. During the eight–week study, I spoke with each student at least twice (once in the first four weeks and once in the second four weeks) about his/her attitude about reading books and visiting the school library. At this time I would also ask students to show me what they were reading and tell me what their book was about. Most of my students could not read the titles of their books nor read the stories.

My only rules are that the students use their "one voices" (low voices) and that they take care of the library. Students read whatever they want, from magazines about animals to books about basketball to thick encyclopedias to basic Spanish picture books. Some read by themselves, others read in groups and others sit around me while I read. Some read at tables, others read on the floor (lying down) and others sit under tables. The whole goal of this activity is to encourage students to enjoy reading and the library, two goals FVR is designed to promote.

In addition to asking the students themselves about their library experiences, I kept a log of personal observations of the students in the library. These accounts of individual students comprise the majority of data used in this study.

The Results

In my class I was able to identify various patterns followed by students. Four distinct classifications emerged. Some students (Group A) preferred reading in small groups, perhaps under a table or in a corner where they felt a little more independent from the class. Some students (Group B) found a book immediately, sat at a table and read quietly for the entire period. Some students (Group C) wandered around the library, switching books frequently and playing with their friends until they were told to read. And, finally, some students (Group D) would follow me wherever I was in the library and mimic the way I read.

Of these groups, I identified 15 students reading in small groups, nine students reading alone, two students wandering, and six students reading around me. I must mention here that these students were not always in these particular classifications. In fact, at the beginning of the study I identified 23 students who were wandering around rather than reading.

I have included my accounts of eight students, two from each of the groups I described above. I find each of the students that I write about here to be fairly representative of their reading groups.

Group A – Edgar

Edgar is one of my brightest students. He is always raising his hand, finishing his assignments before the other students and helping others in the classroom. Since he is eager to help others, I was not surprised to see three other students cling to him in the library. I firmly believe that when he reads aloud to other students (especially Spanish–speaking students), Edgar is helping his classmates through positive modeling and involving their interests.

Although Edgar cannot read according to District definitions (and I must point out here that he has improved tremendously this year), I observed early in the study that he does not permit his illiteracy to get in the way of reading a good book, such as *The Cat in the Hat*, one of his favorites. Whenever Edgar comes to a word he does not know, he puts in the word he thinks should go there. One day he read a story to

The Role of the School Library in the Improvement   165
of Reading Attitudes and Achievement
Among Bilingual Elementary Students

me, and although he did not correctly guess many of the words, he was able to look at the pictures and make his own story. And I thought Edgar's story was better!

His reading group will normally read under a table close to a group of girls who also read under a table. Often, the boys will show the girls pictures of scorpions or snakes that they find in magazines, and predictably they will tattle on each other in a "flirtatious" sort of way.

While I do not encourage students to play in the library, I do want them to have fun there. Edgar tells me practically every day that the library is his favorite place to go. Early in the study I asked him, "Why?"

"Nobody else ever took me there before," he replied.

Group A – Jeanette

On the first day of school, Jeanette arrived to my classroom fifteen minutes earlier than my next student. During that time I was able to talk with Jeanette and her mother for a little bit. Jeanette's mom showed me how Jeanette could add two–digit numbers, read books in English and Spanish, and color elaborate pictures. Jeanette was my first student, and I thought to myself, "Teaching these students might not be that tough after all."

Needless to say, at the beginning of the school year Jeanette turned out to be my only student who could read. She knew it, too.

When I began taking my class to the library, I really counted on Jeanette to pull a couple of her friends aside and read with them. Everyday Jeanette would read with a small group of students. At first, she only read with her friends, but different students started gathering around her at the library. I even began to see a lot of boys, who normally want nothing to do with the girls, trying to read with Jeanette.

For a seven–year–old Jeanette has a wonderfully mature attitude, as she proves time and time again how interested she is in learning, teaching, and helping others.

"I want you to meet Edith," she said to me one day. "She is my best friend, and her friends are my friends."

Jeanette continues teaching her friends, my students. She is helping them all learn how to read much better, and in the process she is making herself a better reader.

Group B – Sandra

One of the most encouraging signs I have seen in our library visits has been an increase in the number of students who look for a place to read independently. I guess I like to see this because when I see them sitting alone and looking at their books, I can truly see them trying to read the words. Sandra has been one of those students who has read on her own from the beginning of the study, and she has made remarkable progress.

When we first started going to the library, I asked Sandra if she liked the library. She told me she did not because there were not many books in Spanish. I did not realize that she could tell the difference between Spanish and English, so I gave her five books (four in English and one in Spanish) and asked her to pick out one she would like to read. She picked the Spanish book.

A few days later I showed Sandra a few more Spanish books and asked her to pick out one she would like to take home and practice reading. She picked *El Patito Listo* (*The Clever Duckling*), and ever since I have seen her reading that book every time we come to the library. One day another girl asked Sandra why she always reads the same book. I was about to tell the girl not to bother Sandra when Sandra began reading a page to the girl, *word for word* (or, in this case, I guess, *palabra por palabra*).

Since that day, I often see different students selecting additional copies of *El Patito Listo* and asking Sandra for help.

Group B – Jonathan

"Are we going to the library today?" Jonathan usually asks when I give him an "early morning high–five" as he walks through the door. Those are the most words I think I ever heard Jonathan say in one sentence.

Jonathan's mother watches over him like a hawk, and she often comes into the classroom to bring him his notebook. She, as well as his abuelito (grandfather), often yells at him in front of the other students. Through it all, Jonathan just listens quietly with a helpless and fearful look on his face. He keeps to himself most of the time in my class, and he does not seem to have any regular playmates.

The Role of the School Library in the Improvement   167
of Reading Attitudes and Achievement
Among Bilingual Elementary Students

As Jonathan's teacher I have tried to boost his confidence as much as possible by giving him important classroom jobs and letting him answer a lot of questions. In fact, I use Jonathan to judge the strength of the lesson plans I teach.

If Jonathan is laughing and smiling I know it is a good lesson; if he shows no expression I know I need to improve the lesson. When he is sleeping I know I need to get my act together or leave the teaching profession. When Jonathan is alert and receptive, however, I know we are going to the library.

"I like getting any books I want and reading them where I want to," Jonathan told me when I asked him about what he likes most about our library visits.

Jonathan has read under tables, in corners, and at desks. I have seen him looking at books about dinosaurs, magazines with football stories, and encyclopedias with animal pictures. He excitedly shows what he is reading to other students sitting near him.

"I think we should go to the library all of the time," Jonathan frequently tells me.

Group C – Jorge

Jorge reminds me of one of my favorite television characters, the brown-nosing and deceitful Eddie Haskell on *Leave it to Beaver*. In front of Beaver's parents, Eddie is a saint and a do-gooder, but when he is around Beaver he is obnoxious.

While I read in the library, Jorge goes around hitting people with books, talking with his friends or disturbing students in some way. Whenever he sees me looking at him, he starts filing books in order or telling people to be quiet.

"I don't like any books in here," Jorge said to me one day early in the study. I began bringing Jorge books I had checked out from my library to see if he liked any of those books. He looked at about 60 different books before he found one that he liked.

I have had to check out Jorge's book three times since the study began. Jorge wanders around the library hitting people with his book, throwing his book and once even chewing his book. When I am keeping an eye on Jorge, however, he sits down, sometimes alone and other times with another student, and quietly reads his book. He knows the

story by heart (although he does not necessarily know how to read all
the words), and I have let him teach other students how to read his
book.

"I like the library better than the other things we learn," Jorge once
said to me. "I like walking around the library because it's a lot bigger
than the classroom."

Maybe Jorge is not always reading, but he does look forward to
going to the library. Sparking an interest in reading, in my opinion, is
the first, and possibly most important, step in developing literacy. I am
confident that Jorge is well on his way to being a good reader. It is like
a teacher of mine used to say: every student is gifted; it just takes some
a little longer to unwrap their gifts.

Group C - Pablo

In the morning I use a hand puppet named Pablo Payaso (Paul, the
clown) that kisses my Latino students who do their work. He is fairly
comical the way he bounces around the room. He reminds me of Pablo,
one of my homeroom students.

Pablo says he wants to learn how to read; he just does not like
looking at one book for too long. He is one of my students who has
been wandering around the library for eight weeks, and by December
23 I estimated Pablo had probably walked about four miles in the
library, searching for the book that would hold his interest forever.

He still has not found that book, but at least he is still looking. At
first I thought Pablo did not understand that I wanted him to choose a
book he liked and eventually read it. I had two other students, Enrique
and Felipe, show him how they found books and then laid down on the
floor in a corner, reading to each other. But Pablo likes to walk around
the library.

As long as he does not bother anyone, I see no harm in his walking
around the library. Good readers are picky readers, as my English
teachers in junior high school used to tell me. When I first walked into
a candy store, I was surrounded by hundreds, maybe thousands, of
delightful items, and my mother told me to pick out one thing I wanted.
I could not do it.

So I let Pablo walk around the library, tasting different books. It
may take him longer than my other students, but eventually I know he

The Role of the School Library in the Improvement   169
of Reading Attitudes and Achievement
Among Bilingual Elementary Students

will find one he likes.

Group D - Monette

Monette is always trying to get my attention. She used to get it by pushing people in line, fighting with other students and coming to school fifteen minutes late. Now she gets it by reading next to me.

Monette amazes me by the way she constantly challenges herself. I often compliment her on how well she reads, especially with different books. She will always look for a book more difficult than the one she read before. She makes sure to show me what she is reading in order to impress me.

"My mama said I've been reading so well that she's going to buy me whatever books I want for my birthday," she said to me.

I am so proud of Monette. She has come a long way in only a short period of time. She has gone from hitting other students to helping them read. I enjoy having Monette sitting and reading next to me. Now if I have students who say they cannot behave, read or sit, all I have to do is point at Monette sitting next to me to show them they can do anything they set their minds to.

Group D - Belinda

Perhaps one of the most gratifying things about teaching is seeing the ways that a teacher influences a child. On most days I want to bang my head against a wall and give up. "They just aren't getting it," I tell myself. When we are in the library, however, my mind relaxes.

Convinced that modeling good reading habits to students produces students with good reading habits, I have read my own books in the library from the first day of the study. One of my biggest surprises has been a reading connection I have made with my worst discipline problem, Belinda.

Belinda, like many of my students, has grown up street smart, with very little use for schools and books. She has been raised by a single mom who, I have observed, is often drunk and abusive to Belinda. Belinda is not exactly honest, and she is pretty intimidating to boys and girls throughout the school (even fifth graders). She is easily the smallest person in my class, and many substitutes have fallen into the trap of believing she is "too small and precious to hurt anyone." They might as well think the same about a bumble bee.

I had practically given up on Belinda. But when we started going to the library every day, something miraculous happened. Belinda would always grab a book right away and sit next to me. In fact, she sat next to me, mimicking the way I read, for the entire eight-week study. If I turned a page in my book, she turned a page in her book. If I sat cross-legged on the floor, Belinda would do the same.

In class now, I hardly ever have any problems with Belinda. She is working much better with other students, and she frantically raises her hand when I ask for volunteers to read. When I asked her how she liked coming to the library, she said it was the best part about coming to school. She loves sitting next to an adult and reading a good book.

The Implications

My study is limited because it focuses solely on my own classroom. I do not have tests to show reading improvement occurred between the time the study began and when it ended. I cannot prove that my students read any better than other second graders at my school. I can say, however, that on a daily basis my students are being exposed to a wide variety of books at various degrees of reading ability. No other teacher at Truman takes students to the school library daily. In fact, many hardly take their students to the school library at all.

"I think it's just great that you take your class to the library every day," Mrs. Turner said to me. "I'm so fixed into my schedule and busy teaching objectives that I don't often get a chance to take my class to the library."

The other second grade teachers at Truman have told me they think my students are benefitting from going to the library every day. We have all observed an enormous amount of progress in my students' reading abilities, which I feel should be at least partly credited to increased library visits. While Mrs. Gatling and Mrs. Hopkins agree with me that going to the library every day is benefitting my students, they, too, do not feel they have the time to take their students to the library.

On the first day of the study, Mrs. Parker, the resource specialist, told some of my students not to look at certain shelves because those books were too difficult for them to read. I informed Mrs. Parker that I was conducting a study and proceeded to tell my students that they

The Role of the School Library in the Improvement   171
of Reading Attitudes and Achievement
Among Bilingual Elementary Students

could read anything they wanted. Many of them selected books from the shelves Mrs. Parker told them not to look at.

Granted, the books Mrs. Parker had pointed to were too difficult for the students to read, but I do not feel it is our place as educators to tell students what they are and are not capable of reading. I fully believe in letting students experience reading for themselves. It is my hope that if students learn to enjoy reading, they will develop lifelong reading habits.

Several problems were brought to my attention as a result of this study. The first, and greatest, problem is that of accessibility to literature. The majority of my students had never been to the school library before, and only three students had ever been in a public library before. Having visited several of my students' homes, I found a heavy lack of reading material of any kind in the home. In addition, many of my students' parents are illiterate.

It has become painfully obvious to me that students need heavy exposure to literature while they are young in order to develop an appreciation for reading as adults. As teachers we can help develop students' appreciation toward reading by (a) taking them to the library daily and (b) modeling good reading habits.

Another great concern of mine is the lack of reading materials in Spanish at my school. Many of my Latino students, and I am specifically convinced about students such as Pablo, would engage in more free reading if there were more books available about their culture (and language is a major part of one's culture).

In conclusion, I agree with Krashen that students who are allowed to read whatever they want will become more interested in reading and, therefore, become better readers. I take my students to the school library every day and allow them to read whatever they want, wherever they want, with whomever they want, as long as they read. I feel the reward of watching students beg me to go to the library and ask me when we will read. I want my students to learn not only how to read but how to enjoy reading.

My attitude has changed from teaching District objectives to teaching my students.

References

Allington, Richard L. (1980). Poor Readers Don't Get to Read Much in Reading Groups. *Language Arts, 57,* 872–876.

Aranow, Miriam S. (1961). A Study of the Effect of Individualized Reading on Children's Reading Test Scores. *The Reading Teacher, 15,* 86–91.

Bilingual Education. (1988). *Encyclopedia of Educational Research.* 6th ed. Washington, D.C.: U.S. Department of Education.

Carrell, Patricia L. (1983). Three Components of Background Knowledge in Reading Comprehension. *Language Learning, 33,* 183–207.

Cleary, Florence D. (1939). Why children read. *Wilson Library Bulletin, 14,* 119–126.

Cohen, Dorothy H. (1968). The Effect of Literature on Vocabulary and Reading Achievement. *Elementary English, 45,* 209–217.

Connor, D.V. (1954). The relationship between achievement and voluntary reading of children. *Educational Review, 6,* 221–227. In Greaney, V. (1980).

Constantino, R. (1994). It's Like a Lot of Things in America–– Linguistic Minority Parents' Use of Libraries. *School Library Media Quarterly,* Winter, 87–89.

Elley, W. (1991). Acquiring Literacy in a Second Language: The Effect of Book-Based Programs. *Language Learning, 41,* 375–411.

Field, M., & J. Aebersold. (1990). Cultural attitudes toward reading: Implications for teachers of ESL/bilingual readers. *Journal of Reading, 33,* 406–410.

Forester, A. (1975). What teachers can learn from natural readers. *The Reading Teacher. 5,* 55–63.

Greaney, Vincent (1980). Factors related to and type of leisure time reading. *Reading Research Quarterly, 15,* 337–357.

Greaney, V., & S.B. Neuman. (1990). The functions of reading: A cross-cultural perspective. *Reading Research Quarterly,* Summer, 172–195.

The Role of the School Library in the Improvement   173
of Reading Attitudes and Achievement
Among Bilingual Elementary Students

Irving, Ann (1980). *Promoting Voluntary Reading for Children and Young People*. Paris: UNESCO, 7. In Morrow, L.M.(1986).

Janopoulos, Michael (1985). The relationship of Pleasure Reading and second language writing proficiency. *TESOL Quarterly*, 763–769.

Krashen, Stephen D. (1987). Encouraging Free Reading. In M. Douglas (Ed.), *Claremont Reading Conference, 51st Yearbook*, 1–10.

Krashen, Stephen D. (1989). We acquire vocabulary and spelling by reading: Additional evidence for the Input Hypothesis. *The Modern Language Journal*, 73, 440–464.

Lamme, Linda L. (1976). Are reading habits and abilities related? *The Reading Teacher*, 30, 21–27.

Long, H., & E.H. Henderson. (1973). Children's use of time: Some personal and social correlates. *Elementary School Journal*, 73, 193–199. In Greaney, V. (1980).

Maxwell, J. (1977). *Reading progress from 8 to 15*. Slough, Bucks: National Foundation for Educational Research. In Greaney, V. (1980).

McDermott, R.P. (1977). Social Relations: Contexts for Learning in School. *Harvard Educational Review*, 47, 198–213. In Allington, R.L. (1980).

McEvoy, George F., & Cynthia S. Vincent. (1980). Who Reads and Why? *Journal of Communication*, 30, 134–140.

Morrow, L.M. (1983). Home and School Correlates of Early Interest in Literature. *Journal of Education Research*, 76, 221–230.

Morrow, L.M. (1986). Voluntary Reading: Forgotten Goal. *The Educational Forum*, 50, 159–167.

Morrow, L.M. (1991). Promoting Voluntary Reading. In J. Flood, J. Jensen, D. Lapp & J. Squine (Eds.), *Handbook of Research on Teaching the English Language Arts*, 681–690.

Morrow, L.M., & C.S. Weinstein. (1982). Increasing children's use of literature through program and physical design changes. *The Elementary School Journal*, 83, 131–137.

Morrow, L.M., & C.S. Weinstein. (1986). Encouraging voluntary reading: The impact of a literature program on children's use of library centers. *Reading Research Quarterly*, 21, 330–346.

Robinson, H.M., & Samuel Weintraub. (1973). Research Related to Children's Interests and to Developmental Values of Reading. *Library Trends*, 22, 81–108.

Sanacore, Joseph (1990). Creating the lifetime reading habit in social studies. *Journal of Reading,* March, 414–418.

Swanton, Susan I. (1984). Minds alive: What & why gifted students read for pleasure. *School Library Journal, 30,* 99–102.

White, Thomas G., Michael F. Graves, & Wayne H. Slater. (1990). Growth of reading vocabulary in diverse elementary schools: decoding and word meaning. *Journal of Educational Psychology, 82,* 281–290.

Whitehead, F., A.C. Capey, & W. Maddren. (1975). *Children's reading interests.* London: Evans and Methuen.

Chapter 8

Tierra Fertil: Making the Soil Rich for Discussion for Young Children in Spanish

Julia Fournier
Cecilia Espinosa

We began our work together, studying children's literature in Spanish, about six years ago. Julia had recently returned from a month in Spain studying at the University of Madrid, and Cecilia had just started working at Machan School. Julia, along with two other teachers who had attended the Summer Institute on Children's Literature in Spanish, was giving a workshop to the district's bilingual educators. The teachers had returned from Spain with suitcases full of books, lists of suggested literature, and a heightened awareness and understanding of the richness of Children's Literature in Spanish. Cecilia, born and raised in Ecuador, had spent the past several years studying at Arizona State University. Although she had studied to be a bilingual teacher, as a newcomer she spent much of her time trying to become versed in English language literature for children. This talk about Spanish literature sparked memories of her own childhood experiences with books and interest in what was available today for her Spanish dominant students.

Our talk surrounding literature started informally, as we hiked Squaw Peak several times a week. Often we would ask each other about books with a particular theme or just share what new books we had stumbled across that had sparked interesting discussion in the class.

When the textbook money in the district was decentralized due to the trend toward site–based/local control, our talks became more focused. We were faced with the exciting prospect of having $900.00 per year, per classroom to spend on books. How would we make informed decisions year after year on what to order?

We began meeting once a week to formally discuss children's literature in Spanish. We began defining good literature, regardless of the language, as well as a list of core or completely necessary books for our classrooms. We debated over translations, discussed regional verb usage and colloquialisms, and developed a broader and deeper knowledge of what was available for our students in Spanish. We pored over catalogs, examining the descriptions. We visited libraries, warehouses and bookstores. We searched for experts to advise us and sources to supply us and found out that we were becoming the best experts for ourselves and that we had to use everything available to get what our students needed and deserved.

What follows here are some of books we use, and books we like very much. In discovering these books for ourselves and sharing them with our students we have learned some things. We will try to give a clear picture of our classrooms, the literature we value and why.

We begin with fairy tale, or more specifically, non-traditional fairy tale. We have always enjoyed the joy that comes from working from these European-based oral traditions. Every child knows at least one. Children enjoy comparing them, contrasting them, arguing over correct endings and over proper characteristics for the traditional roles. There is an abundance of traditional fairy tales available in both English and Spanish. The standards used to determine quality is virtually the same in both languages. We know a good fairy tale when we hear one; the language flows, the story unfolds predictably, but not too, and the illustrations are provocative. Once the criteria have been set in the classroom for what constitutes fairy tale, it is often interesting to move to non-traditional fairy tale. The prior knowledge of traditional fairy tale is essential to understanding what makes the non-traditional just so. Anyone who has ever read Jon Schieska's non-traditional rendition of *The Three Little Pigs* knows this to be true. *The True Story of the Three Little Pigs* would not be funny if we did not know the original version. This book is available in Spanish, and we consider it a good translation. There are, however, so many others we have discovered written in Spanish.

El Asunto de Mis Papás(1991), Regarding My Parents, by Mabel Piárola, is told from the point of view of Red Riding Hood, who is just a little more than disturbed that out of all the things that have happened in her life, people have chosen this one particular incident to remember her by. The illustrations are wonderful and show the text of the book as handwritten pages torn from her notebook.

El Lobito Bueno (1983), The Good Wolf, by J. Goytisolo, explains to us why wolves no longer choose to live among humans and why they prefer to be feared and hated rather than the helpers they once were. This children's book reminds us very much of the poem by Rubén Darío, *Los Motivos del Lobo, The Wolf's Motives,* which would make an interesting comparative discussion.

In *La Niña con los Tres Maridos* (1983), *The Girl with the Three Fiancees,* by F. Caballero, the girl refuses to choose between the three men who have asked for her hand. We are taken along with the three as they compete for the favor of the intended's father. At the end, they must all work together to save the life of the princess. This book may sound serious; however, it is instead very funny and the illustrations by Jesus Gabón are delightful.

El Payaso y la Princesa (1983), The Clown and the Princess, was both written and illustrated by Jesus Gabón. We like this book because the characters refuse to be stereotyped, despite the fact that they are only puppets and should have no control over their lives or the roles they play. With the help of a little magic, the princess is able to escape the boring prince and run away with her true love, the valiant clown.

The heroine in the book *La Princesa y el Pirata (1991), The Princess and the Pirate,* by Alfredo Gomez, has every storybook prince known asking for her hand in marriage. As each one passes by her tower, drawn by her singing, they pledge to give up their respective quests (kiss a Sleeping Beauty, rescue a poisoned girl living with elves, find the owner of a glass slipper, etc.) if she will only marry them. Filomena will not be tied down to any man until she falls for the swarthy pirate Capitán Pirata.

One author of non–traditional fairy tales who is in a class by herself is Adela Turin. This Italian writer has written several fairy tales from a feminist perspective. The stories are interesting, as they contain all we expect from fairy tales, yet the women are strong and smart without taking away from the men or from our sense of fairy tale. The characters and the situations Adela Turin creates add to what we know of fairy tale and provides new possibilities for our students in reading and writing for themselves in this genre. In *La Chaqueta Remendada (1981), The Mended Jacket,* a girl follows in her father's footsteps by becoming a carpenter. Her mother, worried she will never marry, seeks the help of a wise witch who gives her a magic charm to make her daughter more feminine. Through a series of events, a prince ends up with the talisman and becomes very sensitive, creative and communicative. It all ends well when the carpenter and prince are married and travel the world together, happy.

One of our favorite books by Adela Turin is *Arturo y Clementina (1976), Arthur and Clementine.* Although this book is not what we would consider a fairy tale, it does demonstrate that a good ending is not necessarily a fairy tale ending. In this book, the characters are turtles, although they are very human in their actions. The protagonist, Clementina, is courted by Arturo. They fall in love and are married. Once they are wed, Arturo will not allow Clementina to try anything new. When she wants to learn to paint, he scoffs at her and buys her a painting.When she wants to learn to play the flute, he buys her a phonograph. Things continue in this way until finally, Clementina sneaks away, leaving her shell and all the things Arthur has bought for her behind in search of herself.

Literature that explores the theme of self–discovery is very important in our classrooms. The book, *El Primer Pájaro de Piko–Niko (1987), The First Bird of Piko–Niko,* by María de la Luz Uribe, is the story of a bird who hatches and has absolutely no idea of who he is; there are apparently no other beings like him around. As adults we appreciate this book because of our recognition of how important it is to have others to share with and to help us define the world. With children, we see how much they appreciate the humor in knowing something the main character is not aware of--that he is a bird. The Piko–Niko bird finally realizes he is a bird as he is falling off a cliff and other birds suggest to him (not very nicely) that he flap his wings. There are many parallel books to this in English, among them, *Are You My Mother?* and *Stella Luna,* which have both been translated into Spanish. Although the translations are fine, even good, the quality of the language found in the book *El Primer Pájaro de Piko–Niko* written by one of Latin America's foremost poets and writers for children is, we feel, superior, as the expressiveness, flow and humor of the language are more present in this book than the translated ones. A more serious book, *El Aniversario (1983), The Anniversary,* by María Marti i Pol, deals with a man who decides to wear a hat. To us this may seem like a small thing to do, but to him it symbolizes taking a stand. To those around him, it represents a threat. His family is embarrassed, his boss fires him, and the police brutalize him. This book raises important questions about individual rights and freedoms. Like other good books for children, it exists on many levels at the same time; it is simple yet complex, it evokes good dialogue and raises important issues.

Uña y Carne (1990), Inseparable Twins, by Ricardo Alcántara, is another book that encourages important discussions. In this story the brothers Armando and Amado, who have never been apart, learn that spending time away from each other can bring them closer together. When they are accidentally separated, they find it makes the time they are together that much richer as they tell about the adventures they have had.

We define ourselves in different ways. Sometimes it is by who we are surrounded by as in *Uña y Carne,* and *El Primer Pájaro de Piko-Niko,* sometimes it is the stands we take as in *El Aniversario,* and sometimes it is our childhood and the important events that take place during that special time as in *Yo Las Quería (1984), I Longed for Them.* In this book, Marta has long, long hair that her mother brushes and braids for her. When her mother takes ill, she must cut her hair. At first devastated, Marta discovers there is more to her than her braids. After the death of her mother she realizes she is growing up and that with her hair short she looks even more like her mother.

In Spanish language literature, childhood is often treated as a special time, different from past, present or future. We have learned that dreamtime is another separate time, with its own characteristics, and that it is extremely prevalent in Hispanic books. In *La Niña Enlunada, The Moonstruck Girl,* by Carlos Murciano, the main character, Marita, visits a special place that seems to be between childhood and adolescence and between reality and fantasy. She visits this place in her dreams at each full moon. The tension escalates when she must choose between staying in the real world or in the dream world forever.

In the book *¿Dónde Has Estado Aldo? (1986), Where Have You Been Aldo?,* by Ricardo Alcántara, the boy Aldo asks his grandfather what exists beyond the horizon. His dreams give him the answer, and when he wakes up, his grandfather has a question, "Where have you been, Aldo?"

A father telling a story to his daughter as she falls asleep is the backdrop for *El Barco de Camila (1986), Camila's Boat,* by Allen Morgan. Camila's father makes Camila the main character in the story, and as she falls asleep, the story and the dreams become one and the same.

In our multi-age classrooms, layers of meaning are important for the books we read aloud and highlight for discussion. Books with dreams at the center are perfect for reading to groups of children. They will argue over whether the events happened or not, sometimes preferring to attribute the events to magic rather than dreams. *La Luna de Juan (1982) Juan's Moon,* by Carme Solí Vendrell, is one of these books. It is also appealing because the child is very much the hero in this story as he goes to huge lengths to return his father to health.

Another theme that returns again and again in children's literature is nature and art versus humankind. In Carme Solí Vendrell's *La Roca (1990), The Rock,* Marina has a special rock she goes to every day as she herds the cows. This is her favorite place. One day she is shocked to discover that her rock has disappeared. She follows the trail for two days until she finds the rock in the studio of a sculptor who is "discovering what the rock has inside." Although Marina is sad over the loss of her special place, she now looks for possibilities in every rock she sees.

In *Elmekin y la Serpiente (1987), Elmekin and the Snake,* by Rossana Bohárquez Martinez, the Mayan boy Elmekin helps a snake who is trapped. In gratitude, the snake says he will teach Elmekin how to see the world. The snake imparts his wisdom to Elmekin, showing him the beauty of the world and all things that live in it. The snake talks about the "force" in all that surrounds us and tells Elmekin that he has the same "force" inside him. Elmekin discovers his own way to demonstrate his force--by creating with clay the images he sees around him.

The main character in *La danza de Yaxum (1989), Yaxum's Dance,* also by Rossana Bohárquez Martinez, loves the sun so much he wants to perform a dance in its honor. He studies the movements of nature in order to prepare. Yaxum finally offers his dance to the sun and is transformed into a bird. These two books not only address humans versus nature, but they also bring up the theme of art imitating nature.

Las Liebres Blancas (1975), The White Hares, a translation from the French by Janet and Livio Marzot, illustrates these same themes in a beautiful story of an artist who loses his ability to create. He goes away to the forest to be alone in a cabin. Once there, he becomes obsessed with the footprints he sees in the snow. He wants to catch one of these animals or even shoot it. The harder he tries, the more frustrated he becomes, until finally he ends up lost in the middle of the forest. Standing silent underneath a tree, covered by falling snow, he finally sees the hares and realizes you must become one with nature in order to really see it. He begins to paint again as he has learned to respect nature, not control it.

In a similar way, the animals in *La Sequía (1988), The Drought,* by Jesus Zatán, learn the same lesson as they fight over the reflection of the moon in a pool of water. We have used this book in discussing war and conflict. Children respond strongly to the text and illustrations. What is implied comes through just as powerfully as what is actually stated and the children make comparisons to their own conflicts.

The Three Astronauts in *Los Tres Cosmonautas (1989),* by Umberto Eco and Eugenio Carmi, are from three different cultures. They recognize each other only by their differences, and each of them wants to be the first to get to Mars. All three are very brave and arrive at Mars at the same time. Scared when night falls, they all shout the same thing ("Mommy!") in their respective languages. They recognize finally that they have more in common than they thought.

These authors have also brought us another wonderful book, also translated from the Italian, *La Bomba y el General (1989), The Bomb and the General.* In this book there is a General who is determined to further his military career by starting a new war. His plans are ruined when the atoms inside the bombs sneak away. There is nothing left for the general to do in the end but become a hotel doorman (his uniform is perfect for the job), because the people have promised not to have any more wars.

These three books deal with conflict through imaginative story. Although they are not realistic in the sense that they end happily for the good faction and unhappily only for the bad, the children know enough to fill in these gaps. These stories serve as interesting starting places for discussions about real war and real conflict.

Two books that do illustrate the realities of war are *El Destello de Hiroshima (1980), The Destruction Of Hiroshima,* translated from the Japanese, and *Rosa Blanca (1985), Rose Blanche,* translated from Italian. These two books describe the true effects of fear and war on real people, the first in Japan, the second in Nazi Germany. The history behind the story portrayed in *El Destello de Hiroshima* is a fascinating one. The author, Toshi Maruki, was touring Japan with the exhibition of her paintings depicting the aftermath of the bombing of Hiroshima. One day, a woman who had survived the bombing walked in and was horrified that someone had chosen the epitome of human suffering as the subject of her paintings. As the woman toured the exhibition, she told Toshi the story of her own struggle to survive in the days, weeks, months and years following the bombing. This book is the result of the inspiration of this woman. It made even more strong Toshi's conviction to work to ensure that this part of history is never repeated.

The main character of the book *Rosa Blanca* demonstrates to us that kindness and humanity can come in spite of terrible atrocity. Yet in a small German town, Rosa Blanca discovers the concentration camp outside the city limits. We are given a vivid picture of the gradual change the town undergoes from the initial control of the Nazis to the liberation by the Allied forces.

When we elevate the status of a book by selecting it to read aloud to the class or to a group of people, we may do it for several different reasons. Sometimes it is the content or theme of the writing that draws us to it, and sometimes it is the beauty of the language; it could also be that we are drawn by the use of setting or time, or that the characters are well developed and interesting; sometimes the illustrations are beautiful. The books we have mentioned previously fall into categories that authors use frequently. The following books have generated good discussions for their content and are books the children select over and over again. The issues contained in the pages are important, although generally, not highly visible in children's literature.

Two of these books are written bilingually and come to us from Children's Book Press. Although we appreciate the efforts of this publishing company, we have trouble accepting totally the idea of "bilingual books." We feel that picture books serve an important purpose in the development of literacy. The text is what gives our students the starting point for understanding written story, the illustrations provide a window to deeper interpretation of the text. In the best possible situations they go together like a hand inside a glove. When the text is published bilingually, there are things that happen to compromise this important relationship. The first thing is, there is too much text next to the illustrations for the age of the child for which the book is most appropriate. No doubt, it is a smart move economically to purchase these books, as you get, in essence, two books for the price of one. However, one should not attempt to sit down and read these books "bilingually." Just as it is not appropriate to translate directly in bilingual classrooms, for the same reason we see the reading of these books bilingually as an interruption of the transaction taking place between the listener, the illustrations and the text. We would prefer to see these books published separately, to stand on their own in one language.

Friends from the Other Side (1993) is an especially relevant book in these times and strong enough to stand by itself. The story is set on the border in Texas, and as the name implies, deals with illegal immigration and differences within the Hispanic community. Also from Children's Book Press, *The Woman Who Outshone the Sun (1991)*, a Zapotec legend, deals with the unwillingness of people to accept strangers. Both stories show us that it sometimes takes someone from the outside to show us we've become too comfortable and selfish.

Pepín is an imaginative book that brings forward issues surrounding homelessness and giving. On one hand, the story is sweet and endearing, while on the other hand, what is not explicit in the text about the poor and homeless is pointed out by the children in their discussions.

In our experience with young children we have had many discussions around death and loss. In this stage of their lives it is particularly difficult to understand. There have been many books written that deal with this topic in English; among them, *Nana Upstairs, Nana Downstairs* and *The Tenth Good Thing About Barney*. In Spanish, we are fortunate to have the book, *Un Gato Viejo y Triste (1988), The Sad Old Cat*. A philosophical discussion occurs between a young girl and a cat on the verge of dying. The cat explains to the girl the cycle of life and what might happen after death. Following the loss of her friend, the girl is left to contemplate this further as she meets three kittens who appear soon after--the cycle seems to have come full circle.

One of the most important lessons we have learned when examining books for purchase is to use all of our senses when making selections. We have missed or almost missed really fantastic books because we were judging them using the same criteria we use for English books. The world of publishing in English and Spanish differs greatly. We have borrowed a term from the Ethnobotanist Mark Plotkin, that we need to "suspend reality" when working between other cultures. When we look at books in Spanish we do this in order to make better choices for our students. For example, we have made harsh judgments of books because the illustrations were "naive" or simple to our minds. We need to consider the text, our students, and the illustrations together when passing judgment and avoid quick decisions based on one-dimensional thinking. Many books in the Spanish language contain surreal or magical thinking that leads the protagonist or sometimes whole towns to act or believe something. Although this approach to reality is not in our own experience, we should not discount literature or genre that represents the belief and experience of many people. In the same way we have criticized Spanish language literature for not providing us with enough "real life" characters and situations. We have wished for text to exist in Spanish along the lines of Eve Bunting's work—real people real situations. Our experience with Spanish language children's literature had demonstrated to us that these kinds of straight-on books are not easily found. By "suspending reality" we are able to create places for books that are easily found and can be the starting places for the same kinds of discussions that straight-on, real-life books give us.

An example of one of these types of books is *Sapo Enamorado* *(1989), Frog in Love.* Frog is feeling funny, but he doesn't know why. His different animal friends offer suggestions, until he finally realizes it's because he is in love. His friends are shocked to discover it is with the duck. They even tell him he can't love a duck (she is white and he is green, they tell him). Love prevails, and they do live happily ever after. As you might guess, the discussions lead to accepting differences and interracial relationships. This story has also led to discussions about why it's not available in English as the English dominant children absolutely adore this book.

It's great when books cross cultural and language barriers. When the characters are not drawn literally, children seem to be able to include themselves easier in the story. Wordless picturebooks do this so well. *La Expedición (1977), The Expedition,* is one of our favorites of these kinds of books. Besides giving us so much to think about, it is particularly relevant to the culture of the children we serve. The story opens with a ship approaching an island. The captain spots something of interest and lands. The sailors chop through dense jungle vegetation and arrive at a temple plated with gold. The men take apart the temple and carry it back to their ship, only to discover the top of their ship has been dismantled in their absence and now sits in the place of the temple.

When going "in search of" children's literature in Spanish, we have discovered all kinds of ways to get in touch with the kinds of books we are looking for. One of the ways that has worked well is to identify the collections of books we enjoy. In the United States, books are published individually while Spanish language publishers tend to publish books in collections. However, catalog companies in the United States rarely list books in collections, often they don't carry all the books in the particular collection. Many times the ways books are listed in catalogs are not the way the publishers of these Spanish language books intended them to be marketed.

For instance, in becoming familiar with the collection *Asi Vivimos (How We Live)*, by the Venezuelan publishing company, Ekará, we found out about one of these books first and then another. Eventually we realized by looking on the back cover that there were five of these books, and we ordered all of them. They are all wonderful stories of real children. The first book, *La Calle Es Libre (1981), The Streets Are Free,* tells the true story of how the determination of the children in a community in San Juan, Puerto Rico, to make a space to play gets them a park. Although the ending in the book is more optimistic than what actually transpired in real life, the value of non-violent action and uniting in a common cause are real. The main character in the second book in the series, *El Robo de las Aes (1983), The Theft of the As,* deals with his problem in a different way. Upset about the negative publicity his father is getting in the town's paper because of his support of the candidate for mayor who is a poet, a young boy takes all the As from the printer's workshop. His guilt grows and grows until he has to let his father know what he did.

Ni Era Vaca Ni Era Caballo (1984) Neither a Cow Nor a Horse, is the tragic story of a boy from the Venezuelan tribe of the Guajiros. Told in first person narrative, we learn about the daily life of this boy as he herds sheep in the desert. One day, he loses a sheep because he is playing instead of watching the herd. His father is furious. Looking everywhere for the lost sheep, he encounters something that changes his life—a truck. He makes a terrible mistake experimenting with gasoline and runs away from home out of shame. He learns a lesson, too late for him, but not for us—to appreciate what we have and not take too much for granted.

It is difficult to find literature for young children that relates to slavery in Spanish. *La Peineta Colorada (1991), The Red Comb,* deals with slavery in Puerto Rico. Set in the mid-1800s, this book tells with regional vocabulary and beautiful illustrations the story of how a young girl discovers an escaped slave hiding under her house. She turns to Sra. Rosa, one of the wise women of the town for her advice. Instead of turning her in, she decides to help her by feeding her and keeping her location a secret. This book, based on historical fact, gives us much to discuss and to think about.

In the last book of this collection, *Miguel Vicente pata caliente,* we are given a picture of the life and dreams of a shoeshine boy. More than anything else, Miguel wants to travel and see the world. One day he is given a book about Marco Polo, and he sees that it is possible to realize his dreams.

This book, like all the other books in the series, has the child in the center, making important decisions. The children are struggling in some way, and their troubles are real. It is important to note the children in these stories seem to be much closer to the community of children we teach in comparison to the privileged lives or fantasy lives some characters in children's books lead.

In our classrooms we have literally hundreds of books. They are on the shelves or in tubs and available to all children at all times. There are many times during the day when the students have the opportunity to be engaged with books. At different times of the week, month and year, discussions might be centered around an author or genre. There are also different audiences for reading, which may affect the choices the students make.

We have attempted here to give a small example of books that are to us, quality children's literature, and to share our way of seeing them. Because we have had to work so hard at finding books, we have strong feelings about the ones we like as well as the ones we don't like. Not every book has to change our lives. As a matter of fact, we have one category of books we just call "stupid books." We like them because they are so silly and make us laugh.

We make every effort to focus on buying books that were written first in Spanish. We feel it is important not only for children to read in their first language, but to read books authored by writers who have a shared cultural and linguistic history with the children we teach. Some of the books we mentioned were not written in Spanish first. It would be ridiculous to exclude them from our list of favorites for this reason only. The translations are excellent. The language flows and never distracts from the story. This is important to consider when choosing translated literature.

In preparing to write this piece, it was difficult to narrow our selection to only those here. We could go on and on recommending and describing books. Becoming more knowledgeable of children's Spanish literature has made a difference in our lives and in our classrooms. We hope this can serve as a starting point as you continue a journey of discovery on your own, on the road to becoming an expert for the population of children you serve, in the community where you work.

References

Non-Traditional Fairy Tales

Piárola, M. *El asunto de mis papás.* Barcelona, Spain: Ediciones Destino.

Goytisolo, J.A. *El lobito bueno.* (1983). Barcelona, España: Editorial Laia.

Caballero, F. *La niña con los tres maridos.* (1983). Barcelona. España: Editorial Galaxia S. A.

Gomez, A. *La princesa y el pirata.* (1991). México D. F., México: Fondo de Cultura Económica S. A.

Gabón, J. *El payaso y la princesa.* (1983). Barcelona, España: Ediciones Destino S. A.

Turín, A. *La Chaqueta remendada.* (1981). Barcelona, España: Editorial Lumen S. A.

Turín, A., y Bosnia, N. *Arturo y Clementina.* (1976). Barcelona, España: Editorial Lumen

Self-Discovery

Uribe, M. de la L. *El primer pájaro de piko-niko.* (1987). Barcelona, España: Editorial Juventud.

Marti i Pol, M. *El Aniversario.* (1983). Barcelona, España: Ediciones Hymsa.

Alcántara, R. *Uña y carne.* (1990). Barcelona, España: Ediciones Destino S.A.

Martínez y Vendrell, M. *Yo las quería.* (1984). Barcelona, España:
Ediciones Destino.

Dreamtime

Murciano, C. *La niña enlunada.* (1988). Madrid, España: Editorial S.M.
Alcántara, R. *¿Dónde has estado, Aldo?* (1986). Barcelona, España:
Editorial Juventud.
Morgan, A. *El barco de Camila.* (1986). Caracas, Venezuela: Ediciones
Ekará–Banco del Libro.
Solí Vendrell, C. *La luna de Juan.* (1982). Barcelona, España:
Ediciones HYMSA.

Art, Nature and Man

Vendrell, C.S. *La Roca.* (1990). Madrid, Spain: Ediciones S.M.
Bohárquez–Martinez, Rossana. *Elmekin y la serpiente.* (1987). México
D.F., México: Editorial Trillas, S.A. de C.V.
_____. *La danza de Yaxum.* (1989). México D.F., México: Editorial
Trillas, S.A. de C.V.
Marzot, J. and L. *Las liebres blancas.* (1975). Barcelona, Spain:
Editorial Juventud.

Conflict

Zatán, J. *La sequia.* (1988). Madrid, Spain: Ediciones Jucar.
Carmi, E. and Eco, U. *Los tres cosmonautas.* (1989). Barcelona, Spain:
Ediciones Destino S.A.
_____. *La bomba y el general.* (1989). Barcelona, Spain: Ediciones
Destino S.A.
Maruki, T. *El destello de Hiroshima.* (1980). Valladolid, Spain:
Miñon, S.A., and Innocenti, R. *Rosa Blanca.* (1985). Salamanca,
España: 1985.

Big Ideas

Anzaludía, G. *Friends from the other side. (1993).* San Francisco,
California: Children's Book Press.

Zubizarreta, R. *The woman who outshone the sun*. (1991). New York: Scholastic.

Macsolis. *Pepín*. (1987). Barcelona, España: Editorial Juventud.

Zatán, J. *Un gato viejo y triste*. (1988). Madrid, España: Jucar Infantil.

Velthuijs, M. *Sapo enamorado*. (1989). Caracas, Venezuela: Ediciones Ekará.

Baum, W. *The expedition*. (1977). Milano, Italy: Emme Edizioni S.P.A.

Collections

Así Vivimos (Collection in a class by itself). (1981). Caracas, Venezuela: Ediciones Ekará Banco del Libro.

Picó, F., y Ordíñez, M.A. *La peineta colorada*. (1991). Caracas, Venezuela: Ediciones Ekará Banco del Libro.

Canal Ramírez, G. *El robo de las aes*. (1983). Caracas, Venezuela: Ediciones Ekará Banco del Libro.

Kurusa, and Doppert, M. *La calle es libre*. (1981). Caracas, Venezuela: Ediciones Ekará Banco del Libro.

Jusayu, M.A., and Doppert, M. *Ni era vaca ni era caballo*. (1984). Caracas, Venezuela: Ediciones Ekará Banco del Libro.

Araujo, O. *Miguel Vicente pata caliente*. (1992). Caracas, Venezuela: Ediciones Ekará Banco del Libro.

Rimas y Adivinanzas

Uribe, M. de la L. *Doña Piñones*. (1981). Caracas, Venezuela: Ediciones Ekará–Banco del Libro.

Paz Castillo, F. *El Príncipe Moro*. (1978). Caracas, Venezuela: Ediciones Ekará–Banco del Libro.

Darío, Rubén. *Margarita*. (1971). Caracas, Venezuela: Ediciones Ekará–Banco del Libro.

Ponte-Poronte

Barbot, D. *Rosaura en Bicicleta*. (1993). Caracas, Venezuela: Ediciones Ekará.

Berenguer, C. *El Rey Mocho*. (1986). Caracas, Venezuela: Ediciones Ekará.

Rondón, J. *El Sapo Distraído*. (1988). Caracas, Venezuela: Ediciones Ekará.

Narraciones Indigenas

Paz Ipuana, R. *El burrito y la tuna.* (1979). Caracas, Venezuela: Ediciones Ekará.

Paz Ipuana, R. *El conejo y el mapurite.* (1980). Caracas, Venezuela: Ediciones Ekará.

de Armellada, C. *El Rabipelado Burlando.* (1978). Caracas, Venezuela: Ediciones Ekará.

Rivera Oramos, R. *La piedra del Zamuro.* (1981). Caracas, Venezuela: Ekará.

Rivera Oramos, R. *El hojarasquerito del monte.* (1981). Caracas, Venezuela: Ekará.

Los Duros

Menéndez, M. *Concierto de Gatos.* (1990). Madrid, España: Ediciones SM.

Espulga, M. *Un buen día.* (1990). Madrid, España: Ediciones SM.

Alcántara, R., Gusti. *El Pirata Valiente.* (1989). Madrid, España: Ediciones SM.

En Cuento

Roa Bastos, A. *Los juegos de Carolina y Gaspar.* (1976). México D. F., México: Direccion General de Publicaciones del Consejo Nacional para la Cultura y las Artes.

Paz, S. *Las hermanas.* (1993). México D. F., México: Direccion General de Publicaciones del Consejo Nacional para la Cultura y las Artes.

Sarduy, S. *Gatico-Gatico.* (1994). México, D.F., México: Consejo Nacional de Cultura y Artes.

Rincon

Franía, M. *¡A que te pego!* (1992). México D. F., México: Secretaría de Educación Publica.

El Caracol. (1978). México D. F., México: Secretaría de Educación Publica.

Rabo de Gato. (1979). México D. F., México: Secretaría de Educación
Publica.

Rejos De Cuentos

Arredondo, I. *Historia verdadera de una princesa.* (1985). México D.
F., México: Dentro de Informacion y Desarrollo de la Comunicación
y la Literatura Infantiles.
Petterson, A. *El Papalote y el Nopal.* (1988). México D. F., México:
Dentro de Informacion y Desarrollo de la Comunicación y la
Literatura Infantiles.

Relog De Versos

Deltoro, A. *La Plaza.* (1990). México D. F., México: Centro de
Informacion y Desarrollo de la Comunicación y la Literatura
Infantiles.
Sabines, J. *La Luna.* (1990). México D. F., México: Centro de
Información y Desarrollo de la Comunicación y la Literatura
Infantiles.
Paz, O. *La Rama.* (1991). México D. F., México: Centro de
Información y Desarrollo de la Comunicación y la Literatura
Infantiles.

Poetry

Alberti, R. *¡Aire, que me lleva el aire!* (1979). Barcelona, España:
Editorial Labor S. A.
García Lorca, F. *Canciones y poemas para niños.* (1991). México D. F.,
México: Editorial Labor S.A.
Jímenez, J. R. *Canta Pájaro Lejano.* (1981). Madrid, España: Editorial
Espasa–Calpe, S.A
Machado, A. *Yo voy soñando caminos.* (1981). Barcelona, España:
Editorial Labor, S. A.
Mistral, G. *Poesía Infantil.* (1993). Santiago de Chile, Chile: Editorial
Andrés Bello.
Neruda, P. *El libro de las preguntas.* (1974). Santiago, Chile: Andrés
Bello.

Acevedo, M. *Llamo ala luna sol y es de día.* (1988). México D. F., México: Editorial Trillas, S.A.

Serrano, F. *La Luciárnaga.* (1985). México D. F., México: Centro de Información.

Pictureless Books

Nunes, L. *El bolso amarillo.* (1981). Madrid, Spain: Espasa–Calpe, S.A.

Ocampo, C. *Si ves pasar un condor.* (1986). México D.F., México: Editorial Amaquemecan.

Vasconcelos, J.M. *Mi planta de naranja–lima.* (1971). Buenos Aires, Argentina: Editorial El Ateneo.

Uribe, V. *Tres Buches de aqua salada.* (1992). Bogotá, Colombia: Editorial Norma.

Mateos, P. *El cuento interrumpido.* (1984). Madrid, Spain: Editorial Noguer.

Non–Fiction

Bibliographies for Children: Biografías Para Niños

Lopez Chavarría, B.E., y R. Vicarte Solis. *Miguel Hidalgo.* (1992). México D.F., México: Secretaría de Educación Pública.

Pérez Campa, M., y R. Vicarte Solis. *Cuauhtámoc.* (1992). México D.F., México: Secretaría de Educación Pública.

Ruiz Lombardo, A., y R. Vicarte Solis. *Benito Juarez.* (1992). México D.F., México: Secretaría de Educación Pública.

Frutos Prodigiosos

Corona, S. *El chicle.* (1993). México D. F., México: Consejo Nacional para la Cultura y las Artes.

Corona, S. *El Nopal.* (1991). México D. F., México: Consejo Nacional para la Cultura y las Artes.

de Santiago, A. *El Jitomate.* (1991). México D. F., México: Consejo Nacional para la Cultura y las Artes.

Chapter 9

Changing Reading Attitudes: The Power of Bringing Books into the Classroom

Lucy Tse
Jeff McQuillan

Most researchers and educators of language minority students believe that students' own attitudes can help or hinder second language (L2) acquisition. This chapter describes two studies that look at the relationship between language classroom activities and student attitudes toward reading in a second language. The aim of the programs described in both studies was to introduce students to reading materials in their second language, give them opportunities to discuss readings in low-affect situations, and encourage independent pleasure reading. The first study involves an international student enrolled in an intensive English-as-a-second-language program. This case study describes a reluctant second language adult reader introduced to English-language books and encouraged to discuss her questions and reactions with her peers. The student overcame her fear of reading in English and progressed from reading novels on the sixth-grade reading level-- experiencing frustration and low levels of confidence--to reading a tenth-grade level book with enjoyment and ease.

The second study looked at the attitudes of forty-nine second-language (English and Spanish) students toward two language classroom activities: grammar exercises and the extensive reading of popular literature. Students who had participated in courses based on both approaches were asked which activity was more beneficial for language learning and which was more pleasurable. By a significant margin, students favored reading over grammar in both respects.

Before describing these two studies, we will briefly review the literature on the role of reading in language acquisition and the research on L2 reading attitudes. The two studies will then be presented and discussed. Finally, the implications of the studies for language minority students will be explored and pedagogical suggestions offered.

Reading and Language Development

Language acquisition occurs when we are exposed to messages, sometimes referred to as "input," that are comprehensible and that contain elements slightly above our current level of knowledge (Krashen, 1985). Although acquisition can occur through contact with either oral or written input, it is more likely that certain elements in language, such as more sophisticated vocabulary, will be acquired more readily through reading than through listening. Hayes and Ahrens (1988), for example, examined the vocabulary in children's books and found that they included 50% words more rare than in the conversations of college graduates or found in adult television programs. We also know that the more words one encounters, the more opportunities there are for acquisition (Nagy, Anderson, & Herman, 1987; Nagy & Herman, 1987). Nagy and Herman (1987) found that when a reader encounters unfamiliar words, "a small but statistically reliable increase of word knowledge" occurs, giving readers a 5–20% chance of acquiring the new word (p. 26).

In fact, there is substantial research that shows those who read more, either doing free reading in schools or reporting more free reading done out of school, perform better on general language proficiency tests than those who do not. Krashen (1993) reviews several studies in which reading--in this case, self-selected pleasure reading--was compared to skill building and grammar instruction in first and second language classrooms. He found that in thirty-eight of the forty-one studies, students in the reading classes did as well as or better than the comparison skill-building and/or grammar-focussed groups. Elley (1991) conducted a large scale study using book-based programs in Singapore with 3,000 English as a Foreign Language (EFL) students.

The experimental book-based classes outperformed students in skills and grammar-based classes in nearly every area of language performance, including reading comprehension, grammar, listening comprehension, and writing. It is not enough, however, simply to be exposed to messages that contain new language elements. Researchers have also noted that a positive attitude is important in acquiring language. Krashen (1994) has proposed a "Pleasure Hypothesis" for language acquisition, stating that "activities which are good for language acquisition are usually perceived of by acquirers as pleasant" (p. 1). Other theorists have also emphasized the importance of positive affect in language acquisition (Gardner & Lambert, 1972; Mueller & Miller, 1970; Oller, Hudson, & Liu, 1977; and Schumann & Schumann, 1977). There is also a good deal of evidence that reading is perceived of as pleasurable by students who participate in first language literature-based language arts programs (Sperlz, 1948; Gray, 1969; Petre, 1971; Davis & Lucas, 1971). Extensive reading, however, is rarely used in beginning and intermediate second language classrooms, at least in a foreign language setting (Huber, 1993), so there has been little opportunity to determine what students prefer in those types of courses.

Second Language Reading Attitudes

Unfortunately, there has been very little research done on second language students' attitudes toward reading. We do know that despite the well-documented benefits of reading, few second-language students do any reading in their second language in or out of the classroom (Huber, 1993; McQuillan & Rodrigo, this volume). Kaminsky (1992) discovered through observations, interviews, and questionnaires that her twelve elementary ESL students did not elect to read in school when they could choose between reading and drill work, and they did not read recreationally at home. She set out to change those students' attitudes toward pleasure reading by encouraging parents to read with their children, reading to her students during class time, allotting time in class for self-selected sustained silent reading, and allowing students to take books home. As a result, Kaminsky reported dramatic improvement in student attitudes by the end of the school year, as evidenced by the fact that a majority of the students said they would choose reading over television watching in their free time.

To motivate university–level ESL students to get into the habit of reading English language books, Dupuy, Tse and Cook (1996) designed an extensive reading program that introduced students to novels of different levels and genres. The students in the class read thirteen books from six genres of popular literature in four months. Results of a semester–end survey revealed that students found the course enjoyable and worthwhile, though no affective measure was used to determine changes in reading attitudes.

Study 1

The purpose of this study is to examine the impact of an extensive reading course on a second language non–reader in terms of reading attitudes and habits (see Tse, 1996, for complete description). The student participated in an extensive reading course designed to introduce and promote pleasure reading among ESL students by encouraging them to read both assigned and self–selected books in English. Over a period of approximately six months, the subject was presented with a variety of genres of English language books and given the opportunity to discuss those she read in comfortable environments.

Subject

The subject of this case study is a 36–year–old Indonesian woman studying in an intensive English language program at a major American university. Joyce came to the United States with her husband, Tom, and her two children one month before the course began. Her purpose for studying in the program was to improve her English so that she could gain admittance into an American university and successfully complete a master's degree. Her English language learning began in junior high school at about age 12. She recalls grammar and vocabulary drill study about two hours each week until she completed high school. When she entered college, she was required to read health–related textbooks in English, though she explained that she seldom read these texts with much attention because the professors' lectures would cover nearly all of the textbook information, assuming that students had limited comprehension of the texts. She recalled feeling that English language study was stressful, difficult, and uninteresting.

Before coming to the United States, she had never read a book in English other than the textbooks in college. In her first language, she read only for information primarily in newspapers, and she said that she didn't view reading as a leisure activity, adding that "If I had time, I didn't want to spend it reading."

The Course

The 15-week English course was at an intermediate-level, the foundation course of the intensive language program. The students attended the class daily, Monday through Friday, for one and a half hours. In addition, students took vocabulary, grammar, oral skills, and test preparation (TOEFL, GRE, etc.) courses for an average of four hours of coursework total per day.

The purpose of the course was to introduce students to pleasure reading materials and to have students read from several genres, beginning with lower level books and graduating onto more advanced ones. The students in the course began by reading short stories selected by the instructor and were taught some simple reading strategies to help them read faster and with more ease. They were encouraged to read quickly and to guess the meanings of new words, rather than to interrupt their reading to look up words in the dictionary. If they could not guess the meaning, they were encouraged to skip the word all together and move on. The course was based on the belief that students needed to get the maximum amount of comprehensible input possible and that frequent interruptions for dictionary use would slow reading and reduce the amount of input.

Students in the course read four books: the political satire *Animal Farm* by George Orwell (sixth grade reading level), the teenage romance *Forever* by Judy Blume (third grade reading level), the autobiography of a World War II Japanese internee, *Farewell to Manzanar*, by Jeanne Wakatsuki Houston and James D. Houston (sixth grade reading level), and Sue Grafton's modern detective novel *"B" is for Burglar* (sixth grade reading level), in that order (see Table 1). The first two books were selected by the instructor, and the last two books were chosen by the class as a whole from a select number of available books.

Table 1
Grade Level of Books Read by Subject[1]

	Grade Level
Animal Farm	6
Forever	3
Farewell to Manzanar	6
"B" is for Burglar	6
To Kill a Mockingbird	7
You Just Don't Understand:	10
Men and Women in Conversation	

[1]Fry formula used

The majority of class time was spent discussing the novels, an average of 45 minutes per day. The teacher emphasized that their questions and comments would guide the class discussions, resulting in approximately 25% of the discussion time spent on language questions and 75% spent on content questions. The instructor normally had guide questions ready to stimulate conversation but found that they were often not needed. Students were not pressured to speak up in class, and they participated when they felt comfortable and inspired to do so. The discussions followed student interests, and often departed from talk about the book per se. For example, *Forever*, a candid book about a teenager's first romance and sexual experience, prompted a two–day discussion about teenagers' views of love and sex in the students' own countries, and relationships between parents and their children.

Data Collection and Results

Data were collected through teacher observations and student interviews over six months, four months in the classroom and two months in private tutorials. The instructor took notes of student reactions throughout the four–month semester. During the first week, the instructor orally asked the students about their first and second language reading habits and their attitudes toward reading. Joyce continued to be tutored about twice a week by the instructor for two months after the course ended. During four of the tutorial sessions, Joyce spoke about her attitudes toward reading and her reading habits.

When a draft of this paper was completed, a member check was performed where Joyce reviewed a copy of the paper and was asked to confirm the accuracy of the information presented.

Teacher Observations

The students generally completed the assigned reading and attended class with questions and comments for discussion, although some adjustment of the reading schedule was made to provide students with more reading time, based on student suggestions. The class discussions were generally lively and student run, with the instructor answering cultural questions or providing other kinds of background information.

The students, including Joyce, expressed apprehension about reading novels in the early parts of the course. None of the students had ever read a book in English and doubted that they had sufficient language proficiency to do so. The discussions in the first two to three weeks primarily centered around language questions, reflecting students' reliance on form. However, by the time the students had finished the first book, the talk had largely shifted to content and issues presented in the reading. When Joyce began the course, she remained fairly quiet during discussions, though occasionally asking language questions. Very quickly, however, she began to carry much of the discussions by expressing her opinions about the various issues raised by the book and the other students. She appeared to have crossed a juncture near the completion of the second book. She talked about her reading and her reflections on the books with confidence and appeared to enjoy the reading.

Joyce's Observations and Responses

Joyce's comments and responses to questions were collected in four meetings after the completion of the course. Data was gathered and analyzed according to three of Patton's (1980) categories of inquiry: 1) opinion and value; 2) feeling; and 3) knowledge.

Opinion and Value

During one of the interviews, Joyce was asked to recall her belief about the role of reading in language learning before she arrived in the U.S. She said she had believed reading was an important component of language learning that had been excluded from her education, though she believed grammar and vocabulary study were equally important. When asked about her view of reading after taking the course, she said that she believed reading was the most efficient way to learn English and to improve her vocabulary, spelling, and writing. As evidence of this, she had expected her husband to enroll in the same course the following semester as he was studying in the level below hers at the time. When the suggestion was made that another teacher and another curriculum, presumably a traditional textbook-based course, be substituted, she expressed extreme concern. She remarked that she wanted her husband to "know about books" and to learn through them. She believed that her language had improved significantly from reading novels, and she wanted her husband to have a similar experience.

Joyce believed that her view of reading had changed dramatically since she began reading in English. Although she still viewed it as a way to access information, she now realized that books, namely fiction, provided numerous possibilities to gain information and insight.

Feeling

The majority of the questions and collected data falls under the category of feeling, which refers to how subjects respond emotionally to their experiences. Joyce said that she had been afraid to read books, being a non-reader of fiction in her first language. She said that the first book, *Animal Farm*, was particularly difficult because she concentrated on form rather than meaning. She consulted the dictionary often and re-read each page several times. She found this strategy to be frustrating and tiring, and she was tempted to give up many times. However, she persisted because she was determined to give reading a chance. In addition to her inefficient strategies, reading was difficult because she found the vocabulary to be above her level of proficiency and had difficulty following the plot.

By the end of the semester, Joyce said she felt confident about reading. She recalled an incident in which she realized her progress. Her husband enrolled in the extensive reading course the following semester. When he brought home the first assigned book, this time the adult romance *Love Story* by Erich Segal, she examined the book and realized that she could read it with facility and considered it an "easy book." At the time, she was reading Harper Lee's *To Kill a Mockingbird*, a book on the seventh-grade reading level, that has fairly difficult vocabulary and a theme (race relations in the American South) with which she was not at all familiar. She found *To Kill a Mockingbird* to be at a comfortable level for her, and its engrossing plot kept her reading late into the night.

Knowledge

Joyce also felt that reading yielded more than language development, she gained knowledge about American culture and about herself.

Joyce: [The extensive reading course was a] different method to learn English, about reading...not only reading—how to get the main idea, to understand, to guess the new vocabulary—but I learned more than that. [I learned] about American culture. And after I finished these books, I feel that I'm not learning [studying], I can finish this book. That makes me feel excited. I'm not a student.
Interviewer: You mean you felt like everybody else?
Joyce: Yes and that's power in my mind and my feeling that makes me learn more.

Joyce said that she realizes that reading about other people's experience gives her power to widen her outlook on life. In one of the tutoring sessions while discussing *To Kill a Mockingbird*, she said that reading about the African–American experience in the U.S. made her aware of power relationships between majority and minority peoples. As a result, she reflected on the situation in Indonesia where the number of minorities from other Asian countries was steadily increasing. Before reading *Mockingbird*, she had never thought about these types of issues.

Joyce's view of reading and of her own reading competence changed dramatically during the extensive reading course, and it can be argued that her reading proficiency also improved drastically. Joyce began by reading books on the third grade reading level (*Forever*) with fairly familiar themes and moved onto books on the seventh grade reading level (*To Kill A Mockingbird*) with fairly unfamiliar themes. The last book she read within the six months of the study was Deborah Tannen's *You Just Don't Understand: Men and Women in Conversation*, a non–fiction book on the tenth–grade reading level, as determined by the Fry formula. Admittedly, the Fry formula is flawed; it does not take into account background knowledge, which is an essential component of reading comprehension (Dubin, Eskey & Grabe, 1986). However, it provides some rough indication of a book's difficulty level.

Discussion and Implications

Overcoming affective barriers is one of the most difficult challenges faced by second-language learners on the road to fluency. The data presented above show that an introduction to extensive reading in a low-anxiety environment can produce positive affective changes. Joyce's self-reports of her reading improvement and the increase in the difficulty of the books she read provide evidence that an extensive reading course can improve students' reading ability.

There are two likely explanations for Joyce's improvement. First, she may have learned better reading strategies; and while her proficiency did not improve per se, her overall reading ability improved. Second, the large amount of written input caused a dramatic improvement in her English reading proficiency. Regardless of which explanation accounts for the change in Joyce, at the end of the six months she was able to read high-level English books with facility and confidence, replacing previous apprehensions, fear, and stress when reading simpler texts. This study suggests that the introduction of reading in a low anxiety environment and providing students with assistance according to their expressed needs foster positive effects on their reading attitudes and proficiency.

What is especially encouraging is that Joyce has continued to read after the end of the course, confirming the results of McQuillan and Rodrigo (1997, this volume), who found that 75% of his Spanish language learners who had gone through a ten-week extensive reading course continued to read seven months after the completion of the course. If this finding holds true for Joyce, her learning through books has only begun with her formal introduction to extensive reading. She now has the strategies and confidence to tackle adult English language books and to acquire the language and knowledge she desires.

Study 2

The second study summarizes the findings of McQuillan (1994), which looked at the attitudes of second-language students toward grammar study and extensive reading. Two groups of second language students were surveyed. Group 1 consisted of sixteen third semester, university-level English as a Second Language (ESL) students (five men, eleven women; median age = 27.5) studying at an intensive ESL program in the United States. Group 2 was comprised of thirty-three third semester, university-level Spanish as a Foreign Language students (twelve men, twenty-one women; median age = 23). Both the ESL and the Spanish students were enrolled in a ten-week course in the extensive reading of popular literature in their respective second languages. All of the students in the study were assigned to their level based on a placement exam used by their respective programs. Students were not told that their section would be using popular literature as a component of the curriculum prior to signing up for the course.

Both courses consisted of the students reading newspapers, magazines, short stories, graded readers, and (for the Group 1 ESL students) novels in their second language, and discussing them in class. The popular literature was mostly assigned, chosen by the instructors based upon previous experiences with second language classes and student interests. For students in the Spanish foreign language class, the graded readers were selected to conform with the requirements of "narrow reading" (Krashen, 1985), where students read texts from the same author or in the same genre. Narrow reading allows students to capitalize on their background knowledge carried over from text to text, making the books more comprehensible. Several easy-to-read detective short stories written for adult language learners were chosen for this purpose. The Spanish students also read selections from popular Mexican magazines (e.g. *Eres Tu, Variedades*) and local Spanish newspapers. Approximately 15% of class time was spent on grammar explanations.

The ESL students read a variety of adolescent and adult novels, including *Shane, Light in the Forest, The Contender, The Pelican Brief*, and *Love Story*. In addition to the extensive reading, they also read self-selected materials outside of class. Packets of magazine articles were distributed to the class to give students an idea about the range of reading available to them. Selections from *People, Time, Psychology Today, Reader's Digest*, and *Rolling Stone* were included in the packet. The ESL group received no grammar instruction in the ten-week session. All of the students in both groups, however, had been exposed to traditional grammar and skill-building activities in at least one previous or concurrent university second language course, providing them with a basis with which to compare their literature–based course activities.

At the end of the quarter, students were asked to fill out a short survey on their preferences, indicating which activities they found pleasurable and which they found beneficial for language learning. While no survey was given before the class started to the two groups used in the study, previous research in other settings (Harlow & Muyskens, 1994) has found that second–language students ranked reading and grammar about the same in terms of preferred classroom activities. The present survey included closed–end questions in which students were asked to choose only one of the options listed (see questions below). This produced a count for each of the options, which was then used for statistical analysis. The three questions relevant to this study were:

a. Based upon your experience in this class and other second language classes, which do you believe is most pleasurable: assigned readings, self–selected reading, or grammar?

b. Based upon your experience in this class and other second language classes, which do you believe is most beneficial for your becoming fluent in your second language: assigned readings, self–selected reading, or grammar?

c. Given a choice between reading popular literature and studying grammar, which would you prefer to do?

An analysis of the responses of the two groups found no statistically significant differences between them, so the results were combined and are summarized in Tables 2, 3, and 4.

Table 2. Student Attitudes on Reading vs. Grammar: Most Beneficial
(N = 49)

Assigned Popular Reading	51%(25)
Self–Selected Reading	27%(13)
Combined Reading	78%(38)
Grammar Instruction	22%(11)

1 = Assigned Popular Reading plus Self–Selected Responses

*Table 3. Student Attitudes on Reading vs. Grammar: Most Pleasurable
(N=49)*

Assigned Popular Reading	55%(27)
Self Selected Reading	29%(14)
Combined Reading	84%(41)
Grammar Instruction	16% (8)

Table 4. Student Preferences on Reading vs. Grammar (N = 49)

Reading	Grammar Instruction
80% (39)	20% (10)

Table 2 shows which activity students considered most beneficial. Reading is clearly the favorite, with 78% of the students choosing either the assigned popular reading or self-selected categories. The difference between the Combined Reading (assigned popular reading plus self-selected) and Grammar Instruction categories was statistically significant. Table 3 shows that students exposed to both reading and grammar also consider the former to be more pleasurable. Again, the results of the Combined Reading and Grammar categories were compared and found to differ significantly from chance. Finally, Table 4 summarizes student preferences in choosing between traditional grammar instruction and popular reading in the L2 classroom, with reading the favorite of 80% of the students. These results are also significantly different from chance.

Discussion

The instructors for both courses noted that student enthusiasm and interest in learning the second language was greatly improved over the general level shown by students in previous grammar-oriented courses. The preference of students for assigned versus self-selected reading may seem unusual, but the instructors reported that the vast bulk of the assigned texts were well-liked materials that had been popular with previous students. Given a choice between reading enjoyable materials supplied by the instructor and having to search for new reading matter, students may be indicating both their enjoyment of the texts supplied and their convenience. Students were not given a choice among the assigned texts but could do additional reading that they self-selected. In any case, given an opportunity to experience both popular reading materials and grammar instruction, the overwhelming majority of the students found reading to be superior to traditional instruction not only in terms of pleasure, but also in perceived benefits in language acquisition.

It is important to point out that all of the subjects in this study had an opportunity to read popular second-language literature in and outside the classroom, a situation not common in other beginning and intermediate second language courses, as noted above. This may help explain why other measures of student preferences in L2 classroom activities differ from the present study's results. In Harlow and Muyskens (1994), for example, subjects ranked reading 7th and grammar 9th in importance in the FL classroom, suggesting only a marginal preference for reading. There is no indication, however, that students in the survey had much contact with L2 reading in their classes.

Conclusions

The studies reviewed in this chapter provide more support for the notion that students enjoy reading and prefer it over other alternatives when exposed to an extensive reading approach. Given the evidence in support of reading in promoting first and second language acquisition, it seems prudent that second-language instructors consider the use of extensive reading with popular literature in their classrooms in order to foster positive affect and more enjoyable environments for acquiring a second language. Programs such as the ones outlined in this chapter, as well as other approaches to literature-based programs (e.g. MacGillivray, Tse, & McQuillan, 1995), can lead students to forming positive attitudes toward reading and greater success acquiring their second language.

References

Alexander, F. (1986). *California assessment program: Annual report.* Sacramento: California State Department of Education.

Anderson, R., P. Wilson & L. Fielding. (1988). Growth in reading and how children spend their time outside of school. *Reading Research Quarterly, 23,* 285–303.

Davis, F., & J. Lucas. (1971). An experiment in individualized reading. *The Reading Teacher, 24,* 737–747.

Dubin, F., D.E. Eskey, & W. Grabe. (1986). *Teaching second language reading for academic purposes.* Reading, Mass.: Addison–Wesley Publishing Company.

Dupuy, B., L. Tse, & T. Cook. (1996). Bringing books into the classroom: First steps in turning college level ESL students into readers. *TESOL Journal, 5(4),* 10–15.

Elley, W. (1991). Acquiring literacy in a second language: The effect of book-based programs. *Language Learning, 41,* 375–411.

Gardner, R., & W. Lambert. (1972). *Attitudes and motivation in second-language learning.* Rowley, Mass.: Newbury House Publishers.

Gray, G. (1969). A survey of children's attitudes toward individualized reading. In S. Ducker (Ed.), *Individualized reading: Readings* (pp. 330–332). Metuchen, N.J.: The Scarecrow Press.

Harlow, L., & J. Muyskens. (1994). Priorities for intermediate-level language instruction. *Modern Language Journal, 7,* 141–154.

Hayes, D., & M. Ahrens. (1988). Vocabulary simplification for children: A special case of motherese? *Journal of Child Language, 15,* 395–410.

Huber, B.J. (1993). Characteristics of college and university foreign language curricula: Findings from the MLA's 1987–89 survey. *ADFL Bulletin, 24(3),* 6–21.

Kaminsky, D. (1992). Improving intermediate grade level English-as-a-second language students' attitudes toward recreational reading. Unpublished manuscript. (ERIC Document Reproduction Service No. ED 347 509)

Krashen, S. (1993). *The power of reading.* Englewood, Colo.: Libraries Unlimited, Inc.

Krashen, S. (1985). *The input hypothesis: Issues and implications.* London: Longman.

Krashen, S. (1994, March). The pleasure hypothesis. Paper presented at the Georgetown Round Table on Language and Linguistics, Washington, D.C.

MacGillivray, L., L. Tse, & J. McQuillan. (1995). Second language and literacy teachers considering literature circles: A play. *Journal of Adolescent and Adult Literacy, 39,* 36–44.

McQuillan, J. (1994). Reading versus grammar: What students think is pleasurable in language acquisition. *Applied Language Learning, 9,* 107–111.

Mueller, T., & R. Miller. (1970). A study of student attitudes and motivation in a collegiate French course using programmed language instruction. *International Review of Applied Linguistics in Language Teaching, 8,* 297–320.

Nagy, W., R. Anderson, & P. Herman. (1987). Learning word meanings from context during normal reading. *American Educational Research Journal, 24,* 237–270.

Nagy, W., & P. Herman. (1987). Breadth and depth of vocabulary knowledge: Implications for acquisition and instruction. In M. McKeown & M. Curtiss (Eds.), *The nature of vocabulary acquisition* (pp. 19–35). Hillsdale, N.J.: Erlbaum.

Nagy, W., P. Herman, & R. Anderson. (1985). Learning words from context. *Reading Research Quarterly, 20,* 233–253.

Oller, J., A. Hudson, & P. Liu. (1977). Attitudes and attained proficiency in ESL: A sociolinguistic study of native speakers of Chinese in the United States. *Language Learning, 27,* 173–183.

Patton, M.Q. (1980). *Qualitative evaluation methods.* Beverly Hills, Calif.: Sage.

Petre, R. (1971). Reading breaks make it in Maryland. *The Reading Teacher, 15,* 191–194.

Schumann, F., & J. Schumann. (1977). Diary of a language learner: An introspective study of second language learning. In H.D. Brown, C. Yorio, & R. Crymes (Eds.), *On TESOL '77* (pp. 241–249). Washington, D.C.: TESOL.

Sperlz, E. (1948). The effect of comic books on vocabulary growth and reading comprehension. *Elementary English, 25,* 109–113.

Tse, L. (1996). When an ESL adult becomes a reader. *Reading Horizons, 31(1),* 16–29.

Wright, R. (1993). The comic book: A forgotten medium in the classroom. *Reading Teacher, 33,* 158–161.

Chapter 10

Literature-Based Programs for First Language Development: Giving Native Bilinguals Access to Books

Jeff McQuillan
Victoria Rodrigo

The benefits of providing language minority (LM) students access to books in terms of literacy and language development has been persuasively argued by several researchers (Krashen, 1993; Pucci, 1994; Constantino, 1994). More access means more reading, and more reading leads to higher levels of literacy and language acquisition. The problem currently facing teachers is how to provide such access. The method is to build literature-based, extensive and free voluntary reading programs into the language arts curriculum. This chapter will detail three separate program models that have been found to be highly effective in giving LM students more access to texts in their first language, leading to increased vocabulary acquisition, positive attitudes toward reading, and long-term reading habits. We will first describe the elements involved in each program model, followed by a short description of the results of evaluation studies conducted to test the effectiveness of each approach used. It is hoped that by detailing the components of the programs, teachers will be able to set up similar models in their elementary, secondary, or university settings.

Model One: Extensive Reading, Free Voluntary Reading, and Classroom Library

Program Elements

The first model was employed in a fifteen-week, intermediate (fourth semester) Spanish class at a large private university. Among the English speaking students enrolled in the course were six native Spanish bilinguals. There were three important elements in the execution of the course.

Extensive Reading

Extensive reading involves the use of mostly popular, easy-to-read literature which is likely to appeal to students' interests and be comprehensible to them. Students were assigned six graded books and two abridged books (see description below). Before beginning the course, none of the students, with the exception of one of the bilingual participants, had read an entire book in Spanish. The class met twice a week for eighty minutes, during which time students could read quietly and discuss their readings with the instructor. Whole-group sessions were planned for each class period, during which the required readings were examined in more depth. Students were required to turn in a short report about each book they read, giving their reactions to the texts. These reports were not graded for grammatical or content accuracy, but rather used as a tool to allow students to respond in some form to their reading. Students were encouraged to read one assigned and one self-selected book each week, as their grade was determined by the number of texts they completed by the end of the semester. The instructor conducted the class sessions in Spanish, although students could respond in the language they felt most comfortable with.

Free Voluntary Reading (FVR)

In FVR, students are allowed to choose their own texts to read (Krashen, 1993). During the course, students were asked to read three books of their own choosing, keeping a log of the titles and authors and submitting a short reaction report about the book. Students were not required to finish books they did not find interesting or comprehensible. In order to encourage students to find books of their own interest, each week students volunteered to report on their personal reading, commenting on the texts they had chosen. These brief oral reports served to stimulate interest in different texts and create more of a "literacy club" atmosphere among the students (Smith, 1988).

Classroom Library

The use of a classroom library was critical to the success of this model. Morrow (1985) and Routman (1991) (cited in Fractor, Woodruff, Martinez, and Teale, 1993), note that certain features of well–designed classroom libraries increase students' motivation for free reading. These features include:

a. Having a specific place to read: In our program, a special section of the university's School of Education library was employed, called the "Spanish Corner." We were also able to hold class in the library, providing students with immediate access to books.

b. Comfortable atmosphere--Our area was quiet and well lit, and contained enough chairs to accommodate all of the students.

c. Accessibility to books--Students could go directly to the bookshelves to select their texts. Books were displayed in an attractive manner, often with the fronts of the books facing outward.

d. Variety of books--A number of different genres were provided to students in order to satisfy various interests. Texts included children's books, adolescent fiction, literature, history, geography, and comic books.

Types of Materials Used

The type of materials used in this model were typical of those employed in extensive and free reading programs (Cook, Dupuy, and Tse, in press). They included:

a. Graded Readers--Graded readers are books that have been edited, simplified, or written in such a manner as to be more comprehensible to second language learners. The graded readers turned out to be an excellent resource for the native bilingual students, as they allowed them to build up their confidence in reading, an important element found in other programs (Nash and Yun-Pi, 1992/3). This was an excellent "jumping off point" for students into the world of Spanish reading.

b. Light or Popular Literature--By light reading, we mean unabridged texts written for native speakers that are not "classical" literature or technical works. For most students, this type of reading constituted the second stage of their reading, beyond the graded readers. There are a number of different types of popular reading that were used, including:

- Children's books--While easy to understand, some books may not provide interesting topics for students, especially adults, although they might be of use to younger students.
- Adolescent fiction--This proved to be the most popular resource, as the books were both understandable and contained sufficiently adult themes to captivate the students' interest. As with other second language learners (Cho and Krashen, 1994), the *Sweet Valley High* series proved successful with students.
- Comics--Students had a variety of comic books available. This did not prove to be a major source of reading for most students, however, perhaps because of the amount of slang and colloquial expressions found in many of these publications.
- Newspapers and magazines--Students generally enjoyed reading Spanish newspapers and magazines, which had the advantage of providing some comprehensible text for every level and interest (e.g. sports, fashion, politics, etc.).

Literature and Expository Texts

More complex, unabridged books were also used by some students, including short stories, encyclopedias, and history books. This served as the final stage for those students, including many of the native bilinguals, who had passed through the light reading and wanted more adult-level content. The assigned graded readers all focused on a common topic, in this case detective stories. The decision to use a unifying theme considered to be of interest to university students was based on the recommendations for "narrow reading" by Krashen (1985) and Anderson and Pikulski (1992). Narrow reading gives the reader the advantage of context, characters, and recurring vocabulary from book to book, allowing him/her to build upon previous knowledge and thus make the language of the text more comprehensible.

When students were ready for the light reading stage, a common problem was their inability to find books which matched their interests, a key variable in promoting pleasure reading (Nell, 1988). Often, if a book was interesting, it was too difficult, and if it was easy, it was not interesting. The instructor strove to find books that fit both criteria by adopting a method used by Ross (1978) in selecting texts for elementary students. First, the instructor asked each student to make a list of topics they might be interested in reading about. Second, the instructor attempted to find texts on these topics or in these genres, and gave the texts to the students to inspect. Third, students are instructed to flip through the books to see if they are both interesting and comprehensible. Fourth, students showed a book they had selected to the instructor, who could then give the students some background on the topic (if possible) and help them decide whether they wanted to read it. Fifth, students started reading the book, continuing if they found it enjoyable, stopping and selecting a new book if they did not.

Program Evaluation

In order to determine what effect the program had on the six bilinguals who participated in the program, a vocabulary checklist (Rodrigo, 1994) used to measure growth in passive word knowledge as well as an Affective Survey designed by the researchers were administered to the students. The results indicated that all six students made gains in the vocabulary in just one semester, an average of 6% on the checklist. In the affective survey, five of the six students said they enjoyed reading in Spanish more after taking the course, and all six felt that their competency in Spanish reading had improved over the fifteen-week semester. Some comments from open-ended questions on the survey included:

> "I liked the fact that there was no testing...I actually felt the results of my improved reading comprehension as [the program] was going on." "The material was interesting in that it helped me gain a better handle on Spanish." "By reading subjects that interested me, I grew to understand more about Latin American views and learn Spanish writing techniques I was not familiar with."

Model Two: Popular Literature Survey and Literature Circles

Program Elements

The second program model was used in a special Spanish for Native Speakers course in a medium-sized public university in the southwest. Twenty students (six men, fourteen women) enrolled in the ten week course, which satisfied their foreign language requirement at the university. The experimental course had three basic components: a survey of various genres of popular and classic literature, self-selected literature circles, and writing workshops. Class time was divided roughly into equal segments among the three areas. The reading components are described below.

Popular Literature Survey

While the bulk of the course was devoted toward self-selected reading, a packet of twenty assigned readings, which contained examples of a large range of genres, including children's literature, Chicano poetry, newspaper articles, and academic reports, was also included in the curriculum. The instructor also brought in popular materials (newspapers, magazines, adolescent and adult literature) for students to examine and check out. There were three reasons for the assigned reading: First, and most importantly, many of the students had never read for pleasure in Spanish. It was thought that an introduction to various popular and literary forms (such as those described in Model One--comics, short stories, poetry, novels, essays, plays) would provide students with some background to make more informed choices in their free reading. Second, although the level of the assigned reading was at times too difficult for some students, heterogeneous small groups were formed in class to allow lesser proficient readers to discuss the assigned material with better readers, giving them an opportunity to increase their confidence in oral skills as well. Finally, the cultural themes in the readings gave the class common points of discussion each week.

Literature Circles

While the literature survey continued throughout the entire ten weeks, students were asked at the beginning of week two to think about materials they would like to read with other members of the class as part of a self-selected book discussion group called a "literature circle" (MacGillivray, Tse, and McQuillan, 1995). The instructor made grouping suggestions based on approximate reading level of the students as determined by a short English summary of a Spanish newspaper article, but the final decision of grouping was left entirely to the students. Some students chose to group themselves by interest, others according to perceived ability in Spanish reading proficiency or oral fluency. It was up to each group to decide what they were going to read and discuss during the thirty-minute time slot allotted to literature circles during each class period.

As in Model One, students were encouraged to ask the instructor's advice as to possible books, since even after a few weeks of being familiarized with various genres and authors, many students felt unsure of what was available to read. The instructor gave recommendations depending on perceived interest and language proficiency (e.g. *Como agua para chocolate* by Laura Esquivel, the poems of Pablo Neruda, children's stories, *Cosmopolitan* magazine, some adolescent novels). Many groups took the instructor's suggestions, others did not. Two literature circles began by reading nonfiction magazines, but fiction seemed to work better in terms of group discussion, and after a few weeks all of the circles were reading some form of fiction. The amount of reading was determined entirely by the individual groups. The most proficient groups read two novels and several short stories in the ten week span; the less proficient groups read eight to twelve children's, adolescent, or graded reader texts of varying lengths. Students were also encouraged to read outside of class, but no effort was made to measure their outside reading.

The instructor gave students some suggestions as to possible approaches to discussion through whole class sessions based on the assigned readings. Students were asked to talk about whatever they felt comfortable discussing, including personal reactions, comparisons with other texts, and comprehension/language problems. The instructor monitored the groups, providing assistance when asked, but generally left students alone to conduct their circles as they wished. Performance in the groups was never formally evaluated by the instructor, although students did decide to give peer evaluations as part of a student-determined participation grade.

Program Evaluation

As in Model One, changes in vocabulary growth were measured by a vocabulary checklist developed by Rodrigo (1994). The results (reported in full in McQuillan, 1995) indicated that the group made significant gains in word knowledge in just ten weeks of the program, averaging 8%, a considerable feat considering that no formal evaluation or vocabulary instruction was employed. The results are consistent with other data which suggest that vocabulary acquisition is largely incidental and is most efficiently achieved through reading, particularly pleasure reading, rather than direct instruction (Nagy, Herman, & Anderson, 1987; Krashen, 1989, 1993).

An Affective Survey was also administered to the students and, for the purposes of comparison, a control group of nineteen students (nine men, ten women). It was comprised of a combination of traditional grammar exercises and assigned culture readings with essay writing assignments and quizzes. While no measure of reading attitudes was conducted before the course began, there were no significant differences between the two groups as to their pleasure reading habits at the beginning of the semester. Students responded to statements on their attitudes and practices on a Likert–style scale of 1 ("strongly agree") to 5 ("strongly disagree"). Due to the small numbers in each cell, responses were collapsed into two categories, Agree/Yes (1 and 2) and Disagree/No (3, 4, and 5), and statistical tests were conducted on the resulting figures for comparison and experimental groups. Given that the forms were completed anonymously, there was little incentive for the students to "please" the instructor with their responses.

The results of the survey of attitudes toward Spanish literacy of the experimental and control groups are shown in Table 1 (from McQuillan, 1995). As noted above, neither group reported much pleasure reading (Question 1) before enrolling in the SNS course (less than 17% from both groups), with no significant difference between the two classes. Both groups reported having significantly more positive attitudes as a result of taking the SNS course. The difference between the two groups at the end of the quarter was not statistically significant (Question 2 only). VR methods, then, were as effective as assigned readings and traditional skills instruction in improving students' attitudes toward Spanish reading. Both classes reported that the SNS courses improved their confidence in reading (75% of the total), while again there was no difference between the two groups (Question 3). It should be emphasized that the control group, like the experimental group, also used some cultural readings in class, which may have contributed to those students' positive attitudes toward reading after the course.

Table 1. Reading Habits and Attitudes of Native Spanish Bilinguals (n=39)

1. Before taking this class, I would read in Spanish for pleasure.

Experimental		Control	
Yes	No	Yes	No
10%(2)	90%(18)	16%(3)	84%(16)

2. I am more likely to read in Spanish for pleasure after completing this course than before I started.

Experimental		Control	
Yes	No	Yes	No
80%(16)	20%(4)	63%(12)	37%(7)

3. As a result of taking this class, I feel more confident as a reader in Spanish.

Experimental		Control	
Yes	No	Yes	No
80%(16)	20%(4)	68%(13)	32%(6)

4. I would recommend this course to a friend to help them improve their reading and writing in Spanish.

Experimental		Control	
Yes	No	Yes	No
85%(17)	15%(3)	89%(17)	11%(2)

5. As a result of this class, I know more about types of popular and literary reading material in Spanish.

Experimental		Control	
Yes	No	Yes	No
75%(15)	25%(5)	53%(10)	47%(7)

Moreover, the treatment period was extremely short in comparison to other FVR programs reported on in the literature. Krashen (1993) has noted that most sustained silent reading programs, for example, need at least seven months for the full effects to take place. Longer periods of

FVR exposure, or comparisons to a more strictly skills–oriented course, may have produced results more clearly favoring the free reading students, as in other studies.

Students were asked if they would recommend the course to a friend to help them improve their Spanish reading and writing (Question #4). Again, the overwhelming majority said "yes." Finally, students were asked if the course improved their knowledge of sources of popular and literary reading material. More than three fourths of the experimental group answered affirmatively (76%), as did a little over half from the control group (53%), although these differences did not reach statistical significance.

The experimental group was also asked to fill out an additional survey on a number of specific points related to the functioning of their literature circles. While no control group comparisons are possible, the results are illustrative of the positive attitudes developed by the use of the reading groups and give us additional information on the effectiveness of this method of FVR. The results are shown in Table 2. Again, the "Agree" figures correspond with those who answered either 1 or 2 on the Likert Scale, and "Disagree" with either 3, 4, or 5.

Table 2. Attitudes Toward Literature Circles by Experimental Group (n=20)

	Yes	No
1. Literature Circles (LCs) made Spanish reading more enjoyable.	85%(17)	15%(3)
2. LCs increased my confidence in reading in Spanish.	90%(18)	10%(2)
3. LCs increased my reading comprehension in Spanish.	95%(19)	5%(1)
4. Hearing the views of others helped me understand the text more.	90%(18)	10%(2)
5. I did all of the reading for my LC.	90%(18)	10%(2)
6. Having the instructor observe my LC inhibited our conversation.	15%(3)	85%(17)

As shown in Table 2, the large majority of students indicated that the literature circles had a very positive impact on their experience of Spanish reading, increasing their enjoyment, confidence, and comprehension (Questions 1, 2, and 3). The opportunity to hear the views of fellow students in a low stress environment is also perceived as beneficial (Question 4). Literature circles seem to combine the best of two effective strategies for classroom reading: self–selected, free voluntary reading and cooperative groups (Kagen, 1986). It is also important to point out that almost all of the students reported doing the reading for their literature circles. This is indeed an interesting finding: Students enrolled in a compulsory course will read without formal evaluation if they are allowed to select their own texts. The draw of FVR and literature circles seems to be particularly strong in motivating students to read.

Students did not find the presence of the teacher observing their circles to be inhibiting (Question 5). This is perhaps because they knew there was no teacher evaluation of the groups, and that the instructor made an attempt only to "listen in" without interfering with the flow of the discussion.

Model Three: Popular Literature Survey, Outside Reading, and Inquiry Learning

Program Elements

The third program model was also used in a similar class as that employed in Model Two, a university Spanish for Native Speakers course. There were ten students (three men, seven women) who enrolled in the course and agreed to be evaluated for the study (McQuillan, 1995). The main elements of the course were:

Popular Literature Survey

The same method as described in Model Two was used.

Weekly Free Voluntary Reading

Students were asked to read an average of ten articles per week from either *La Opinion* newspaper, a Spanish language magazine, or an equivalent amount of reading from children's, adolescent, or adult literature books. Each student selected his/her own reading materials, and was asked to keep a weekly log with the title of the selection and a brief reaction to the piece, similar to that done in Model One. Students were asked to comment on what they were reading, and were given time in class to ask questions about material they did not understand. This component provided the bulk of the FVR in the course. Students who had a very low reading level began with simple newspaper texts (ads, horoscopes, the comic section) and with children's books. More advanced readers chose short stories or popular novels.

Individual Inquiry Learning Project

Each student carried out a ten-week project related to some aspect of interest in Spanish language or Latino culture. The only requirement was that the project have some extensive reading and writing in Spanish connected to it. A wide variety of projects resulted. One student read extensively on Mexican rodeos and wrote a report on his findings. Several students who worked as bilingual aides or teachers in local elementary schools did reading and writing in relation to their work. Others decided to read a novel or short stories in Spanish in addition to their weekly FVR. Although a grade was assigned to the project, the topics and texts were chosen by the student.

The course also included short lectures on Mexican and Mexican-American history to provide further background knowledge for some students' self-selected reading. Some very limited grammar instruction was also included, usually comprising less than 10% of class time.

The grade was determined in the following manner:

Student reading log:	25%
Inquiry Learning:	50%
Lecture Quizzes:	15%
Grammar Quizzes:	10%

Note that 75% of the grade was related to self-selected, extensive reading.

Program Evaluation

Approximately seven months after the end of the course, the experimental course students were asked to fill out a Literacy Practices Survey created by the researchers. For the purposes of comparison, a control group of eighteen SNS students (five men, thirteen women) who had not participated in the FVR course were also surveyed. This was done in order to determine if those who had been exposed to FVR had significantly different reading habits than those who had not. Table 3 summarizes the results of the experimental and control group survey. The difference between the two groups was found to be statistically significant. Among the experimental group, 90% said that they continued to do some form of free reading seven months after the end of the course. Only 45% of the control group, which had no exposure to FVR, reported any sort of pleasure reading. These results are similar to those reported by Greaney and Clarke (1973), who also found that FVR has long–term effects. In their study of sixth–grade boys, they discovered that those who had participated in an FVR program were reading more than those who had not *six years* after the end of the course.

Table 3. Self–Selected Pleasure Reading in Spanish

Group	Yes	No
Experimental	90%(9)	10%(1)
Control	44%(8)	56%(10)

When the experimental participants were asked if they were free reading in Spanish more, less, or about the same now than before taking the SNS experimental course, 75% responded "more."

While the number of subjects was admittedly small, the results from the experimental group were impressive given the short period of exposure to an FVR approach. It should be noted that ten weeks may be too short for some students to "get into the habit" of reading. One student noted that, "I continued reading for the next quarter but as time went on it became less and less." Still, students reported noting improvements both in their understanding of Spanish and in their attitudes toward pleasure reading. "I enjoyed [the course]. I could tell my comprehension and fluidity were improving in Spanish." Participants also expressed satisfaction with the wide selection of readings assigned, which gave them exposure to avenues for further reading.

Implications: Providing More Access

The three models presented here of providing language minority students with access to print are by no means exhaustive. Other ideas to expose and encourage literacy have been suggested that were not used in these models, including Sustained Silent Reading (e.g., Pilgreen and Krashen, 1994) where students are provided fifteen to thirty minutes each day to read self-selected materials; and Read Alouds (Trelease, 1982), where stories are read to students during class to encourage interest in books. These models have been successful in getting LM students interested in reading, resulting in gains in vocabulary and increased interest in improving their Spanish literacy.

There is an important obstacle to the implementation of any book-based program of the type advocated here--namely, obtaining a supply of books! Teachers will need to be creative in their solutions, perhaps appealing to local public libraries and finding other low-cost alternatives. What is certain from the experience of the teachers who participated in the programs outlined in this chapter is that, after a certain investment of time at the beginning of the project, the rewards were not only greater interest by students in reading, but a lessened workload for the teacher. Most of the elements in the models do not require a great deal of teacher time, since students take responsibility for reading. There are no worksheets to correct and no exams to grade. More importantly, teachers have the satisfaction of knowing that students will continue reading on their own long after they leave their classrooms.

References

Anderson, R., & J. Pikulski. (1992). *Independent reading: The key to success. Reading and Language Arts Series.* New York: Houghton Mifflin.

Cho, K.S., & S. Krashen. (1994). Acquisition of vocabulary from Sweet Valley High series: Adult ESL acquisition. *Journal of Reading, 37,* 654–662.

Constantino, R. (1994). Pleasure reading helps, even if readers don't believe it. *Journal of Reading, 37,* 504–505.

Cook, T., B. Dupuy, & L. Tse. (in press). Learning English through the extensive reading of popular literature in a university–level academic English ESL Program. *School Library Media Quarterly.*

Fractor, J.S., M. Woodruff, M. Martinez, & W. Teale. (1993). Let's not miss opportunities to promote voluntary reading: Classroom libraries in the elementary school. *The Reading Teacher, 46,* 476–484.

Greaney, V., & M. Clarke. (1973). A longitudinal study of the effects of two reading methods on leisure–time reading habits. In D. Moyle (Ed.), *Reading: What of the Future?* (107–114). London: United Kingdom Reading Association.

Kagen, S. (1986). Cooperative learning and sociocultural forces in schooling. In *Beyond language*. In California State Department of Education (Ed.), *Social and cultural factors in schooling language minority students* (231–298). Los Angeles: Evaluation, Dissem–ination, and Assessment.

Krashen, S. (1985). *The input hypothesis: Issues and implications.* London: Longman.

Krashen, S. (1989). We acquire vocabulary and spelling by reading: Additional evidence for the input hypothesis. *Modern Language Journal, 73 (4),* 440–464.

Krashen, S. (1993). *The Power of Reading.* Englewood, Colorado: Libraries Unlimited.

MacGillivray, L., L. Tse, & J. McQuillan. (1995). First and second language teachers considering literature circles: A play. *Journal of Adolescent and Adult Literacy.*

McQuillan, J. (1995). How should ethnic languages be taught? The effects of a free voluntary reading program. *Reading Teacher, 39(1),* 36–44.

Nagy, W., P. Herman, & R. Anderson. (1987). Learning words from context. *Reading Research Quarterly, 20,* 233–253.

Nash, T., & Y. Yun Pi. (1992/93). Extensive reading for learning and enjoyment. *TESOL Journal, 2,* 27–31.

Nell, V. (1988). *Lost in a book: The psychology of reading for pleasure.* New Haven, Conn.: Yale University Press.

Pilgreen, J., & S. Krashen. (1994). Sustained silent reading with ESL high school students: Impact on reading comprehension, reading frequency, and reading enjoyment. *School Library Media Quarterly, 22,* 21–23.

Pucci, S. (1994). Supporting Spanish language literacy: Latino children and free reading resources in schools. *Bilingual Research Journal,*

18, 67–82.

Rodrigo, V. (1994). *Spanish vocabulary checklist for intermediate students.* Unpublished manuscript. University of Southern California.

Ross, P. (1978). Getting books into those empty hands. *The Reading Teacher, 31,* 397–399.

Smith, F. (1988). *Joining the literacy club.* Portsmouth, N.H.: Heinemann.

Trelease, J. (1982). *The Read–Aloud Handbook.* New York: Penguin Books, Limited.

Chapter 11

Libraries, Books, Attitudes and Tests. . . . Case Studies

Implementing Free Voluntary Reading With ESL Middle School Students – Improvement in Attitudes Toward Reading and Test Scores

Fay Shin

Many English as a Second Language (ESL) teachers use different strategies to meet the needs of students with diverse backgrounds and varying English proficiency levels. A common concern ESL teachers share is: How does one provide students with a meaningful and authentic curriculum that will meet the needs of these second-language learners? In particular, what if some students read at a first-grade level and others read at a fifth-grade level (which is very typical of any middle school ESL class)?

Implementing a free reading program into the language arts curriculum has been supported by many researchers (Krashen, 1993; Trelease, 1982; Jenkins, 1957). Recent research in language arts supports a whole language philosophy (Goodman, 1986). The whole language philosophy of teaching English is based on the principle that students learn language, learn about language, and learn through language by reading (Harste, Woodward, and Burke, 1984).

Krashen (1993) argues that free voluntary reading is the "missing ingredient in first language 'language arts' as well as in intermediate second and foreign language instruction" (p. 1). He further states that free voluntary reading (FVR) is beneficial for language acquisition and literacy development, even more beneficial than direct instruction. He concludes that in–school FVR works as long as the programs are for a long period (about one school year).

Research has shown that students in reading programs with sustained silent reading have higher reading comprehension and vocabulary test scores than students without SSR (Krashen, 1993; Elley & Mangubhai, 1983). In addition, students have been found to have a much more positive attitude about reading (Nagy, Anderson, & Herman, 1987; Aranha, 1985). More recently, Pilgreen and Krashen (1994) found high school ESL students who participated in a sixteen–week sustained silent reading program showed gains in reading comprehension, reported greater frequency and enjoyment of reading, and utilized more sources of books after the program.

Another important component of a successful reading program is providing the students with a variety of different reading materials. Jenkins (1957) and Krashen (1993) believe that one of the most important factors to consider in a self–selected reading is providing children with access to a variety of reading materials such as trade books, magazines, comic books, newspapers, and journals.

The purpose of this study is to examine the effects of a free reading program using both sustained silent reading and self–selected reading with an English as a Second Language middle school class. There were two research questions investigated: If ESL students at various levels (beginning, intermediate and advanced) were given access to a variety of reading materials and time for free reading, (a) would their attitude towards reading change, and (b) would there be any improvement in reading scores?

Subjects

The subjects of this study included fifteen ESL students in grades 6–8. Because this school did not have a large second language learner (or limited English proficient) middle school population, this ESL class consisted of students at various English proficiencies. Two students had lived in the U.S. for less than four months (beginning level); four students had lived in the U.S. for an average of 1.4 years (intermediate); and the other students had lived in the U.S. for at least four years. Five students were born in the United States and learned English as a second language; however, they never fully attained cognitive academic language proficiency in English or their first language. Because their standardized test scores were below the required minimum to be reclassified as Fluent English Proficiency (36th percentile), they were required to receive support in an English language development program.

The first language of the students represented their diverse backgrounds--five Russian, one Korean, one Cantonese, and eight Spanish-speaking students. The school was located in the inner city and in an ethnically diverse community in Los Angeles. The school average Comprehensive Test of Basic Skills (CTBS) reading scores are below the national average.

Limitations

The majority of the ESL students are exempted from taking the standardized tests because of the lack of English proficiency or LEP classification; thus, many test scores were not available.

This class was smaller than a typical class (average class size is thirty students) and there was much more individual attention. Although English Language Development (ELD) support, smaller class size, specialized instruction and interaction with native speakers may have influenced any positive changes in attitudes towards reading and test scores, other factors *limiting or interfering* with growth in English language development or proficiency need to be considered.

The majority of the students were in classes that were not sheltered for most of the day. They had only one out of seven classes in a sheltered environment. Because their core subject classes were not sheltered, they had difficulty in these classes. Since the students were at the middle school grade level, most of the subject matter was too difficult for the students to participate in. The students had the basic interpersonal communicative skills (BICS), but they lacked the cognitive academic skills in English that were needed to succeed in their classes.

Research suggests it takes five to seven years to develop cognitive academic language proficiency (Cummins, 1981; Krashen, Long & Scarcella, 1979). Thus, many of the students were "barely surviving" in their other classes (this was documented from their past report card grades). The beginning students were often "bored" and felt "left out" of their core subject classes.

Unfortunately, as too often heard, these students were not receiving the extra academic support they needed because of lack of resources and the small number of second language learners at the school (unfortunately, sheltered classes for fifteen students in grades 6–8 was not a practical or realistic alternative).

Before this class was created, the researcher was aware of the fact that five of the students had attended school in the U.S. since kindergarten. Because of past experiences, the researcher was concerned about the affective variables affecting these students. There has always been a negative stigmatization attached to being in an ESL classroom, particularly for middle school students when peer pressure is most prevalent. Therefore, after individual conferences with each student, they were given the opportunity either to transfer to another classroom where an individualized program would have been implemented or to stay in this ESL class. All the students chose to stay in this class.

Instrumentation and Methodology

Students were given a pre- and post-reading survey at the beginning and end of the 1993–94 academic year, September 1993 and June 1994. They were informed that the survey was completely voluntary and anonymous, and their answers would not affect their grades in any way.

Students had one class period (50 minutes) one day a week for free reading. An additional ten to fifteen minutes of free reading time were added to the curriculum approximately twice a week. No tests, book reports, or follow-up activities were required for their reading. The students were encouraged to bring in reading materials of their choice (comic books, magazines, etc.). In addition, there were magazines, comic books, novels and newspapers available for the class every day.

The materials available included fifteen daily copies of the *Los Angeles Times*, current monthly issues of *Sports Illustrated for Kids*,

Teen, Sassy, People, Time, and *US* magazines. There was also a wide range of more than one hundred donated magazines that were both current and old (*Car and Driver, Seventeen, Glamour, Good Housekeeping*, etc.). There were approximately 200 novels, 20 children's books (grades K–4), 20 reference books, 15 comic books, and 50 student–published books. In addition to the classroom materials, the class went to the library approximately three times a month for a full 55–minute period. The school library had approximately 3,000 trade books or novels, magazines, reference books, and Spanish language books.

The regular curriculum included reading a class novel and discussion, writing in dialogue journals, creative writing assignments, a newspaper project, writing and "publishing" a book, and interactive group work. At the end of nine months, in June 1994, the students were asked to fill out the same survey.

Results

Table 1. Do you ever read for pleasure?

	Never/Sometimes	Always
Pre:	13 (77%)	3 (23%)
Post:	6 (44%)	9 (56%)

Table 2. Reading is fun.

	No	Yes
Pre:	12 (75%)	4 (25%)
Post:	5 (33%)	10 (67%)

The change in total students responding to the pre–survey (16) and post–survey (15) was because one student moved to another school. As shown in Table 1, only 3 (or 23%) of the students reported they "always" read for pleasure in the pre–survey (before the program). In the post–survey after the nine month program, this percentage doubled to 9 (56%) of the students reporting they always read for pleasure. In addition, 10 (67%) indicated they felt reading was "fun," a significant increase from a dismal 4 (25%) reported on the pre-survey. The survey results indicate a significant change in attitude towards reading.

Although the survey results showed students definitely read for pleasure more often and felt reading was more enjoyable, the observational data of the students' reactions were even more supportive. Many students always preferred free reading time over regular class time. Many of the students showed up before class (nutrition/recess) time to read the newspaper or magazines. One male student in particular consistently showed up early in the morning (thirty minutes before school started) to read the daily Sports Section of the *Los Angeles Times*. Because he did not have access to the daily newspaper, the researcher brought in the Saturday and Sunday Sports Section for him to read on Monday (at the student's request).

The fact that this class was fortunate enough to have fifteen copies of the daily newspaper (donated by the *Los Angeles Times*) was an additional benefit to the reading program. This meant there were enough copies for everyone in the class. Many students commented on how surprised they were to find out there was "actually interesting stuff to read" in the newspaper. The boys often read the Sports page, and the girls liked the View Section, which had articles on celebrities, current fashions and trends. The students discovered the Metro Section often had news about "their neighborhood" events.

Another significant observation was the impact on students who tended to be "at risk" or "highly unmotivated to work." A tremendous difference was observed in their attitudes and behavior during the free reading times because it was a rare but consistent time period where they "stayed on task" by simply reading what they wanted to read. There was an incident when one teacher walked into the room and was very surprised to actually see Mike (not his real name) reading quietly. She commented on how he often talks and disrupts her class. The researcher noted that although it took more time to find something Mike was interested in, once he found it, he was hooked.

Another factor that undoubtedly contributed significantly to this change in attitude towards reading was the fact that there were no assignments, accountability, or *strings attached* to the reading. At the beginning, the students had a difficult time adjusting to the fact that they would be allowed to read *anything* (particularly comic books and magazines), and that there were no book reports or writing assignments required. It took students some time to become comfortable with the notion that reading was for pleasure and not just a school assignment. It was obvious that many students held the belief that reading was only for studying or learning.

Although the majority of the students' test scores were not available, the researcher obtained scores from the students who did take the tests (five students). As mentioned earlier, students in an English Language Development program are not required to take the CTBS. However, the cumulative files of students A through D show they have taken the test since the second grade, and because their scores were below the 36th percentile (California's minimum requirement), they never were reclassified. Therefore, these students remained in an English Language Development program and test scores were available. The following table shows the results of all ESL students who took the tests in 1993 and 1994.

Table 3 : *Percentile scores of CTBS (Comprehensive Test of Basic Skills) 1993 to 1994*

Student	Reading		Spelling		Language	
	'93	'94	'93	'94	'93	'94
A	5	4	1	19	6	38
B	14	14	3	12	23	29
C	6	37	*	27	*	24
D	32	39	22	49	25	37
E	*	29	*	81	*	57

* indicates scores were not available

Average percentile gain from 1993 to 1994 for students A–D.
Reading   + 9.7
Spelling   + 18.0
Language   + 17.0

Because there was no comparison group, norm–based comparisons cannot be made in program evaluations because they represent student growth, not program effects. However, we will consider the fact that these test scores showed that substantial growth did occur during the one-year period for students A through D.

As indicated in Table 3, the percentile scores were significantly increased from 1993 to 1994. Although only five students took the tests, the results were phenomenal for all five of these students. All the students showed incredible gains in spelling and language: Student A went from the 1st to 19th and 6th to 38th percentiles; Student B went from the 3rd to 12th and 23rd to 29th percentiles; and Student D went from the 22nd to 49th and 25th to 37th percentiles, respectively. Although Student C did not have available scores in spelling and language, her scores in reading showed tremendous growth. She went from the 6th to 37th percentile in reading.

Student E was in the United States for only two years; this explains why she did not have scores for 1993. Her results were added to the table because of her impressive achievement for her second year studying English as a second language. She is an avid reader and has always enjoyed reading, which probably is the main reason for her above-average scores in both spelling and language in such a short time period.

Conclusions and Implications

Although we cannot state unequivocally that the conclusions of this study were caused by a sustained silent reading program, it is rational to surmise that the SSR program was a major contributing factor. This study showed phenomenal growth in standardized test scores. The survey and observations demonstrated students had a more positive attitude towards reading and enjoyed reading much more than before the program started.

The implications of this study support other studies that have shown free voluntary reading in any language arts or ESL program can be beneficial to the students. When children are allowed the opportunity to self-select literature and are exposed to a print-rich environment, they develop positive attitudes towards reading.

References

Aranha, M. (1985). Sustained silent reading goes east. *Reading Teacher*, *39* (2), 214–217.

Cummins, J. (1981). The role of primary language development in promoting success for language minority students. *Schooling and Language Minority Students: A Theoretical Framework*. California State University, Los Angeles: Evaluation, Dissemination and Assessment Center, 3–49.

Elley, W., & F. Mangubhai. (1983). The impact of reading on second language learning. *Reading Research Quarterly*, 19, 53–67.

Goodman, K. (1986). *What's whole in whole language?* Portsmouth, N.H.: Heinemann.

Harste, J., V. Woodward, and C. Burke. (1984). *Language Stories and Literacy Lessons*. Portsmouth, N. H.: Heinemann Educational Books.

Jenkins, M. (1957). Self-selection in reading, *Reading Teacher*, *10*: 84–90.

Krashen, S. (1993). *Power of Reading*. Englewood, Colo.: Libraries Unlimited Inc.

Krashen, S., M. Long, and R. Scarcella. (1979). Age, rate, and eventual attainment in second language acquisition. *TESOL Quarterly*, *13* (4), 573–582.

Nagy, W., R. Anderson, & P. Herman. (1987). Learning word meanings from context during normal reading. *American Educational Research Journal*, *24*, 237–270.

Pilgreen, J. & Krashen, S. (1994). Sustained silent reading with English as a second language high school students: Impact on reading comprehension, reading frequency, and reading enjoyment. *School Library Media Quarterly*, Fall, 21–23.

Trelease, J. (1982). *The Read–Aloud Handbook*. New York, N.Y.: Penguin Books Limited.

Effect of Library Use on Standardized Test Scores of Language Minorities

Donald Singleton

The purpose of this study was to document the effect of consistent library use on the standardized test scores of linguistic minorities.

The subjects used in the study were 170 high school students who were labeled linguistic minorities. Ninety-seven students or almost 57% of the total group spoke Spanish as a first language. Sixty-eight students or almost 40% of the students spoke Ebonics or Black dialect and were not proficient in Standard English, and five of the students (almost 3%) spoke Samoan or Tongan as their first language.

The classes were divided into five groups of approximately thirty-four students in each section. One group of students was sent to the library one day per week. They were instructed to find a library book within the first seven to ten minutes, sit down, and read. The other four groups did not go to the library at all. They read from a teacher-selected book, *Heart of Aztlan*. This book was read to them every class period.

At the beginning of the project, the students failed to find a book immediately. They used the library time as a social event, talking among themselves. I explained to them that library behavior was quite different from classroom behavior, and that they would lose valuable class points if they did not find a book, sit down and read. Most of the males began to pick up car and sports magazines and look at the pictures. Although I did not quiz any students on their reading selection, I observed that the boys tended to select action magazines, while the girls tended to select fashion magazines. Occasionally, students of both sexes used the library time to complete class assignments in my class, or other classes.

After the third week of library attendance, I observed a shift in the attitudes of my students. Whenever I failed to take them to the library at their appointed time and day, the students would clamor for their library time. I reminded them that their library attendance was predicated upon their good library behavior, i.e., finding a book and reading it immediately. The results were promising. The students went to the library, picked out books, magazines and newspapers of their choice, and read. I did not suggest reading material for them, I did not criticize their choice of material, and I did not test them on the material that they read. The class experienced a 95% library time participation. The students became very interested in library time.

Results

In order to test the effect of library attendance on linguistic minorities, I administered a SAT pre-test to all 170 students. The pre-test consisted of twenty questions that tested a student's ability to recognize analogies, and vocabulary. The average score among students was 20% correct.

The students were re-tested after six weeks. The students who attended the library regularly improved their scores by an average of 17%. The students who did not attend the library regularly showed an increase of about 2%. The students who attended the library also performed better on their classroom final exams. Twenty-three percent of the students in the subject class received excellent grades, compared to an average of 4% to 6% in the other classes.

There was another unexpected result of constant library attendance. The students who went to the library reported an increased desire to go to the library on their own. Seventy-eight percent of the students who went to the library with the class stated that they now read more often. I gave all 170 students a library questionnaire which asked a series of questions about their library attendance. Excluding the thirty students used in the experiment, only 3% of the other students went to the library on a regular basis, either with a class or on their own. The students who did not go to the library on a regular basis also did not read independently at home. Thus, the students sent to the library were the only students who engaged in any regular reading.

The study suggests that encouraging students to read for pleasure can result in increased literacy development and, perhaps even more importantly, more reading. By providing an opportunity for students to read, we increase their literacy and learning, and, hopefully, improve the quality of their life.

Attitudes Toward Reading and Library Use by Fifth Grade Students

Erika Seeman

The last two decades have been filled with studies that delve into the affects of reading on students' academic achievement (Krashen, 1993; Adams, 1972; Goelman, Oberg, and Smith, 1984; Koga and Haroda, 1989). Frank Smith (1988) has conducted extensive research on the factors that encourage the development of literacy. He discovered that it is a process that occurs when children are surrounded by books and are given alternate ways to improve reading comprehension; for example, magazine activities, producing class newscasts, and writing from a character's point of view—thereby allowing them to experience learning that reaches beyond skill and drill. True literacy entails more than the ability to decode words, and it can be achieved only by making books and other resources accessible to our school children (Smith, 1988).

Accordingly, Krashen (1994) found a clear link between pleasure reading and literacy development and language acquisition. The first ingredient, however, is access to books. Unfortunately, books are expensive, and children in poor neighborhoods do not often understand that libraries are free and for everyone (Constantino, 1993). Since studies show that the richer the print environment, the better the literacy development (Krashen, 1993), it is evident that children with more access to books will be more successful in achieving literacy. Libraries play a vital role in ensuring that all children have opportunities to succeed, especially since students with access to books were among the best readers in school (Elley, 1992). By providing all children access to libraries—public, school, and classroom—we are making their opportunities to achieve literacy more equal.

This study was conducted to answer the following question: Do students who are allowed to take their school library books home have better attitudes toward reading and school than their peers who must leave books at school? The subjects were members of one fifth–grade class in School A and one fifth–grade class in School B. Because they were all fifth–grade students, their ages ranged between ten and eleven years old. Both classes were primarily Latino students who had been in the United States for various lengths of time. Other ethnicities were Anglo and African–American. Community demographics reflected the school in that the people were primarily low socio–economic Latinos. School B's community also had middle and high socio–economic status people of varying races. Although the majority spoke English fluently, only half spoke the language in their home environments. The students' access to books was equal in that they all visited the school library once a week, the rooms had classroom libraries of about fifty books, and few parents in either area provided regular public library visits. The major difference was the fact that the students in School B were able to take home their school library books freely, enjoying regular library privileges. The students in School A were not allowed to take their school library books out of the classroom. Therefore, the only time that they could use their books was at the teacher's discretion.

In order to measure the students' attitude toward reading and school, the researcher conducted one–on–one interviews with children whom the teacher selected from each class. The only people present during the interview were the researcher and the student, and the interviews were conducted in a separate room where no one else could hear the responses. Because all variables were equivalent except for the full library privileges accorded to the students in School B, the researcher concluded that moving school library books freely between school and home is vital in creating positive attitudes toward library use and pleasure reading.

Research Question: Is there a link between taking library books home and attitudes toward school and public library use?

The research found that students who were able to take their library books home had a positive attitude toward both school and libraries. Kristie said, "I go to the library because it is nice and quiet and I like to read," while Jennifer went to the library "because you can learn things." Students from School A generally had no opinion of libraries because they have never experienced regular library use. "I never think about libraries" (Diana), and Kosmin says that "libraries are good only to get books for book reports." Because neither group of students had easy access to public libraries, the difference of opinion can be attributed to the difference in their school library experience. Even the students in School B who said they like the library were frustrated that they were allowed to check out only two books at a time. A conclusion that can be drawn is that students need to experience the full range of library privileges--taking books home, checking out as many as they desire, and using the other resources that the library offers--in order for them to appreciate fully the richness of a library experience.

In spite of the fact that the majority of the students from School B liked the library and had a positive attitude toward its possibilities, only 30% visited the public library regularly. Jennifer would like to go to the public library in her town but cannot because it is not within walking distance and her mom doesn't have time to take her. Erika's mom works and is not able to take her, while Didier does not know where it is and does not have anyone to take him. Sadly, these three students are representative of the majority (70%) of the School B students. Their experiences in school do not extend into their home lives.

Educators cannot control the conditions of the student's home life, but they can make sure they provide every possible opportunity within the school environment, which includes offering full library privileges to the students. Although 70% of the School B students do not visit any library other than the one in their school, they appreciate the freedom to take their school library books home; Ellie from School B said, "I read three hours a week at home from my school library books." Although the School A students do not view the library with the same expectations as the School B students, they also do not see it in a negative light. Joe said, "I like it when we go to the library with our class. . . . I wouldn't go without my class, though." If given the opportunity to take their library books home, they could conceivably begin to look at the library as a resource at their disposal that will benefit them immeasurably in school. In other words, the potential for library use among the School A students is great.

Research Question: Do students who are able to take their library books home engage in more pleasure reading than students who must leave their books at school?

Very few of the students from School A engaged in pleasure reading largely because they did not have access to books at home. Ninety–five percent of the School A students chose activities ranging from television to sports to listening to music instead of reading for their extracurricular time. Although their classroom teacher has built her curriculum around books and promotes reading as an integral part of everyone's lives, the School A students rarely engage in pleasure reading. "I like to read, but I don't have any books at home" (Nina), and Joe says that he "would rather do something else" when he is at home. Conversely, when asked how they felt about reading in general, 80% of the students view reading in a positive light. The researcher interpreted this dichotomy to mean that the students have been given positive reading experiences in school but do not transfer those experiences into their daily lives. In other words, reading is fun for school but not an activity to be chosen over other opportunities. Nina (School A) said, "I like to read in school, but I don't have many books at home and my mom can't take me to the library so I don't really read anywhere else." Nina's sentiments were echoed by the majority of her classmates. Since their teacher promotes reading and they have access to books in the classroom and school libraries, the students would appear to benefit greatly from being able to take their library books home. If allowed to enjoy full library privileges, the students might start internalizing the idea that reading is not just a school activity.

Summary of Findings

The research found two groups of students who were the same age, had the same access to books in the classroom and home environments, and had teachers with similar philosophies of teaching. The major difference was that one group enjoyed full school library privileges while the second group was exposed to school library books solely at the discretion of their classroom teacher. Both groups liked the idea of reading, but only one set of students chose reading over other activities; in other words, only one set engaged in pleasure reading. Additionally, the same group that engaged in pleasure reading possessed a deeper understanding of the purpose of libraries beyond using them to get books for school work. Because the other variables were constant and the students from School A liked the idea of reading in general, the researcher concluded that taking school library books home creates better attitudes toward reading and library use. Although there is no one means to creating literate individuals, if our students are given the tools to use reading in their daily lives and feel welcome in all types of libraries, they will begin to be able to read, write, speak and listen--to communicate effectively.

References

Adams, J. (1972). *A study: Library attitudes, usage, skill, and knowledge of junior high school age students.* Salt Lake City, Utah: Brigham Young University: Graduate Department of Library and Information Science.

Constantino, R. (1993). Immigrant ESL high school students' understanding and use of libraries: Check this out! *Scope Journal,* Vol. 2, pp. 15–20.

Elley, W. (1992). *How in the World do Students Read?* Hamburg: International Association for the Evaluation of Education Achievement.

Goelman, H., A. Oberg, & F. Smith. (1984). *Awakening to Literacy.* New York: Heinemann.

Koga, S., & T. Haroda. (1989). The impact to school library services on student achievement. Livermore, Calif: Pervin Press

Krashen, S. (1993). *The Power of Reading.* Englewood, Colo.: Libraries Unlimited, Inc.

Smith. F. (1988). *Joining the Literacy Club.* New York: Heinemann.

Spaulding, A. (1992). *Beyond decoding: Literacy and libraries.* Albzny: New York State Library.

Index

Books in Spanish

About the Authors

After completing her Master's in Teaching English as a Second Language, **Stephanie Asch** moved to Israel, where she teaches English. She is interested in adult education and literacy development.

Danny Brassell is a 1994 Teach for America corps member in Los Angeles and is currently working on his doctorate in literacy. He is the founder and director of "Assignment Books," a non-profit group that obtains book donations for school libraries in the Compton Unified School District.

Kyung-Sook Cho, while an Assistant Professor at Pusan National University of Education in Korea, implemented new reading methods into the teacher education program. Her research interests are free reading and second and foreign language development.

While completing her doctorate in Language, Literacy and Learning, **Rebecca Constantino** began publishing in the area of literacy development, second language learning, and equity in education. She has taught in several countries for various populations. Currently, she is assistant editor of the *TESOL Journal.*

Originally from Ecuador, **Cecilia Espinosa** is a bilingual kindergarten teacher in Phoenix, Arizona. She publishes articles in the area of bilingual literature.

Widely published in the areas of bilingual and second language education, **Chris Faltis** is an Assistant Professor of Education at Arizona State University. His numerous books and articles have contributed greatly to the education of language minority students. Currently, he also serves as the Associate Editor of the *TESOL Journal*.

Julia Fournier is a third grade bilingual teacher in Phoenix, Arizona. She is interested in Spanish literature and has published articles on the subject.

Barry Gribbons is project director at the Center of the Study of Evaluation/CRESST, University of California, Los Angeles. He specializes in research and evaluation methodology, especially related to "at–risk" students.

As development officer for Washoe County Libraries, Reno, Nevada, **Sharon Honig–Bear** combines public relations, writing and fund raising in her position. She helped develop several success joint–use libraries and has published in the field of library science as well as literature.

Currently, **Sally Kinsey** is the president of the Nevada Library Association. While developing and overseeing several joint libraries, she has published articles in library journals.

Stephen Krashen is the author of more than 160 articles and books in the fields of bilingual education, neurolinguistics, second language acquisition and literacy. His publications have received numerous awards. He is an Associate Professor of Education at the University of Southern California.

Jeff McQuillan became interested in second language acquisition and learning while teaching in Mexico. While an Assistant Professor of Education at California State University, Fullerton, he publishes widely in the field of literacy as well as second language acquisition.

As a 20–year veteran high school ESL teacher, **Janice Pilgreen** implemented a successful free reading program for her students. She completed a doctorate in Language, Literacy and Learning, and currently is the Director of Reading at the University of LaVerne. Her research interests include the effects of free reading on ESL students' comprehension and motivation as well as models for literacy development.

After living and teaching English in several countries, **Sandra Pucci** returned to the U.S. and earned a doctorate. Trilingual herself, she teaches bilingual education at the University of Wisconsin, Milwaukee.

Victoria Rodrigo's research interests lie in second/foreign language development and reading. Currently, she is an Assistant Professor of Spanish at Louisiana State University.

Erica Seeman teaches middle school in East Los Angeles and serves as a mentor teacher. She completed a Master's degree at the University of Southern California.

Fay Shin is an assistant professor in the School of Education at California State University, Stanislaus, where she teaches courses in Cross-Cultural Language and Academic Development Teaching Training Program. She received her Ph.D. in Education at the Univeristy of Southern California. She has published articles on public perceptions and attitudes toward bilingual education.

After leaving a successful law practice, **Donald Singleton** returned to graduate school where he studied education. He currently teaches high school in Compton, California.

Lucy Tse is an Assistant Professor of Education at Loyola Marymount University. She has conducted research in the areas of second language reading, heritage language development, and ethnic identity formation. Currently, she is acquiring Chinese.

Addresses

Daniel Brassell
312 N. Francesca
Redondo Beach, CA 90277

Kyung-Sook Cho
Department of English Education
Pusan National University
263 Koje-dong, Yonje-ku
Pusan, 611-736

Rebecca Constantino
975 Joaquin Miller Drive
Reno, NV 89509

Cecilia Espinosa
3831 E. Camelback Road, #130
Phoeniz, AZ 85018

Chris Faltis
4564 E. Corral Road
Phoenix, AZ 85044

Julia Fournier
2323 N. Evergreen
Phoenix, AZ 85006

Barry Gribbons
12618 Mitchell Avenue, #2
Mar Vista, CA 90066

Sharon Honig-Bear
Box 2151
Reno, NV 89509

Sally Kinsey
Box 2151
Reno, NV 89509

Stephen Krashen
Department of Education
Univ. of Southern California
Los Angeles, CA 90089-0031

Jeff McQuillan
3175 Hoover St.
Los Angeles, CA 90007

Janice Pilgreen
5103 Castle Road
La Canada, CA 91011

Sandra Liliana Pucci
Bilingual Education
Univ. of Wisconsin at Milwaukee
Enderis 329
Milwaukee, WI 53201

Victoria Rodrigo
Dept. of F.L. and Literature
Prescott Hall 222
LSU
Baton Rouge, LA 70803

Fay Shin
1923 Douglas Road
Stockton, CA 95207

Donald Singleton
630 North Grand, #409
Los Angeles, CA 90012

Lucy Tse
Loyola Marymount University
School of Education
7900 Loyola Blvd.
Los Angeles, CA 90045-8425